BEBOP
GUITAR IMPROV SERIES

VOLUME 1
Workbook

RICHIE ZELLON

v.5.1

Cover Design by Isabel Robalo

Band in a Box is the registered trademark of PG Music Inc.

ABOUT THE GUITAR IMPROV SERIES

Developed over a 10 year period by its author and used as an instructional method in various music schools, *The Bebop Guitar Improv Series* consists of two volumes with multi-media materials. It is intended as a guide to lead both the player with little or no formal improvisation skills, as well as the player who does so exclusively by ear, on the journey to becoming a seasoned jazz improviser. Each volume is comprised of 3 books: the *Lesson Book*, *Workbook*, and *Scale & Arpeggio Book*.

Volume 1 is devoted to teaching the rudimentary principles of jazz improvisation in theory and practice. It initially focuses on learning how to systematically develop a vocabulary to improvise over chord changes from a guitar-oriented technical perspective. A variety of essential harmonic progressions found in jazz are covered in order of difficulty. Each new progression is taught through a series of short etudes, and gradually introduces one or more of the chord/scales required to improvise over most jazz standards. Various melodic concepts and syncopated rhythms commonly used in the swing/bebop idioms, are covered as well.

Volume 2 builds on the principles explored in Volume 1 and explores various applications over «Rhythm Changes», as well as major, minor and extended tonalities. The technical focus is on multi-positional playing using the entire fretboard.

Be sure to check out the **Bebop Guitar Improv Series Online**! Featuring 150+ instructional videos, it is the perfect compliment to the book series.

For more info please visit *https://bebopguitar.richiezellon.com*

NOTE: This series focuses solely on the development of linear improvisation. A working knowledge of basic 7th chords is presumed throughout, as guitar oriented instruction on their construction is beyond its scope.

ABOUT THE AUTHOR

Richie Zellon, guitarist, composer, and music educator, has held teaching positions as professor of jazz guitar at Florida International University (Miami) the University of South Florida (Tampa) The Music Workshop (Orlando) and his own venue, Miami Jazz Guitar.

With several critically acclaimed recordings under his name, Zellon has recorded and/or performed with some of the most influential musicians both in the mainstream and Latin jazz genres. Among them, Paquito D' Rivera, David Leibman, Jerry Bergonzi, Sam Rivers, George Garzone, Danilo Perez, Jeff Berlin, Abraham Laboriel, Alex Acuna and Ignacio Berroa to name a few.

Due to his innovations in the field of jazz and latin music he has been profiled in several important books such as «*The Great Jazz Guitarists*» by Scott Yanow, «*The Jazz Guitar: Its Evolution, Players and Personalities Since 1900*"» by Maurice J. Summerfield, «*El Diccionario de Latin Jazz*» by Nat Chediak , «*Caliente: A History of Latin Jazz*» by Luc Delanoy and «*Jazz Jews*» by Michael Gerber.

For almost a decade, he wrote an instructional column for Jazz Improv magazine. In addition to his dedication to mainstream jazz, his ongoing research on the music of various Latin American cultures and their fusion with contemporary music has been a sought after topic by musicians at international clinics and workshops as well.

For more information please visit *www.richiezellon.com*

CONTENTS

PART 5: BEBOP CALISTHENICS #4

PART 6: BEBOP CALISTHENICS #5

PART 7: BEBOP CALISTHENICS #6

APPENDIX 1

APPENDIX 2

BEBOP
PREPARATORY EXERCISES
VOICE LEADING WITH GUIDE TONES

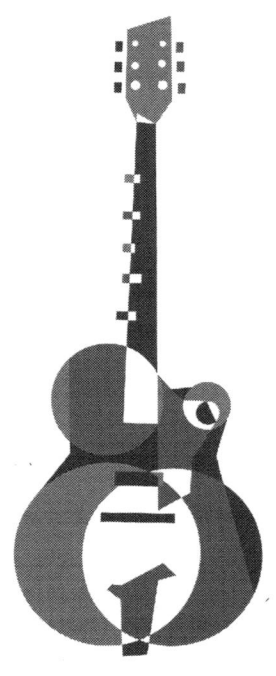

MIXOLYDIAN ARPEGGIOS
PAT 1 / PAT 4 / PAT 5

VOICE LEADING WITH GUIDE TONES IN THE BLUES

The upcoming 2 exercises serve to train your mind and hands to resolve to the closest primary guide tone (3 or b7) at the point of chord change in a blues progression. Here are some voice leading principles to keep in mind:

*When transitioning from the I7 to the IV7, the «3» resolves 1/2 step down to the «b7» .
*When transitioning from the I7 to the IV7, the «b7» resolves 1/2 step down to the «3».
*When transitioning from the I7 to the V7, the «3» moves 1/2 step up to the «b7» .
*When transitioning from the I7 to the V7, the «b7» moves 1/2 step up to the «3» .

The following exercises are written using intervallic script (see p.20 in Lesson Book). Please make sure you have memorized Mixolydian patterns 1,4 & 5 in the «Bebop Improv Series: Scale - Arpeggio Fingerings» before continuing.

COMMON GUIDE TONE RESOLUTIONS WITHIN BLUES PROGRESSIONS

I7-IV7-I7 (PATTERNS 1 AND 4)

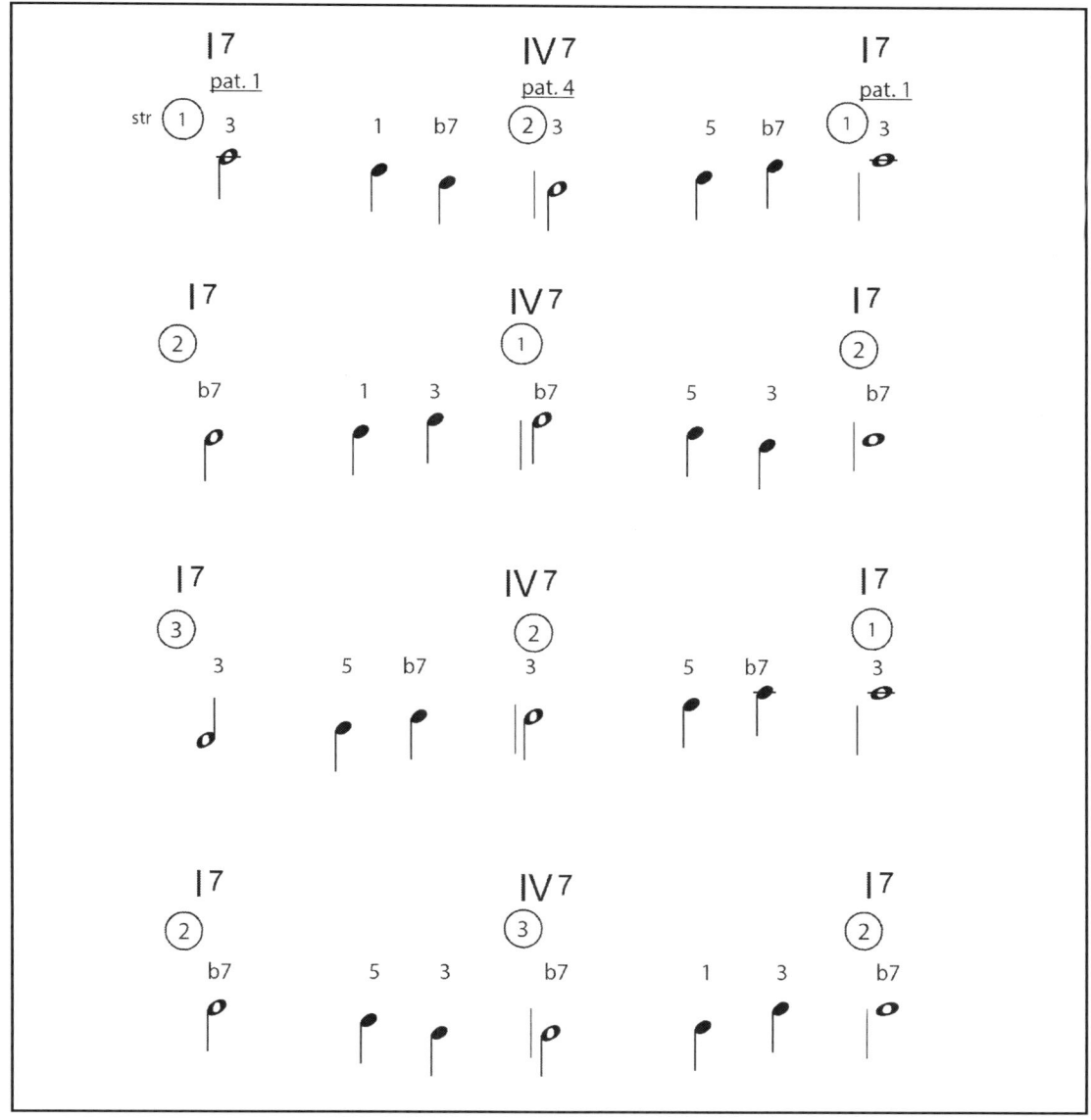

COMMON GUIDE TONE RESOLUTIONS WITHIN BLUES PROGRESSIONS

I7-V7-I7 (PATTERNS 1 AND 5)

Notice that the V7 to IV7 sequence that takes place in bars 9 and 10 of a traditional 12 bar blues, is not covered in the previous exercises. Because of the close proximity between the 2 chords, guide tone resolution at the point of chord change is limited to a parallel descending movement which can be summed up as follows:

*When transitioning from the V7 to the IV7, the «3» resolves 1 whole step down to the «3» of the IV7 .
*When transitioning from the V7 to the IV7, the «b7» resolves 1 whole step down to the «b7» of the IV7 .
Let's limit ourselves to these principles for the time being. Other options will be explored as new melodic resources are introduced.

The following 2 exercises consist of a 12 bar blues progression comprised solely of dominant 7 chord tones (1,3,5b7) in diverse inversions. This is referred to as the *arpeggio framework* and is based here on mixolydian fingering patterns: 1, 4 and 5. In preparation for the etudes in the main Lesson Book, your goal is to better familiarize yourself with the location of each chord tone and its corresponding numerical scale degree. In addition you want to program your mind to spot the closest guide tone at the point of chord change.

The 1st page of each exercise displays it in both tab and regular notation in the key of F. The 2nd page features the same exercise notated employing intervallic script. It should be played in different keys throughout the fretboard. <u>NOTE:</u> *Similar exercises for all upcoming progressions in the Lesson Book are available for download at: https://bebopguitar.richiezellon.com/downloads.html*

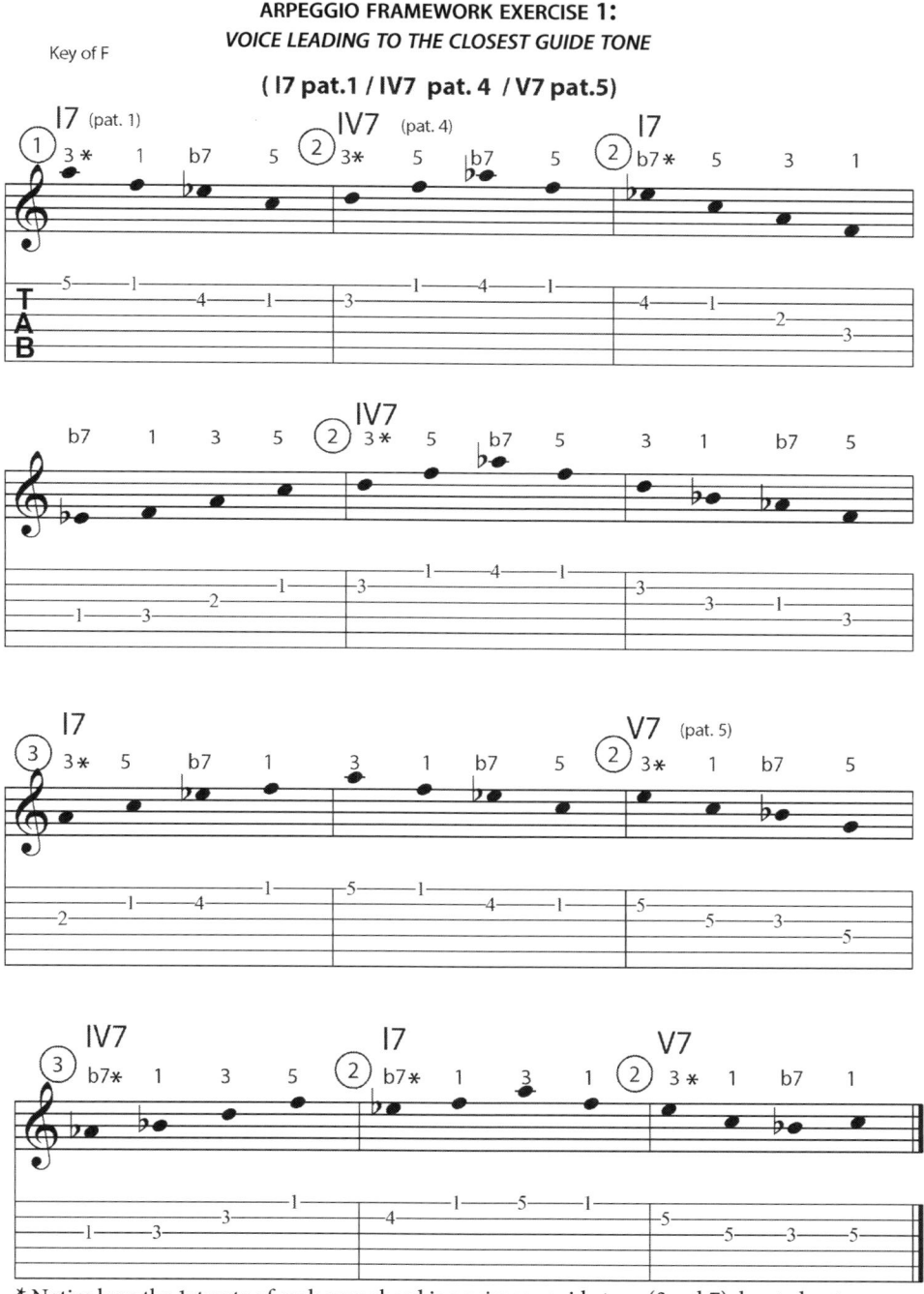

ARPEGGIO FRAMEWORK EXERCISE 1:
VOICE LEADING TO THE CLOSEST GUIDE TONE

(I7 pat.1 / IV7 pat. 4 / V7 pat.5)

Key of F

* Notice how the 1st note of each new chord is a primary guide tone (3 or b7), located a step away from the preceding note. This exemplifies the smooth voice leading principle we want to observe.

ARPEGGIO FRAMEWORK EXERCISE 1:
VOICE LEADING TO THE CLOSEST GUIDE TONE
(I7 pat.1 / IV7 pat. 4 / V7 pat.5)

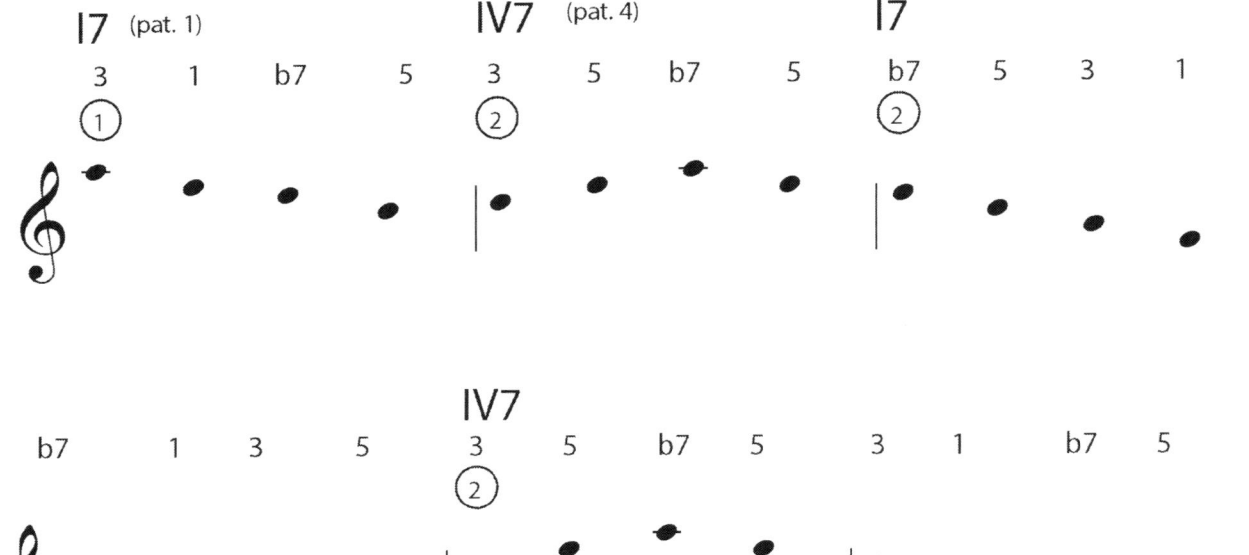

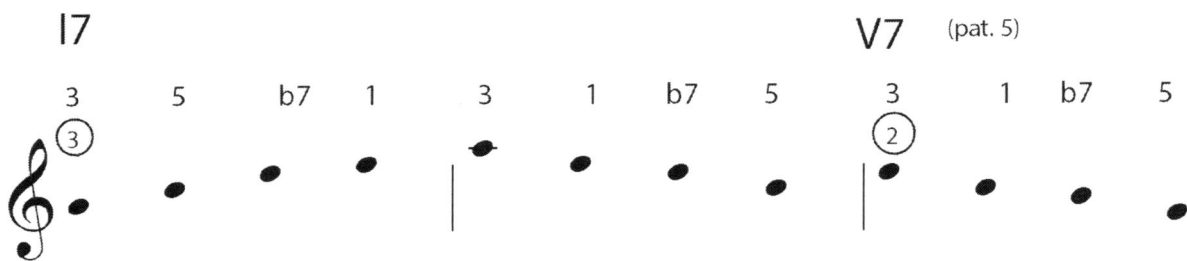

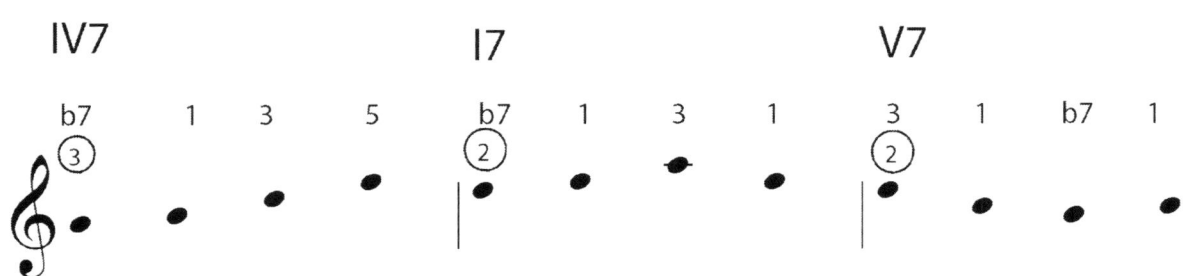

ARPEGGIO FRAMEWORK EXERCISE 2:
VOICE LEADING TO THE CLOSEST GUIDE TONE
(I7 pat.1 / IV7 pat. 4 / V7 pat.5)

Key of F

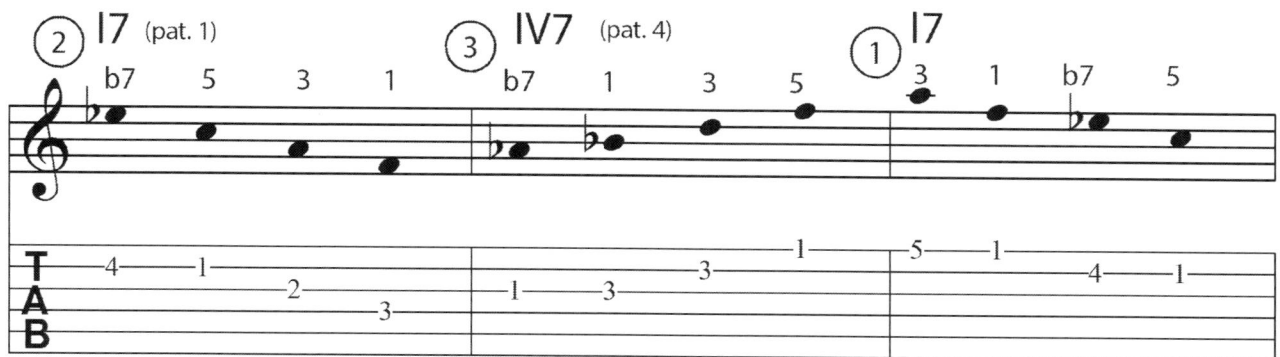

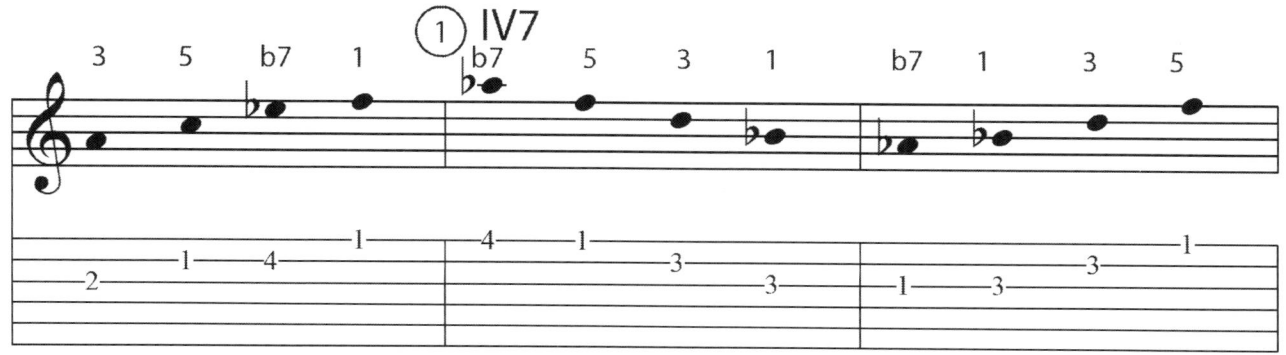

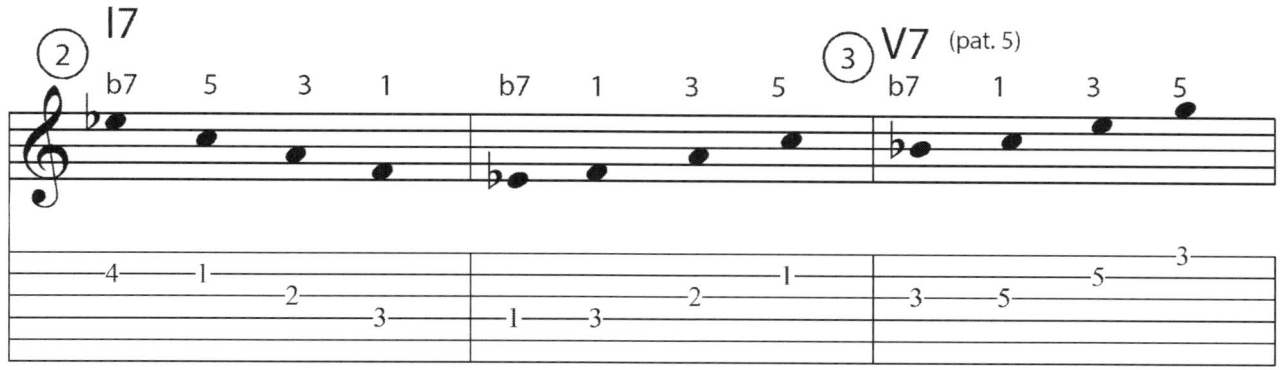

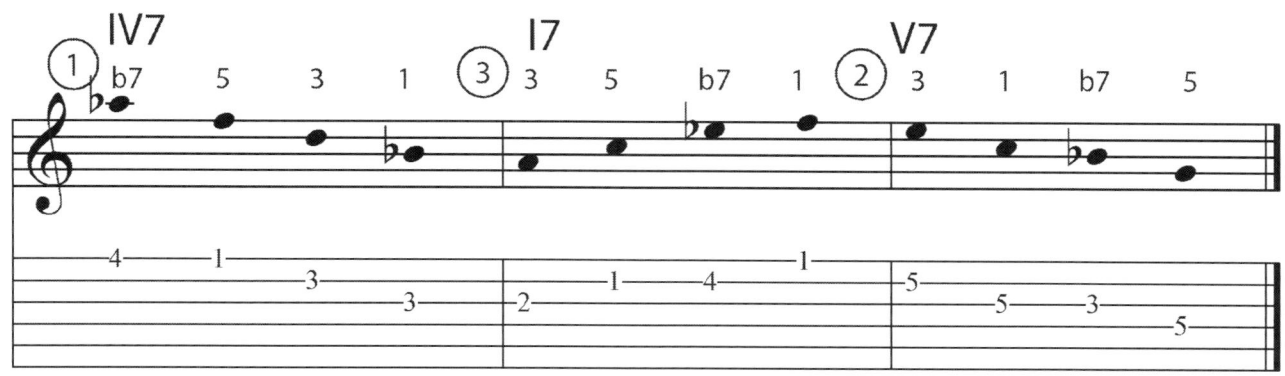

ARPEGGIO FRAMEWORK EXERCISE 2:
VOICE LEADING TO THE CLOSEST GUIDE TONE

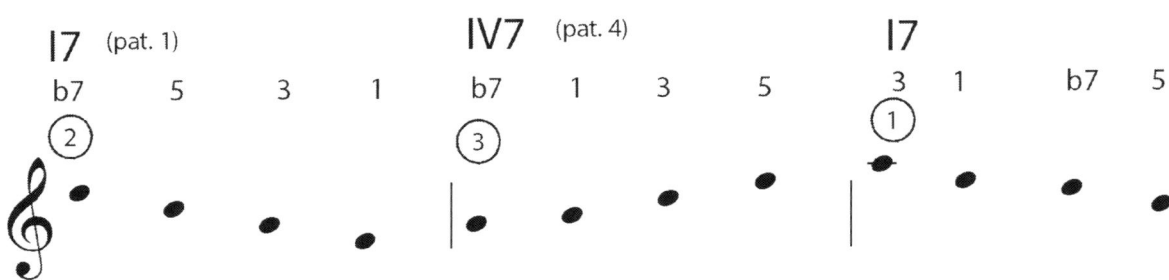

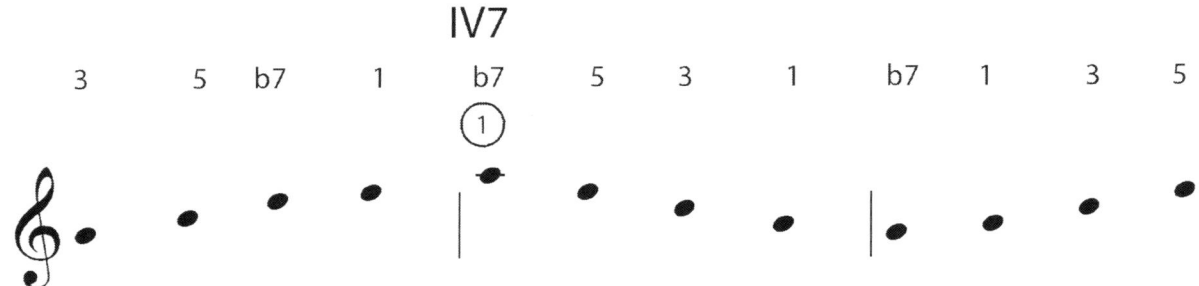

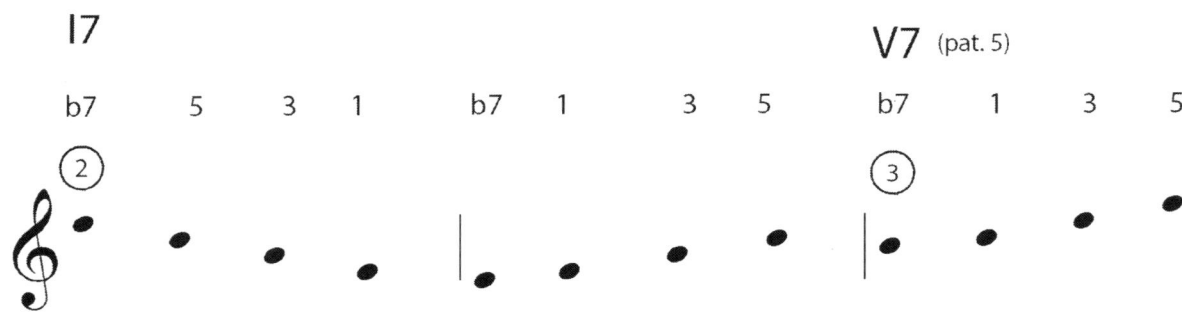

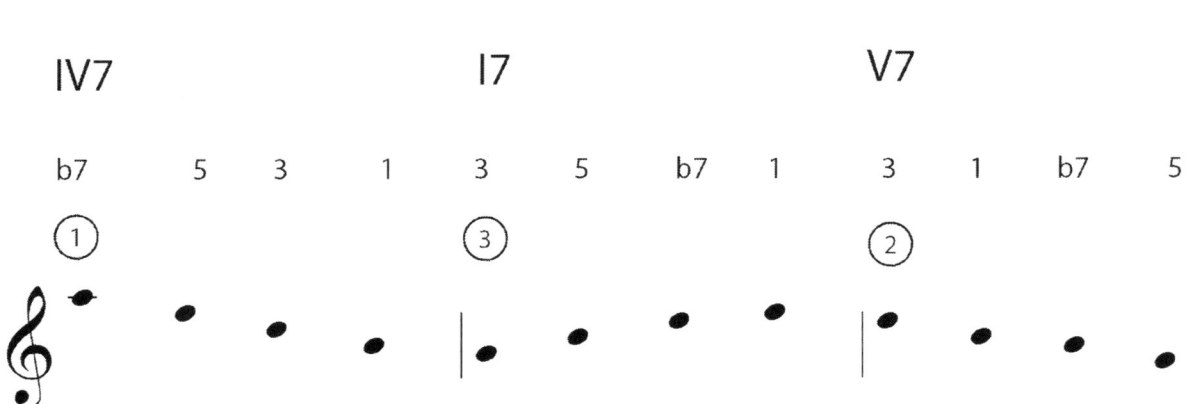

RHYTHM LAB 1: SWING EIGHTH NOTES

When playing swing eighth notes in pairs, the first eighth note (known as the «downbeat») should last longer than the second one (known as the «upbeat»). The best way to interpret this is to imagine a set of eighth note triplets in which the first 2 eighth notes are tied together as in the following example:

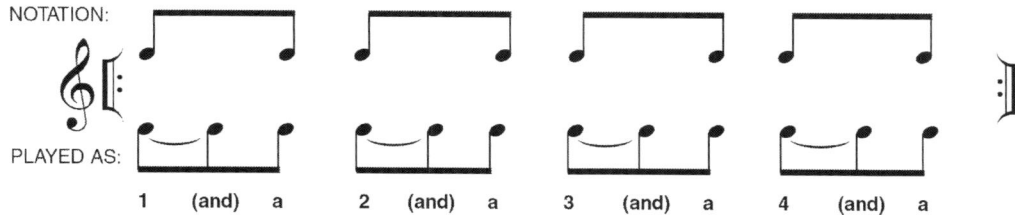

When playing swing in 4/4 time in a slow to medium tempo, we should feel an imaginary underlying continuum of 12/8 at all times. This is crucial if we want to play and accent the 8th notes properly. (Note that when playing at a real fast tempo, the 8th notes go by too fast and therefore this concept is no longer applicable.) The following example illustrates this concept:

In the following exercise we want to mentally subdivide in swing 8th notes even as we play larger note values such as quarter and half notes. Set a metronome at a comfortable tempo and be sure to tap your foot on every «downbeat» (1, 2, 3, 4). Conversely, make sure your foot is in an upward position on every «upbeat» (the second 8th note of each beat).

Your goal is to synchronize every note you play to the clocklike motion of your foot and not vice-versa. Use alternate picking and for now make sure that your pick always plays a downstroke on every downbeat and an upstroke on every upbeat. Simply put, your pick should be synchronized with the downward and upward motion of your foot.

BASIC RHYTHMS IN 4/4

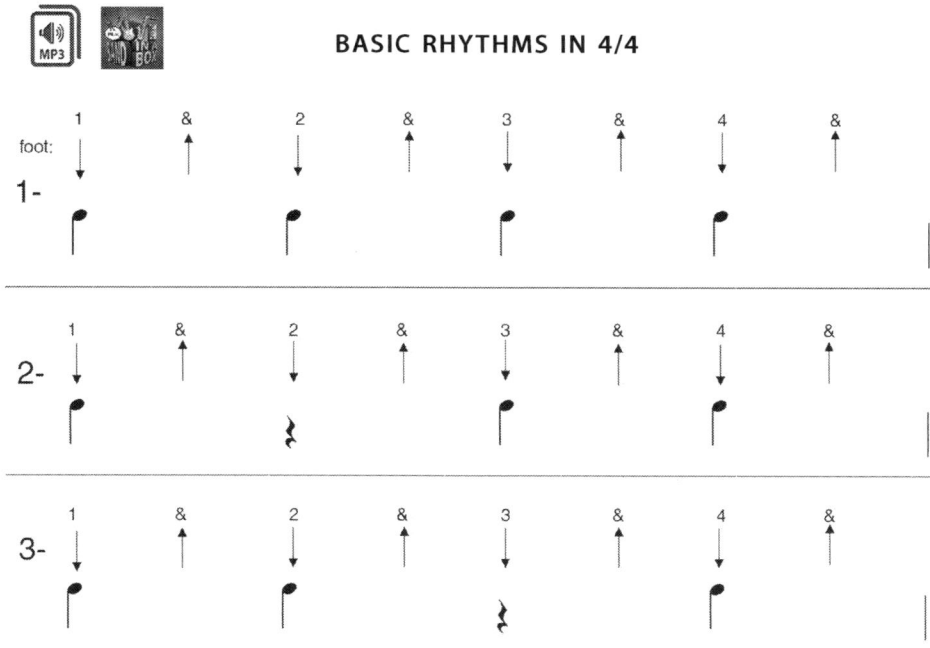

(BASIC RHYTHMS CONTINUED)

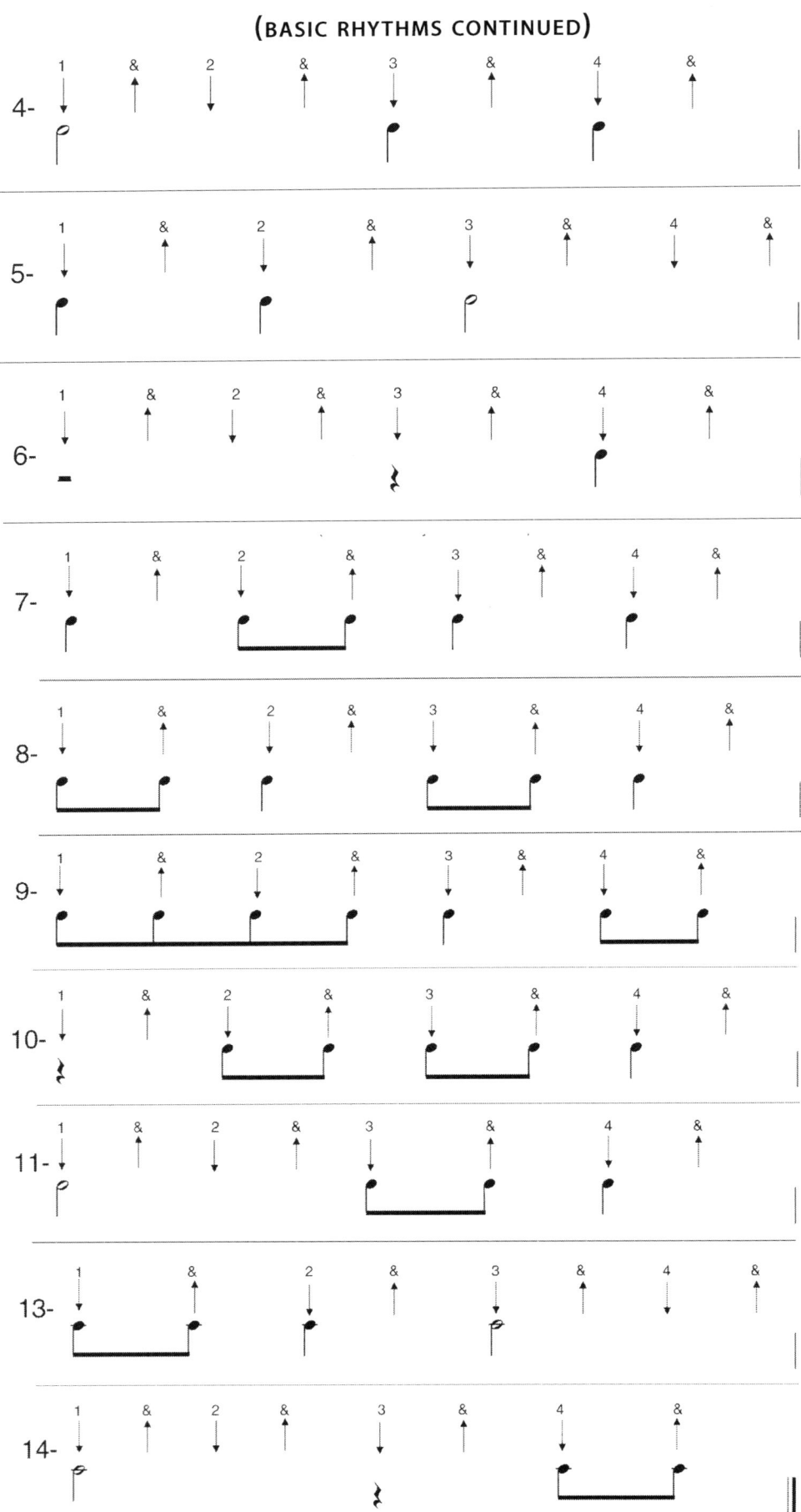

INTRODUCING THE BEBOP CALISTHENICS

The Bebop Calisthenics make up the perfect warm up to begin your regular practice routine with. These exercises have been carefully structured to simultaneously work on the following levels, both consciously and subconsciously:

1. TECHNICAL LEVEL

Each exercise explores one or more arpeggio fingerings with different «approach note» permutations. The fingering patterns appear here in the order that they are introduced in the etudes featured in the main lesson book. The given melodic formula for each exercise moves sequentially either descending from the highest available note in the fingering pattern or vice versa.

The same sequence of notes will present different fingering challenges as it is transposed from one pattern to another. You will notice that some exercises will feel natural and come easy, while others will initially feel awkward and require more effort to master. Ultimately, the ongoing practice of the same melodic phrase employing the different fingering patterns, will create the technical flexibility necessary to allow you to play an idea anywhere you find yourself on the fretboard. This skill is an invaluable resource in our quest to achieve total freedom of expression when improvising.

2. THEORETICAL LEVEL

Technical skill alone will not enable us to improvise a melodically coherent solo. We must be aware of where our target notes lie within each fingering, as well as what notes we can use to approach said targets for the creation of interesting melodic lines. Fortunately, since each exercise is focused on a specific chord arpeggio and «approach note» concept, this information is being continually reinforced throughout.

3. CREATIVE LEVEL

All the 7th chord arpeggios with diverse «approach note» combinations presented here, constitute the melodic foundation of the Bebop idiom. After going through each set of calisthenics and playing the associated etudes in the main lesson book, you will notice that various fragments of these exercises are present in the lines therein. If you don't find this obvious, it is only because they are rhythmically disguised. In fact, that statement holds the key to creating new melodic lines from each exercise. Simply put— by extracting a fragment of any exercise and assigning new rhythmic values to the notes, you can create new vocabulary instantly! Upon becoming familiar with the sound of an arpeggio and a selected approach, you will start to incorporate them spontaneously into your solos.

4. AURAL LEVEL

Last but not least is the importance of pre-hearing in our mind, what we are going to play. Although these exercises are no substitute for formal ear training, with continued practice the various sonorities of the interval combinations repeated throughout each arpeggio, should eventually become mentally audible. It is only when we can «pre-hear» what we are going to play, that we are in total control of our note choices and play what we truly hear in our heads. This is akin to singing through our instrument. If you can sing a simple melody fairly in tune even without having a trained voice, you intuitively know what the notes produced by your vocal cords are going to sound like a split second before they are produced. As a matter of fact, those that already posses this ability are a substantial amount closer to achieving the same skill on the guitar, than those that don't!

HOW TO PRACTICE THE BEBOP CALISTHENICS

The goal with these exercises is to be able to play them by simply glancing at the formulas for each exercise that appear on the final page of each section, entitled «Summary of Bebop Calisthenics». In order to accomplish this, be sure to follow these guidelines:

*1. Before attempting to play any set of exercises— make sure you have committed to memory the prescribed fingering patterns for the scales/arpeggios being used, as taught in the «BEBOP GUITAR IMPROV SERIES: Scale & Arpeggio Fingerings» book .*This means that you must be able to comfortably play the pattern starting from the highest available chord tone on the 1st string and descend to the lowest available chord tone on the 6th string. In addition, you must be able to identify all the chord tones in the arpeggio as you play them. The tablature included here should only be used as an initial reference to check whether or not you are using the proper fingering. Relying on it each time you play an exercise will defeat the purpose of what you are trying to achieve.

2. Focus on just reading the interval script on top of the regular notation, after initially reading the tablature and making sure you are using the proper fingering . Remember, to improvise you need to visualize the fingering pattern in terms of numerical degrees (intervals), each with a unique harmonic function. In practice these intervallic patterns are easier to recall and transpose on the fly than their alphabet based counterparts (eg. A, Bb, B, etc.).

3. Practice the same version of each exercise for all the fingering patterns featured in the section (eg. Ex#1 for pat.1, Ex#1 for pat. 4 and Ex#1 for pat.5). Do this instead of completing all the exercises for a given pattern before moving to the next pattern in the section. The reason for this is that you want to learn and reinforce all the current fingerings evenly within each section. If you concentrate on just playing all the exercises over the initial pattern before attempting to cover any that follow, when you finally do so, your mind will already be tired. As a result you will have a harder time assimilating the additional fingerings.

4. Alternate the order in which you practice each exercise for the given patterns. That is, if today you practice each single exercise first for pat.1, then pat. 4 and finally pat.5; tomorrow invert the order to pat.5, pat.4 and pat.1. Give even attention to all the fingerings in a section as all will be required equal attention when the time comes to play music!

5. Practice the exercises by solely glancing at the «Summary of Bebop Calisthenics» page at the end of the section.

- Let's break the process down into manageable parts. To demonstrate the procedure we will use the 1st exercise on p.31; «Descending Dominant 7 Arpeggio w/ Lower NT for 3 and b7» over Mixolydian Pattern 1.

PROCEDURE

1. Isolate and play only the target notes. In this case we want to play only all the 3's and b7's within the specified pattern and arpeggio.

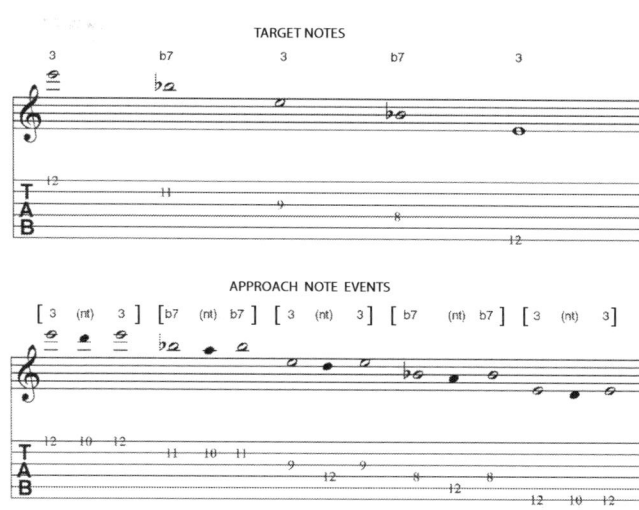

2. Play just the approach notes and target resolution notes. Now we would play all the 3's and b7's with their lower neighboring tones. From here on, any group of approaches resolving to their target will be refered to as an *approach note event.*

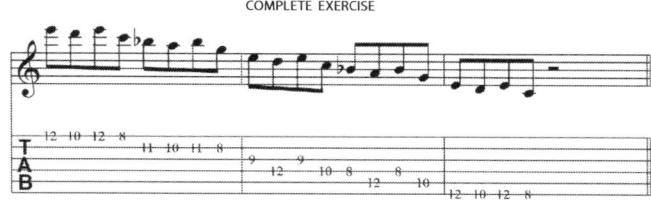

3. Once familiar with the locations of the events taking place in relation to each target note, you are ready to play the full arpeggio and incorporate said events with much more ease.

- To initially help you keep track of where you are in the arpeggio, as you play each note, say the chord tone degree you are playing (eg. 1, 3, 5, b7). For any approach note, rather than saying 2, 4 or 6, it is preferable to say «approach» . For example if playing a descending arpeggio with lower neighboring tones for the 3rd and 7th, you would say: «b7–approach–b7–5–3–approach–3–1» and so on. An alternative is to say «b7–lower–b7–5–3–lower–3–1». This will help you mentally reinforce the chord tones numerically as target notes and further differentiate them from the remaining degrees which are acting as approach notes.

- *Notice that each exercise is usually made up of the same sequence of notes repeated in 2 octaves.* When you are aware of this, it is much easier to both remember the sequence and pre-hear what it is supposed to sound like as you are playing it again in the 2nd octave.

- **GOAL:** *After playing the exercise using the above procedure, attempt to play it as fast and consistently as possible without saying the numbers.* Rely exclusively on your ear and finger memory. If you find that you can't retain the sound of the exercise along with a mental map of how to execute it on the fretboard, go back and play it slower than you did previously and then attempt to play it again without «thinking» of the numbers. The goal of this final step is to «let go» and just play! When we improvise, we don't have time to stop and think. Instead, we have to just let our ears guide us while our fingers do the walking. The outcome will depend on how well our ears have been programmed to dictate what our fingers play on the spur of the moment.

IMPORTANT: For lack of space and to avoid redundancy, only a few fingerings will be featured for each arpeggio and approach concept introduced in the «Bebop Calisthenics». It is your responsibility to adapt and apply the «Summary of Bebop Calisthenics» at the end of each section, to any new fingering patterns that you learn in the future! To better understand how to practice these exercises, please be sure to check out *APPENDIX 1: How to Practice using the Summary of Bebop Calisthenics (p.113).*

BEBOP
CALISTHENICS 1
ARPEGGIOS with NEIGHBORING TONES

MIXOLYDIAN: PAT 1 / PAT 4 / PAT 5

**Summary for Mixolydian / Dorian /
Ionian / Locrian / Super Locrian**

PAT. 1 MIXOLYDIAN ARPEGGIO w/ NEIGHBORING TONES

C7

Descending dom. 7th arpeggio w/ lower neighboring tones for 3 & b7

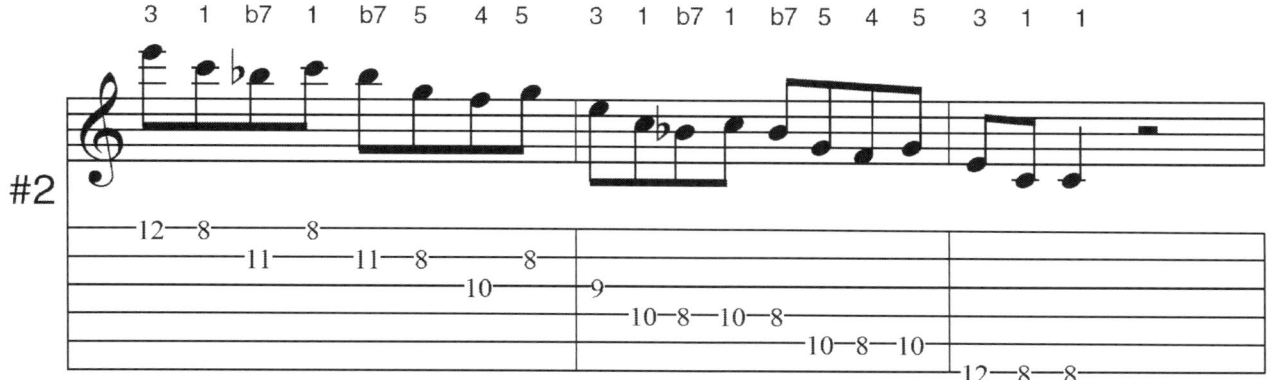

Repeat exercise #1 using lower chromatic NT of 3 instead of "2"

Descending dom. 7th arpeggio w/ lower neighboring tones for 1 & 5

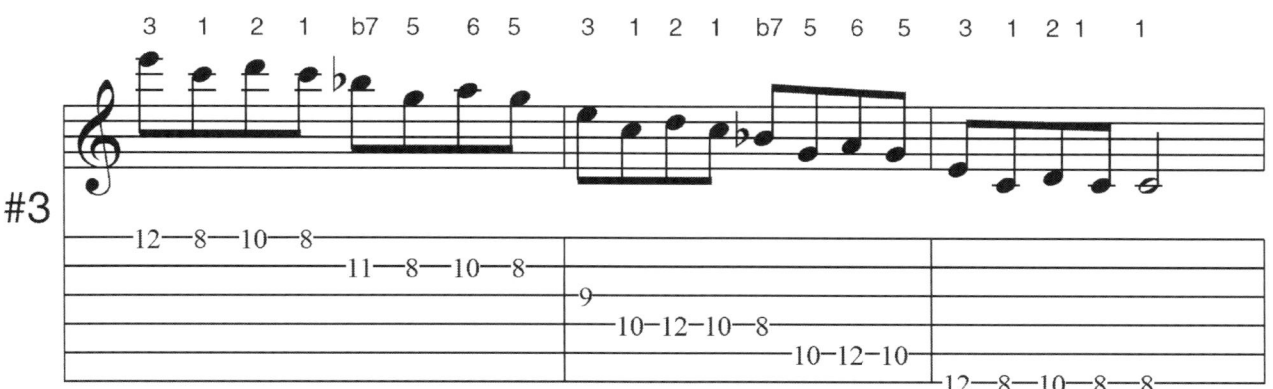

Repeat exercise #2 using lower chromatic NT of 5 instead of "4"

Descending dom. 7th arpeggio w/ upper neighboring tones for 1 & 5

19

PAT. 1 MIXOLYDIAN ARPEGGIO w/ NEIGHBORING TONES

Ascending dom. 7th arpeggio w/ lower neighboring tones for 3 & b7

Repeat exercise #4 using lower chromatic NT of 3 instead of "2"

Ascending dom. 7th arpeggio w/ lower neighboring tones for 5 & 1

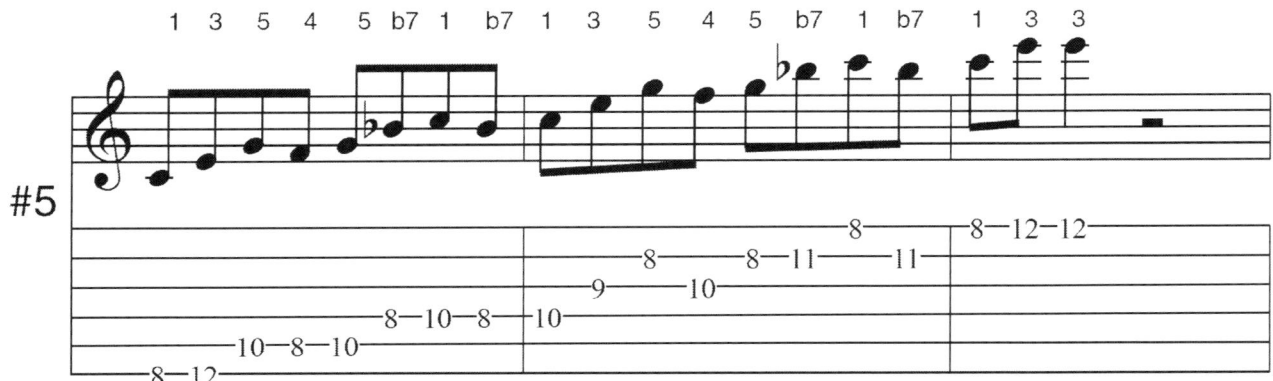

Repeat exercise #5 using lower chromatic NT of 5 instead of "4"

Ascending dom. 7th arpeggio w/ upper neighboring tones for 1 & 5

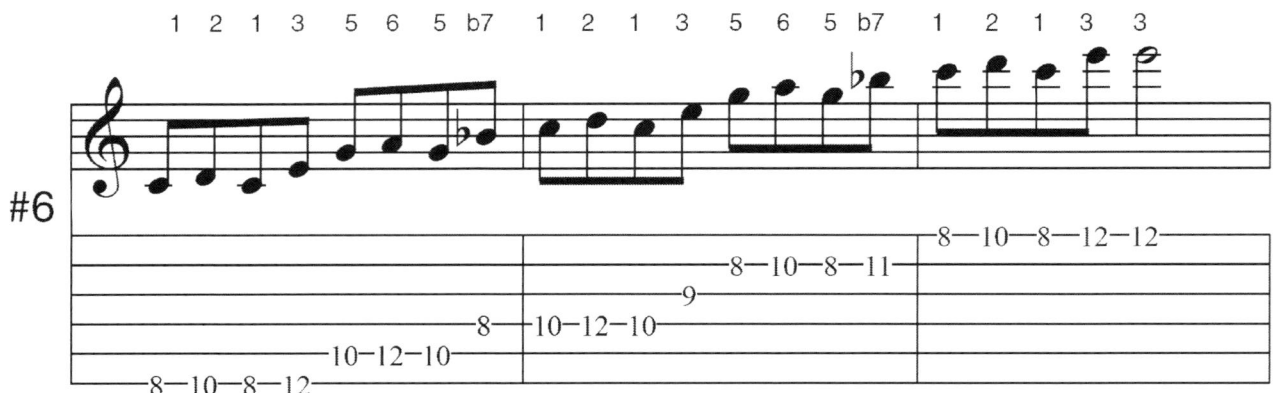

PAT. 1 MIXOLYDIAN ARPEGGIO w/ NEIGHBORING TONES

Ascending dom. 7th arpeggio w/ upper neighboring tones for 3 & b7

Ascending dom. 7th arpeggio w/ lower neighboring tone for 3 & upper for 5

Repeat exercise #8 using lower chromatic NT of 3 instead of "2"

Ascending dom. 7th arpeggio w/ upper neighboring tone for 3 & lower for 5

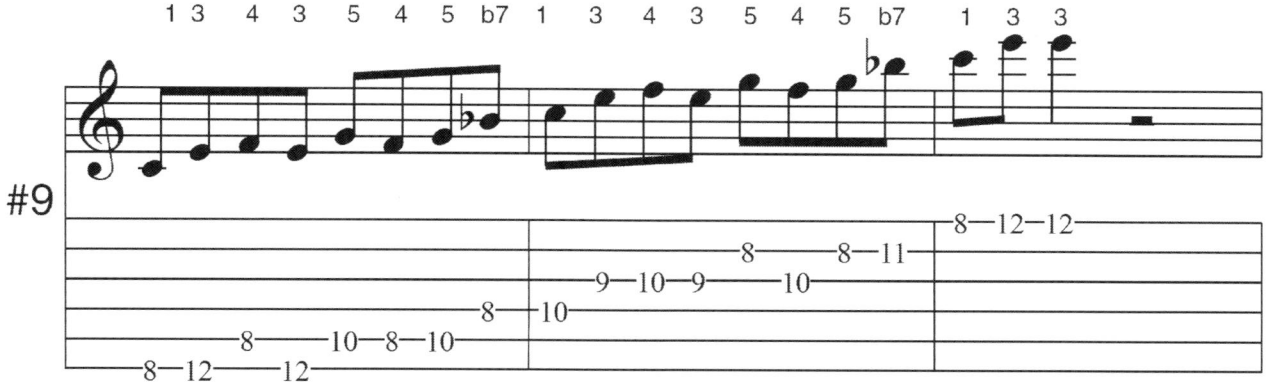

Repeat exercise #9 using lower chromatic NT of 5 instead of "4"

PAT. 1 MIXOLYDIAN ARPEGGIO w/ NEIGHBORING TONES

Descending dom. 7th arpeggio w/ lower neighboring tone for 3 & upper for 5

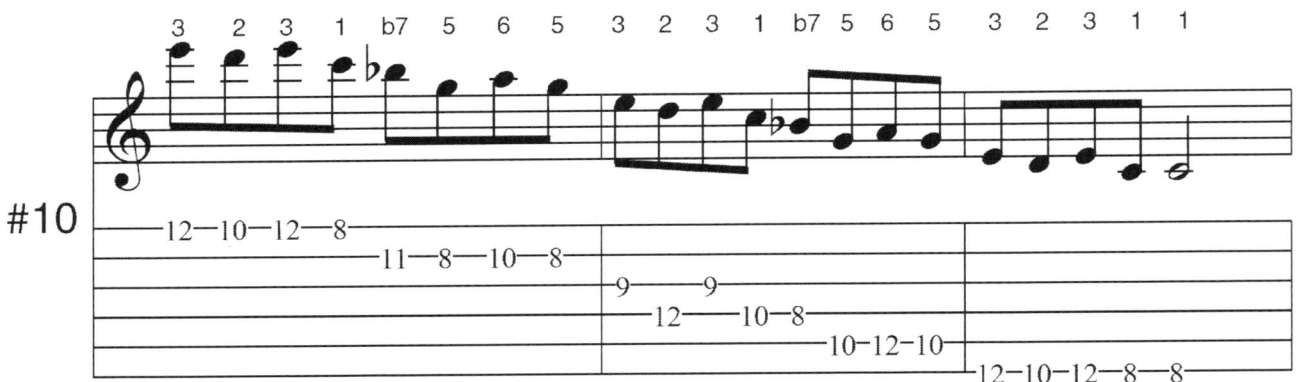

Repeat exercise #10 using lower chromatic NT of 3 instead of "2"

Descending dom. 7th arpeggio w/ upper neighboring tone for 3 & lower for 5

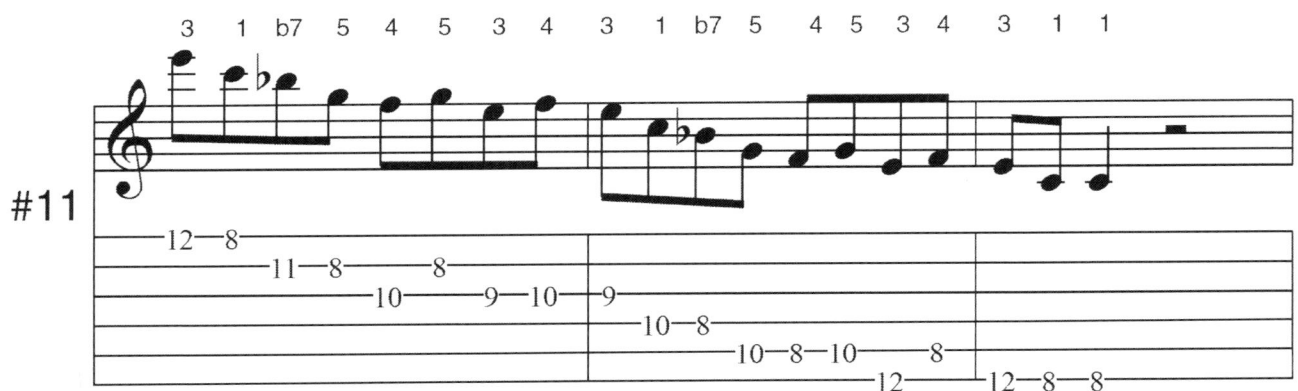

Repeat exercise #11 using lower chromatic NT of 5 instead of "4"

Descending dom. 7th arpeggio w/ upper neighboring tone for 1 & lower for b7

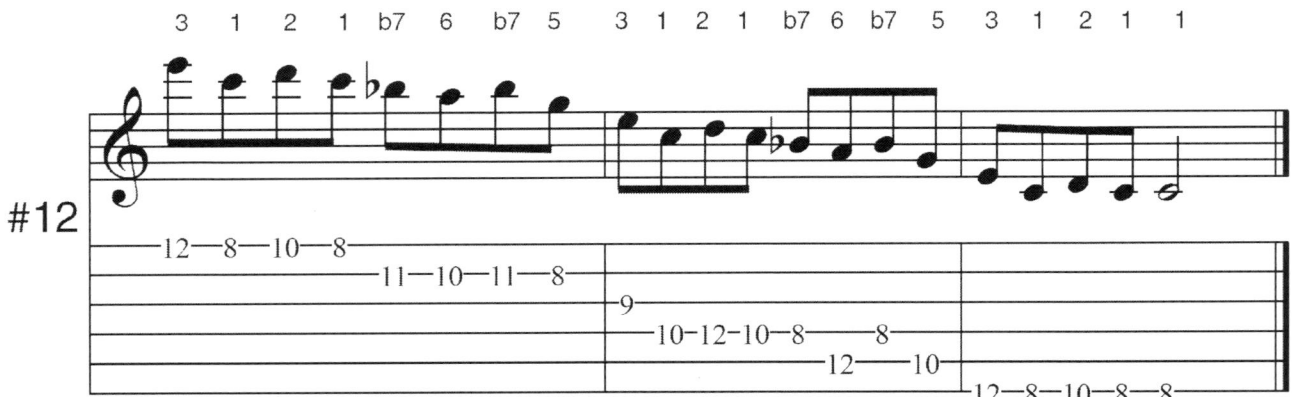

PAT. 4 MIXOLYDIAN ARPEGGIO w/ NEIGHBORING TONES

F7

Descending dom. 7th arpeggio w/ lower neighboring tones for 3 & b7

Repeat exercise #1 using lower chromatic NT of 3 instead of "2"

Descending dom. 7th arpeggio w/ lower neighboring tones for 1 & 5

Repeat exercise #2 using lower chromatic NT of 5 instead of "4"

Descending dom. 7th arpeggio w/ upper neighboring tones for 1 & 5

23

PAT. 4 MIXOLYDIAN ARPEGGIO w/ NEIGHBORING TONES

Ascending dom. 7th arpeggio w/ lower neighboring tones for 3 & b7

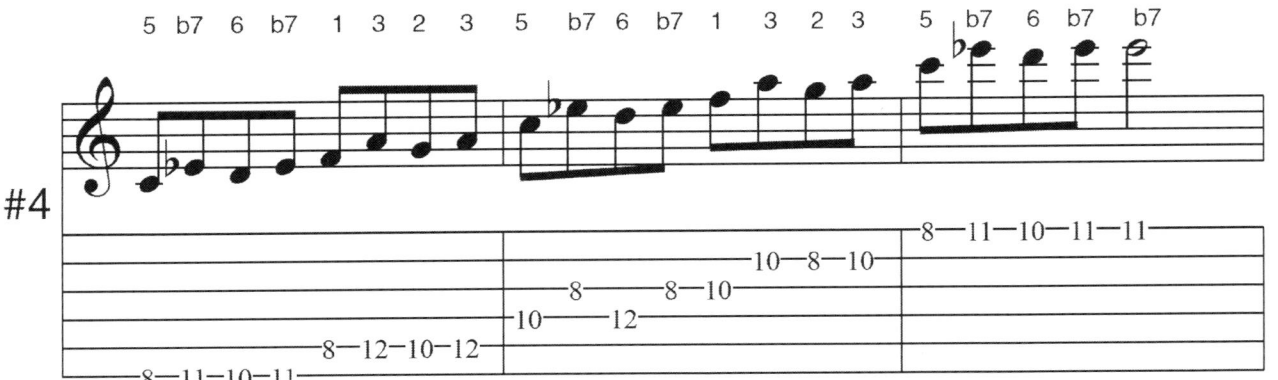

Repeat exercise #4 using lower chromatic NT of 3 instead of "2"

Ascending dom. 7th arpeggio w/ lower neighboring tones for 5 & 1

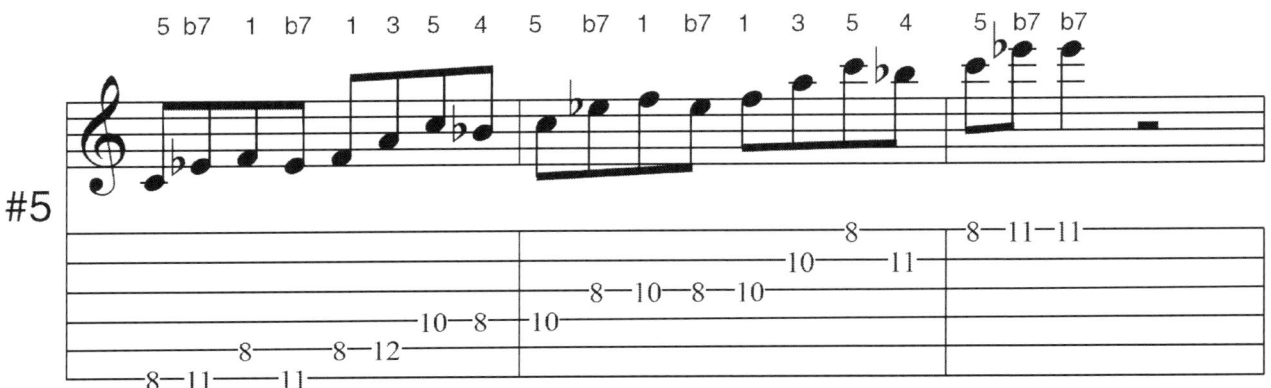

Repeat exercise #5 using lower chromatic NT of 5 instead of "4"

Ascending dom. 7th arpeggio w/ upper neighboring tones for 1 & 5

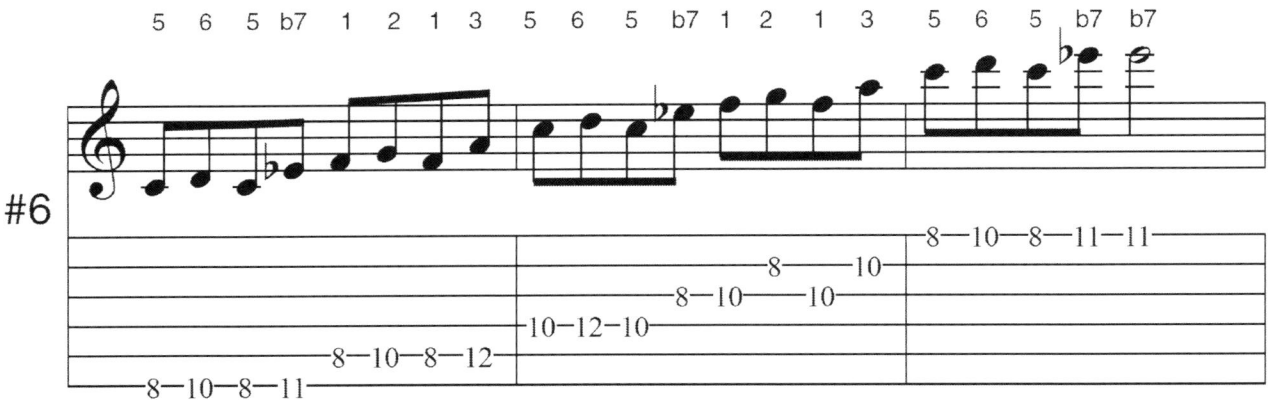

PAT. 4 MIXOLYDIAN ARPEGGIO w/ NEIGHBORING TONES

Ascending dom. 7th arpeggio w/ upper neighboring tones for 3 & b7

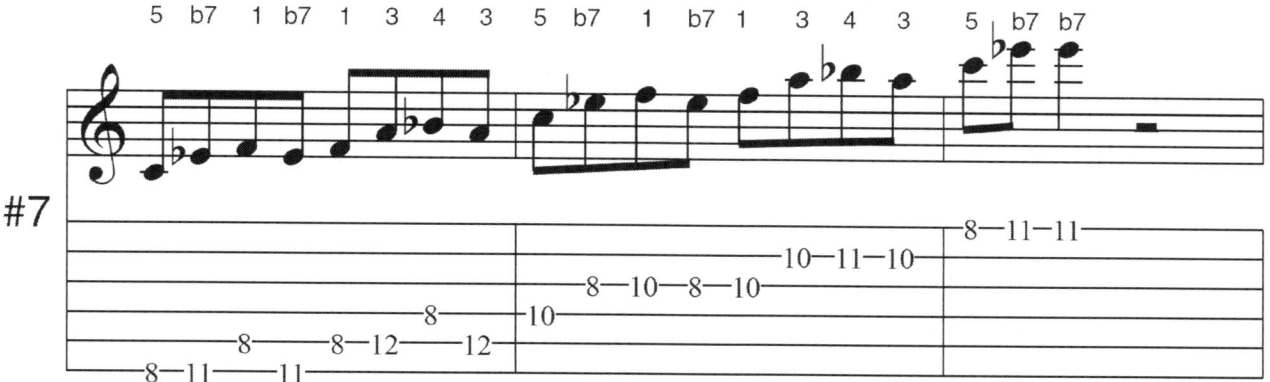

Ascending dom. 7th arpeggio w/ lower neighboring tone for 3 & upper for 5

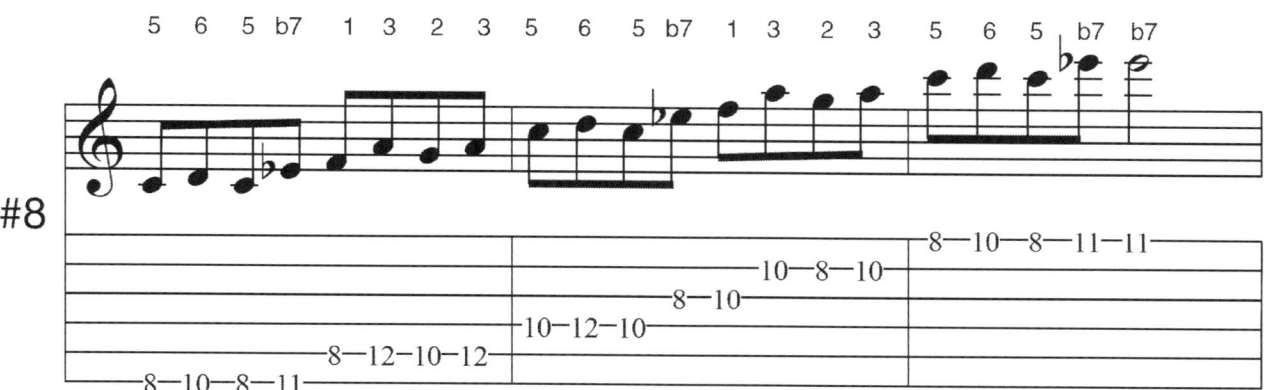

Repeat exercise #8 using lower chromatic NT of 3 instead of "2"

Ascending dom. 7th arpeggio w/ upper neighboring tone for 3 & lower for 5

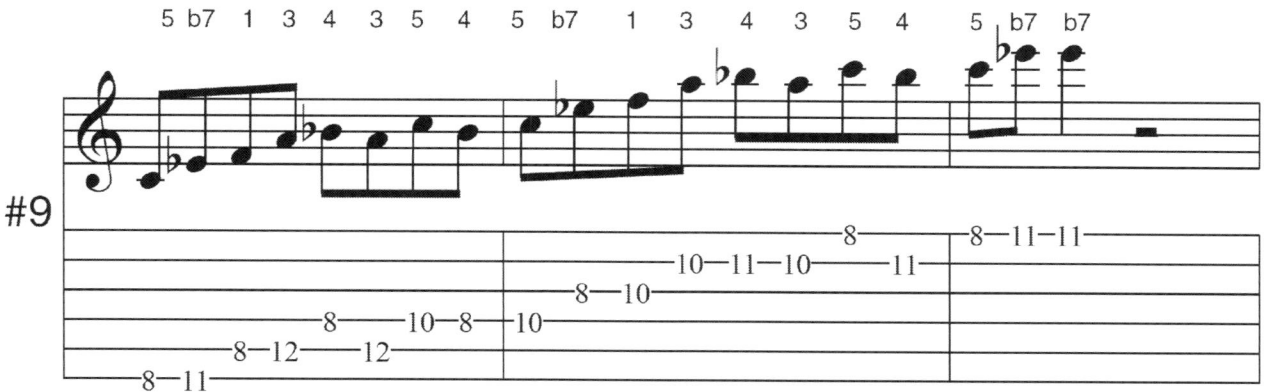

Repeat exercise #9 using lower chromatic NT of 5 instead of "4"

PAT. 4 MIXOLYDIAN ARPEGGIO w/ NEIGHBORING TONES

Descending dom. 7th arpeggio w/ lower neighboring tone for 3 & upper for 5

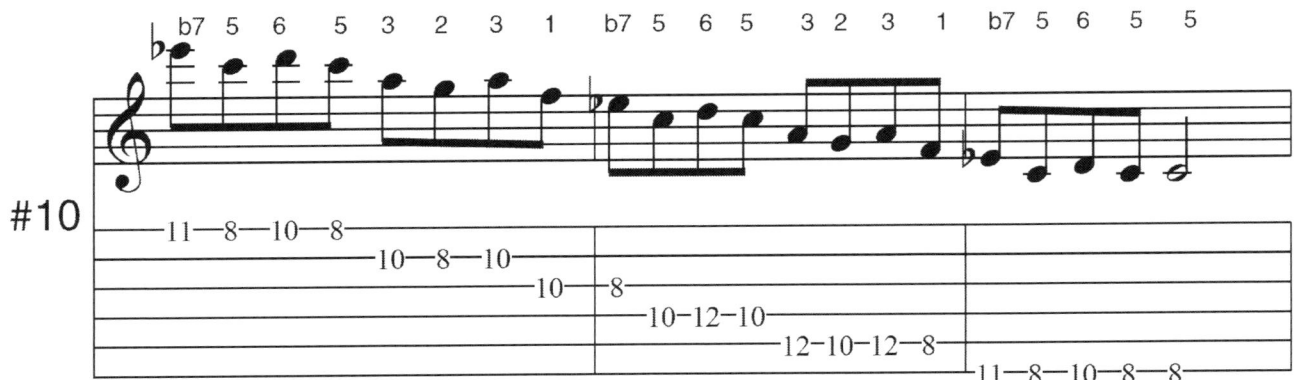

Repeat exercise #10 using lower chromatic NT of 3 instead of "2"

Descending dom. 7th arpeggio w/ upper neighboring tone for 3 & lower for 5

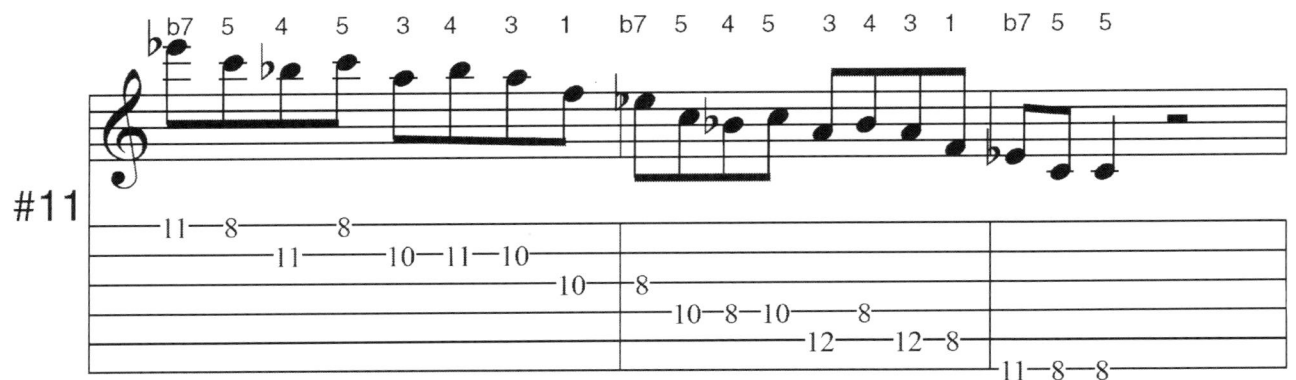

Repeat exercise #11 using lower chromatic NT of 5 instead of "4"

Descending dom. 7th arpeggio w/ upper neighboring tone for 1 & lower for b7

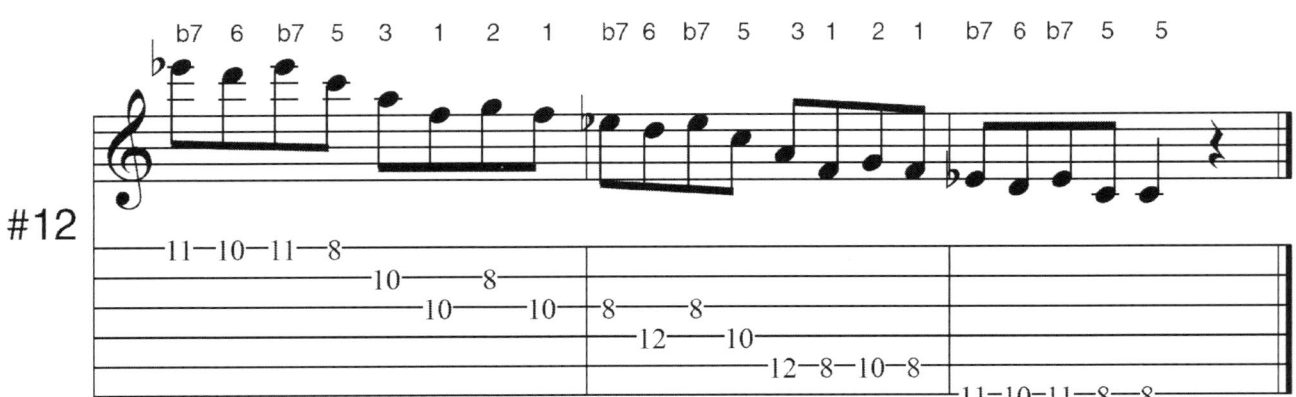

PAT. 5 MIXOLYDIAN ARPEGGIO w/ NEIGHBORING TONES

Descending dom. 7th arpeggio w/ lower neighboring tones for 3 & b7

Repeat exercise #1 using lower chromatic NT of 3 instead of "2"

Descending dom. 7th arpeggio w/ lower neighboring tones for 1 & 5

Repeat exercise #2 using lower chromatic NT of 5 instead of "4"

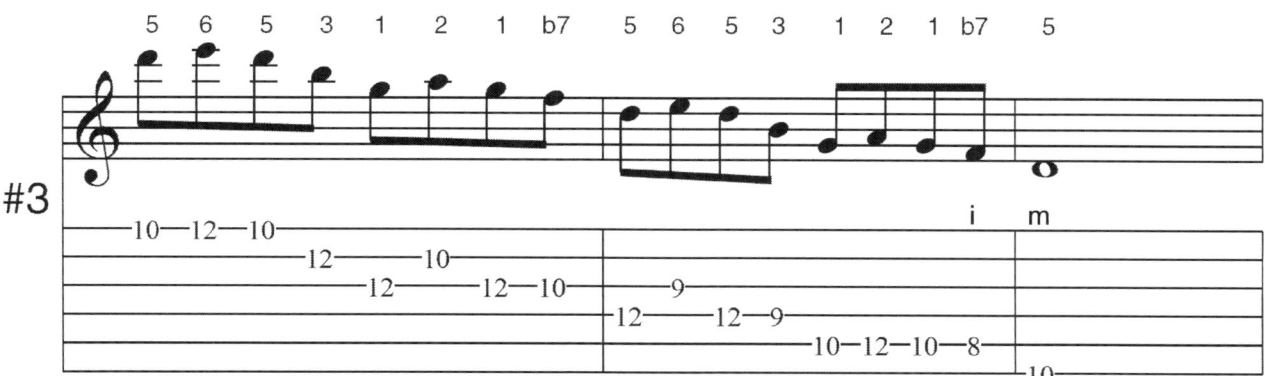

Descending dom. 7th arpeggio w/ upper neighboring tones for 1 & 5

PAT. 5 MIXOLYDIAN ARPEGGIO w/ NEIGHBORING TONES

Ascending dom. 7th arpeggio w/ lower neighboring tones for 3 & b7

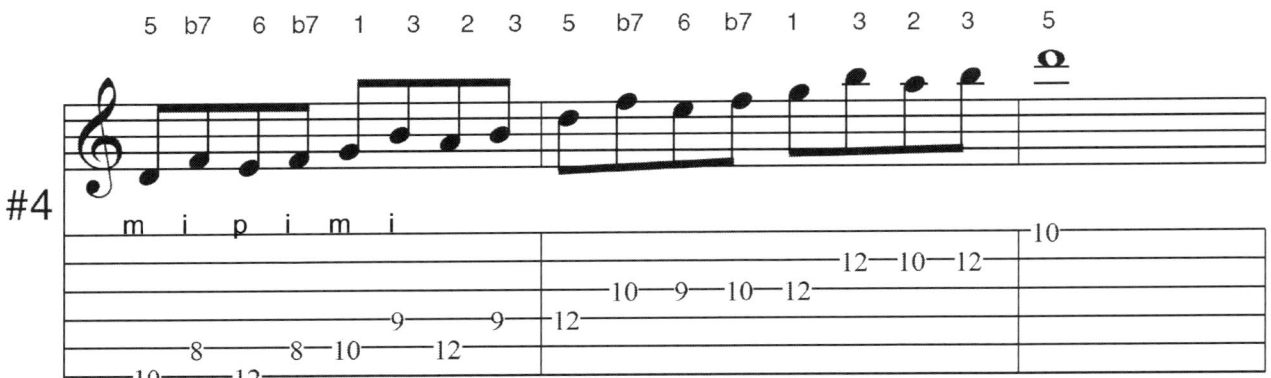

Repeat exercise #4 using lower chromatic NT of 3 instead of "2"

Ascending dom. 7th arpeggio w/ lower neighboring tones for 5 & 1

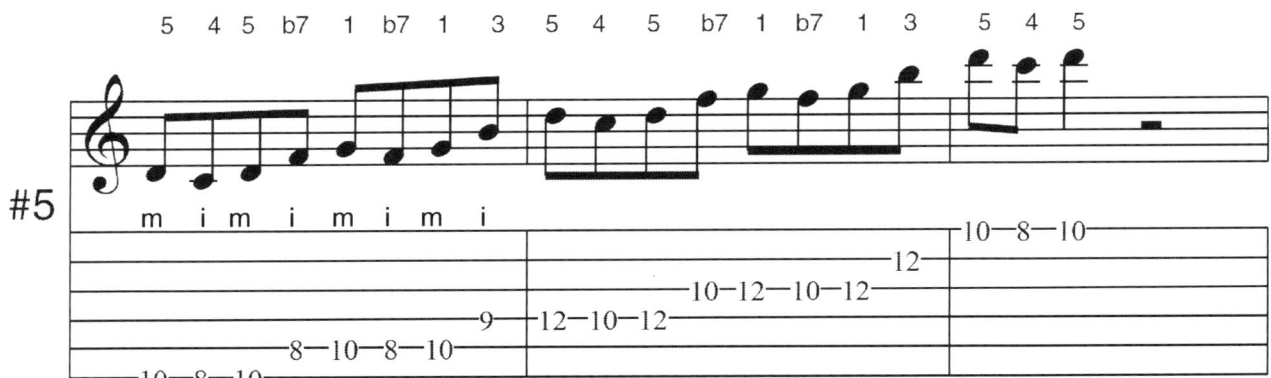

Repeat exercise #5 using lower chromatic NT of 5 instead of "4"

Ascending dom. 7th arpeggio w/ upper neighboring tones for 1 & 5

PAT. 5 MIXOLYDIAN ARPEGGIO w/ NEIGHBORING TONES

Ascending dom. 7th arpeggio w/ upper neighboring tones for 3 & b7

Ascending dom. 7th arpeggio w/ lower neighboring tone for 3 & upper for 5

Repeat exercise #8 using lower chromatic NT of 3 instead of "2"

Ascending dom. 7th arpeggio w/ upper neighboring tone for 3 & lower for 5

Repeat exercise #9 using lower chromatic NT of 5 instead of "4"

29

PAT. 5 MIXOLYDIAN ARPEGGIO w/ NEIGHBORING TONES

Descending dom. 7th arpeggio w/ lower neighboring tone for 3 & upper for 5

Repeat exercise #10 using lower chromatic NT of 3 instead of "2"

Descending dom. 7th arpeggio w/ upper neighboring tone for 3 & lower for 5

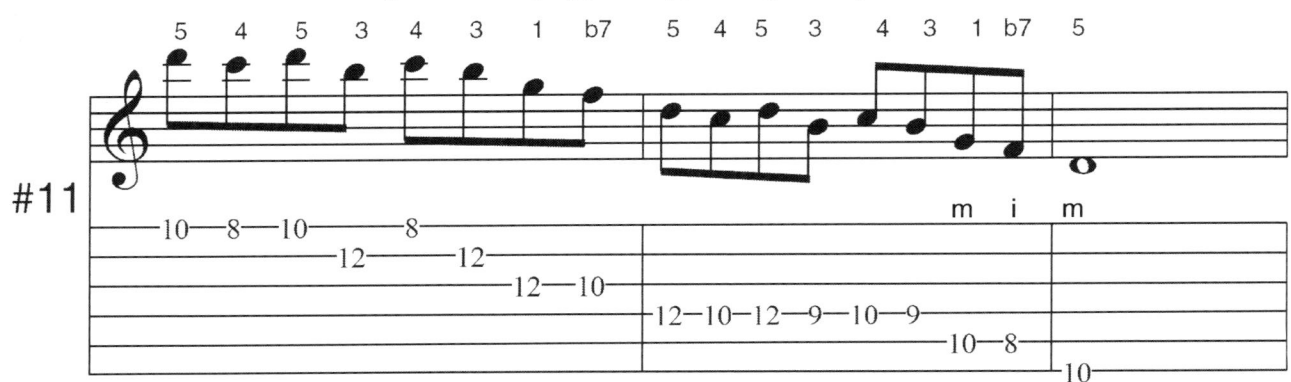

Repeat exercise #11 using lower chromatic NT of 5 instead of "4"

Descending dom. 7th arpeggio w/ upper neighboring tone for 1 & lower for b7

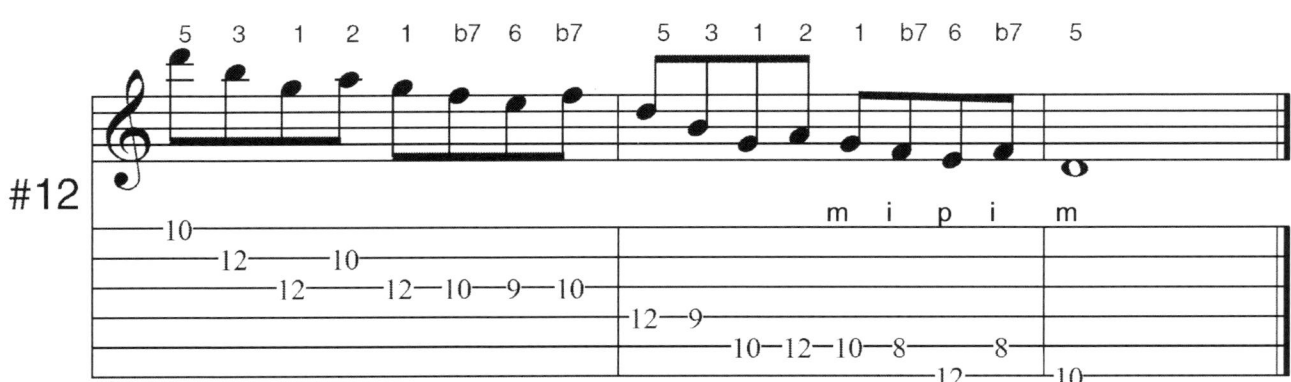

SUMMARY OF BEBOP CALISTHENICS 1A

ARPEGGIOS WITH NEIGHBORING TONES

For further instructions see APPENDIX 1: How to Practice using the Summary of Bebop Calisthenics (p.113).

Mixolydian (1 - 2 - 3 - 4 - 5 - 6 - ♭7) Play each exercise descending and ascending 🡇 🡅

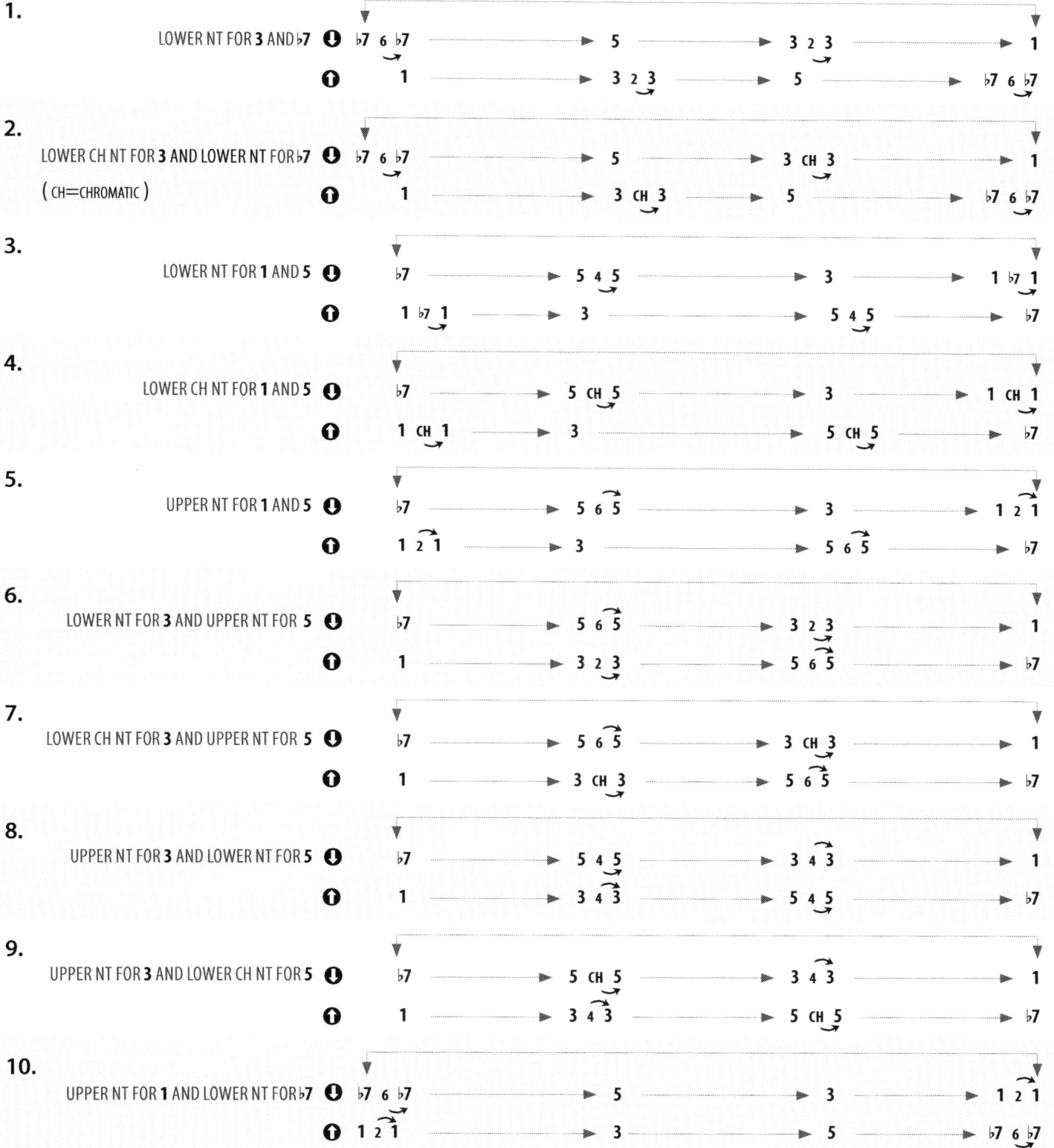

SUMMARY OF BEBOP CALISTHENICS 1B

ARPEGGIOS WITH NEIGHBORING TONES

Dorian (1 - 2 - ♭3 - 4 - 5 - 6 - ♭7) Play each exercise descending and ascending ⬇ ⬆

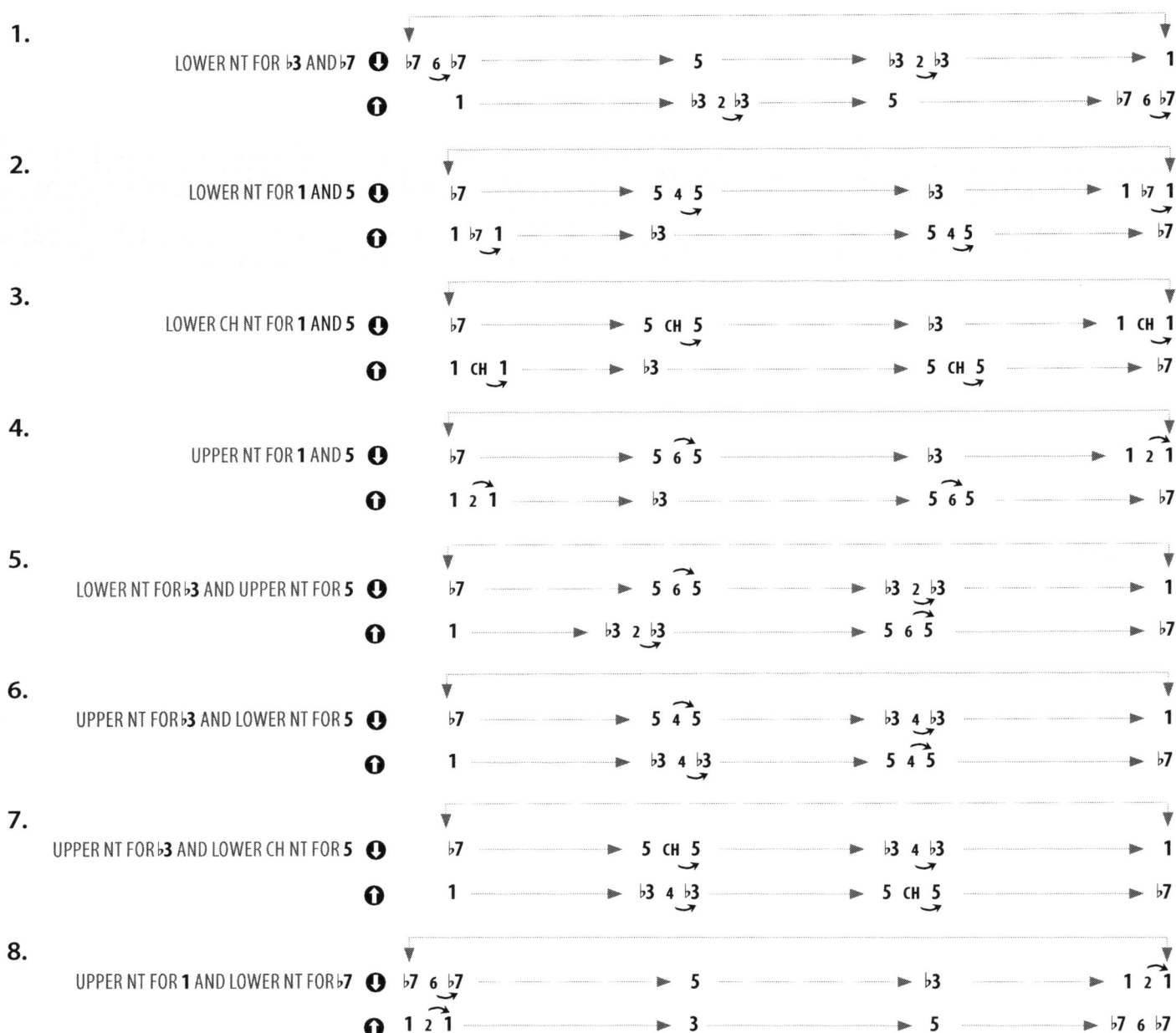

SUMMARY OF BEBOP CALISTHENICS 1C

ARPEGGIOS WITH NEIGHBORING TONES

Ionian (1 - 2 - 3 - 4 - 5 - 6 - 7) Play each exercise descending and ascending ⬇ ⬆

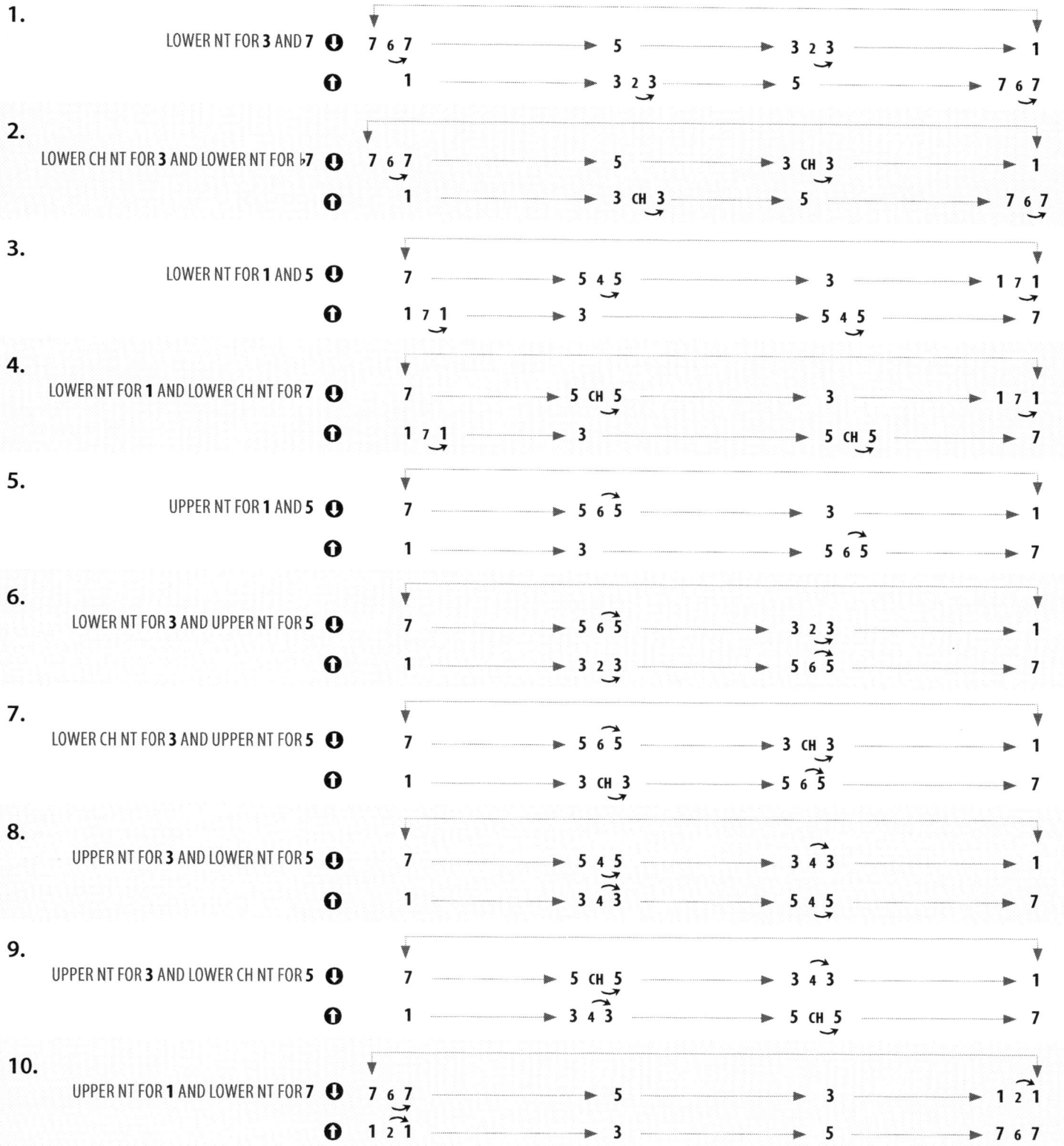

SUMMARY OF BEBOP CALISTHENICS 1D

ARPEGGIOS WITH NEIGHBORING TONES

Locrian (1 - ♭2 - ♭3 - 4 - ♭5 - ♭6 - ♭7) Play each exercise descending and ascending ⬇ ⬆

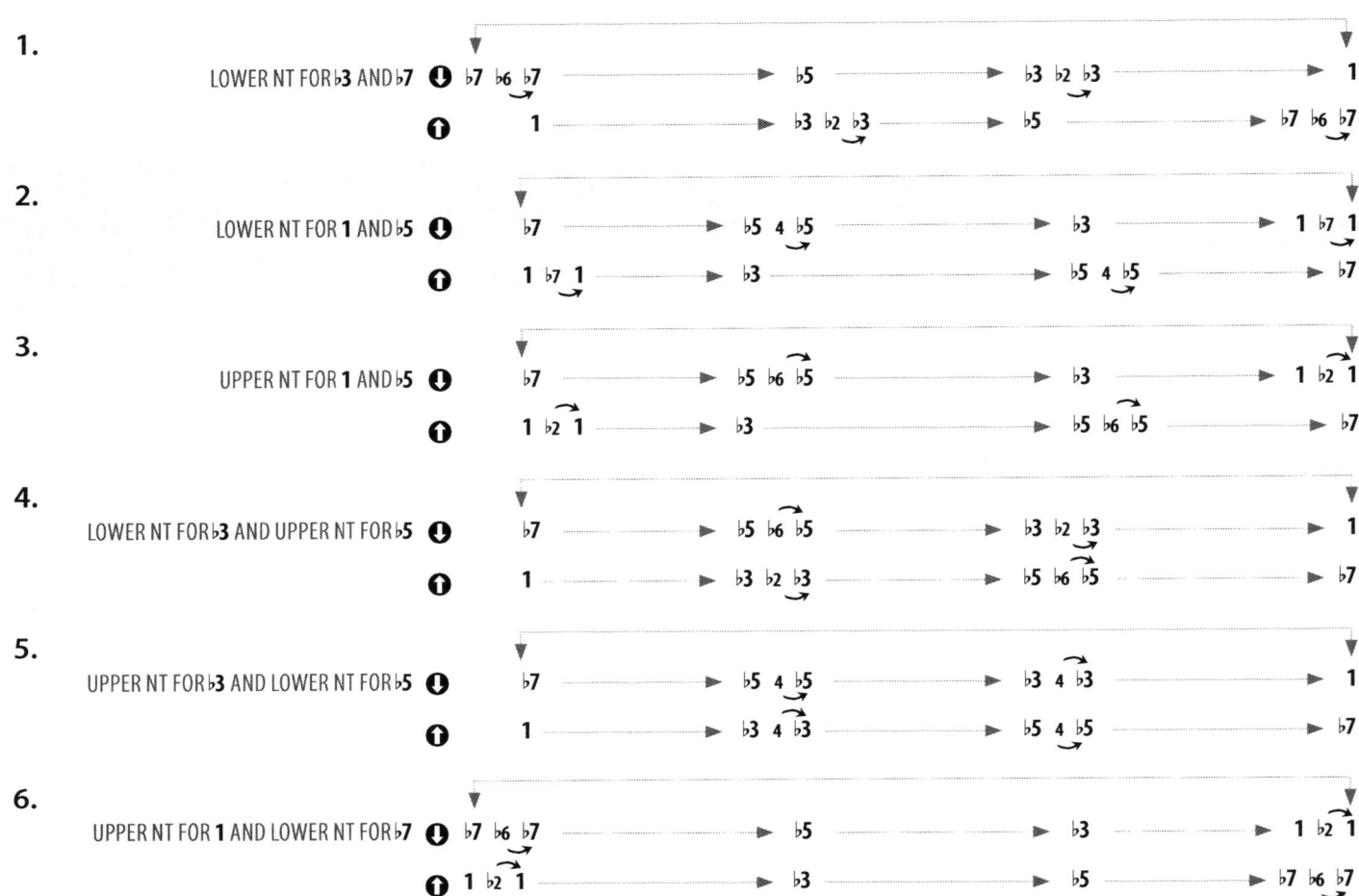

SPECIAL NOTE ON ALTERED DOMINANTS

As noted in the main lesson book (Lesson 6), the Super Locrian or Altered Dominant Scale has no «avoid» notes which in turn allows its derivative chord and arpeggio to include any of its tones. As a result, the nomenclature employed for its extensions varies depending on how the function of the 5th is understood within the underlying 7th chord formation (eg. dom7b5 or dom7#5). The following diagram illustrates the reasoning behind each label.

In the case of the exercises that follow, our underlying 4 part chord arpeggio will be comprised of the following scale degrees: 1 - 3 - #5 - b7 (configuration 2). Left over are the b2, #2 and #4. Although all can function as upper extensions within the chord, they will be used as neighboring tones for now. However, in the interval script the b2 and #2 will be labeled b9 and #9, regardless of their duration. This is done in the interest of reinforcing the location of these 2 tones when functioning as upper extensions. Not only is their nomenclature consistent within any configuration of the altered dominant, but they are also essential in portraying the characteristic sound of this chord.

It is assumed that at this point the student has a good grasp of the mixolydian mode. Therefore, if we use it as our initial reference we can easily derive an altered dominant scale from it by respectively altering all its degrees with the exception of the 3 and b7.

MIXOLYDIAN		ALTERED DOMINANT
1		1
2	alter to	b2 (b9) and #2 (#9)
3		3
4	alter to	#4 (#11)
5	alter to	#5 (b13)
6		(not available)
b7		b7

Initially it can be helpful to keep in mind that within the altered dominant scale:

the b9 is a 1/2 step above the 1
the #9 is a 1/2 step below the 3
the #11 is a whole step above the 3

The following pages demonstrate the Super Locrian-Pattern 6 arpeggio (introduced in Lesson 6), using its upper and lower neighboring tones. Its «Bebop Calisthenics Summary» applicable to all 7 fingerings, is available at the end of this section.

PAT. 6 ALTERED DOMINANT ARPEGGIO w/ NEIGHBORING TONES

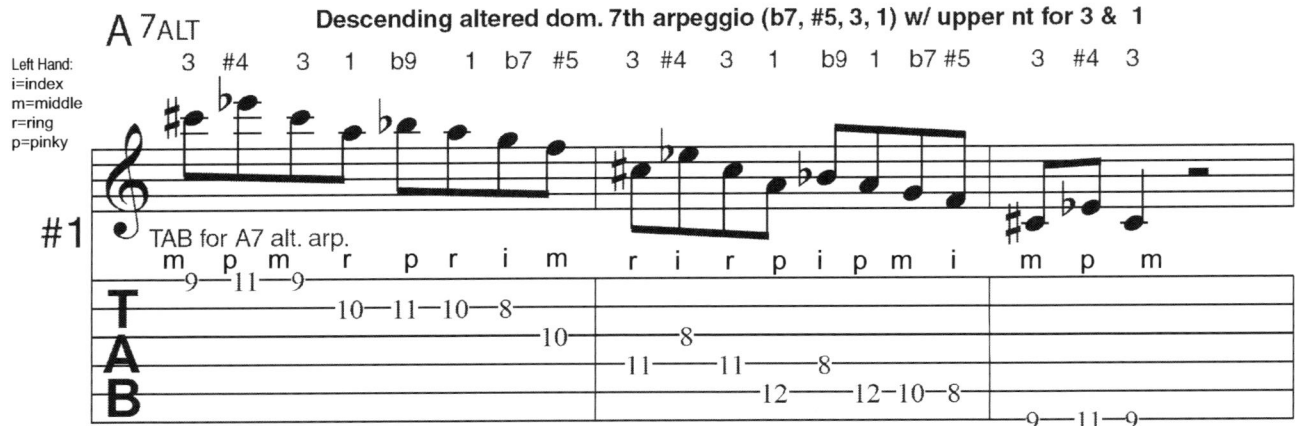

Descending altered dom. 7th arpeggio (b7, #5, 3, 1) w/ upper nt for 3 & 1

Descending altered dom. 7th arpeggio (b7, #5, 3, 1) w/ upper nt for #5 & b7

Descending altered dom. 7th arpeggio (b7, #5, 3, 1) w/ lower nt for 3 & b7

PAT. 6 ALTERED DOMINANT ARPEGGIO w/ NEIGHBORING TONES

Descending altered dom. 7th arpeggio (b7, #5, 3, 1) w/ upper nt for #5 & 1

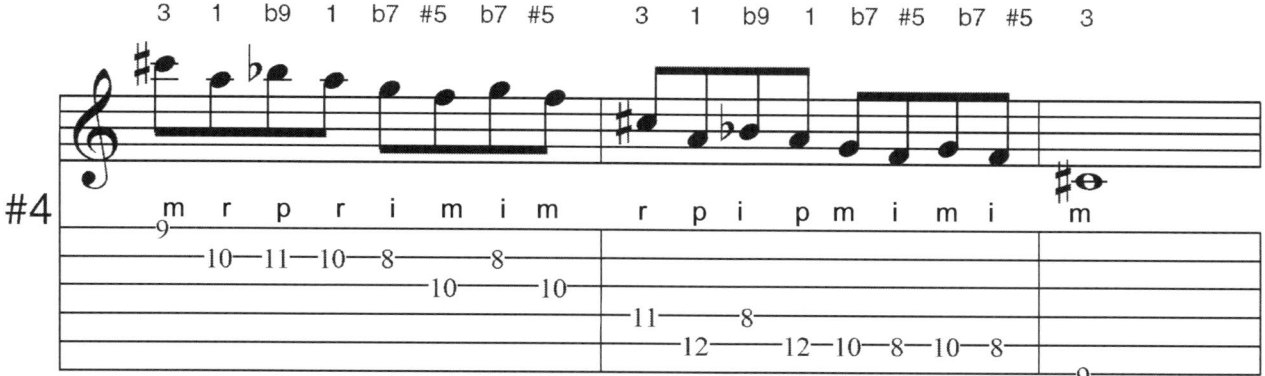

Ascending altered dom. 7th arpeggio (b7, #5, 3, 1) w/ upper nt for 3 & 1

Ascending altered dom. 7th arpeggio (b7, #5, 3, 1) w/ upper nt for #5 & 1

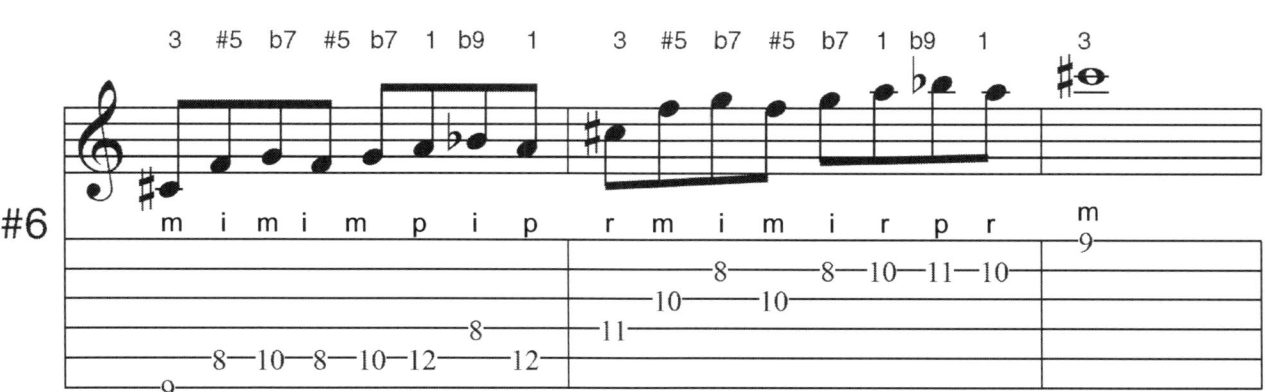

PAT. 6 ALTERED DOMINANT ARPEGGIO w/ NEIGHBORING TONES

Ascending altered dom. 7th arpeggio (b7, #5, 3, 1) w/ lower nt for 3 & upper for 1

Ascending altered dom. 7th arpeggio (b7, #5, 3, 1) w/ lower nt for #5 & upper for 1

Descending altered dom. 7th arpeggio (b7, #5, 3, 1) w/ lower nt for 3 & #5

PAT. 6 ALTERED DOMINANT ARPEGGIO w/ NEIGHBORING TONES

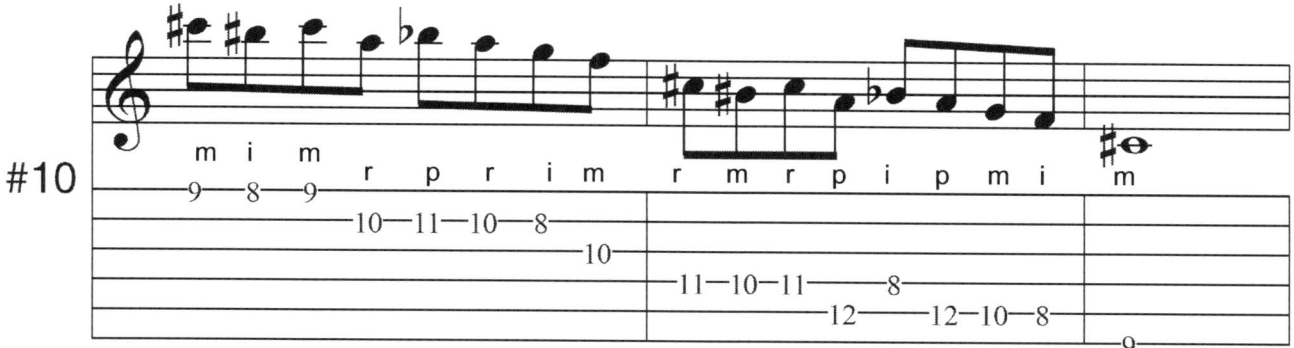

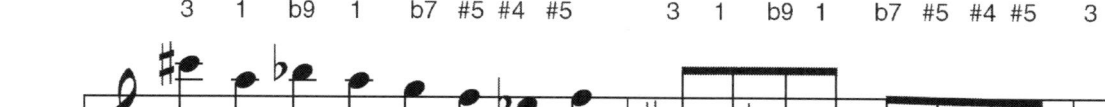

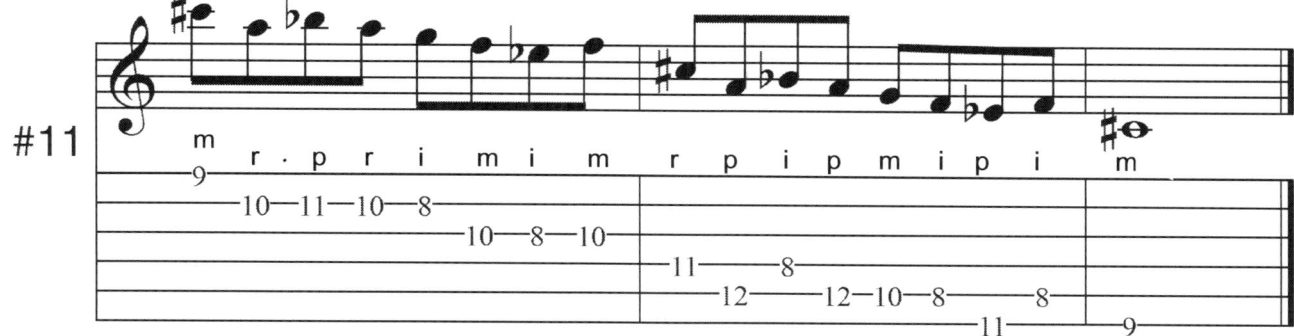

39

SUMMARY OF BEBOP CALISTHENICS 1E

ARPEGGIOS WITH NEIGHBORING TONES

Super Locrian (1 - ♭2 - ♯2 - 3 - ♯4 - ♯5 - ♭7) Play each exercise descending and ascending ⬇ ⬆

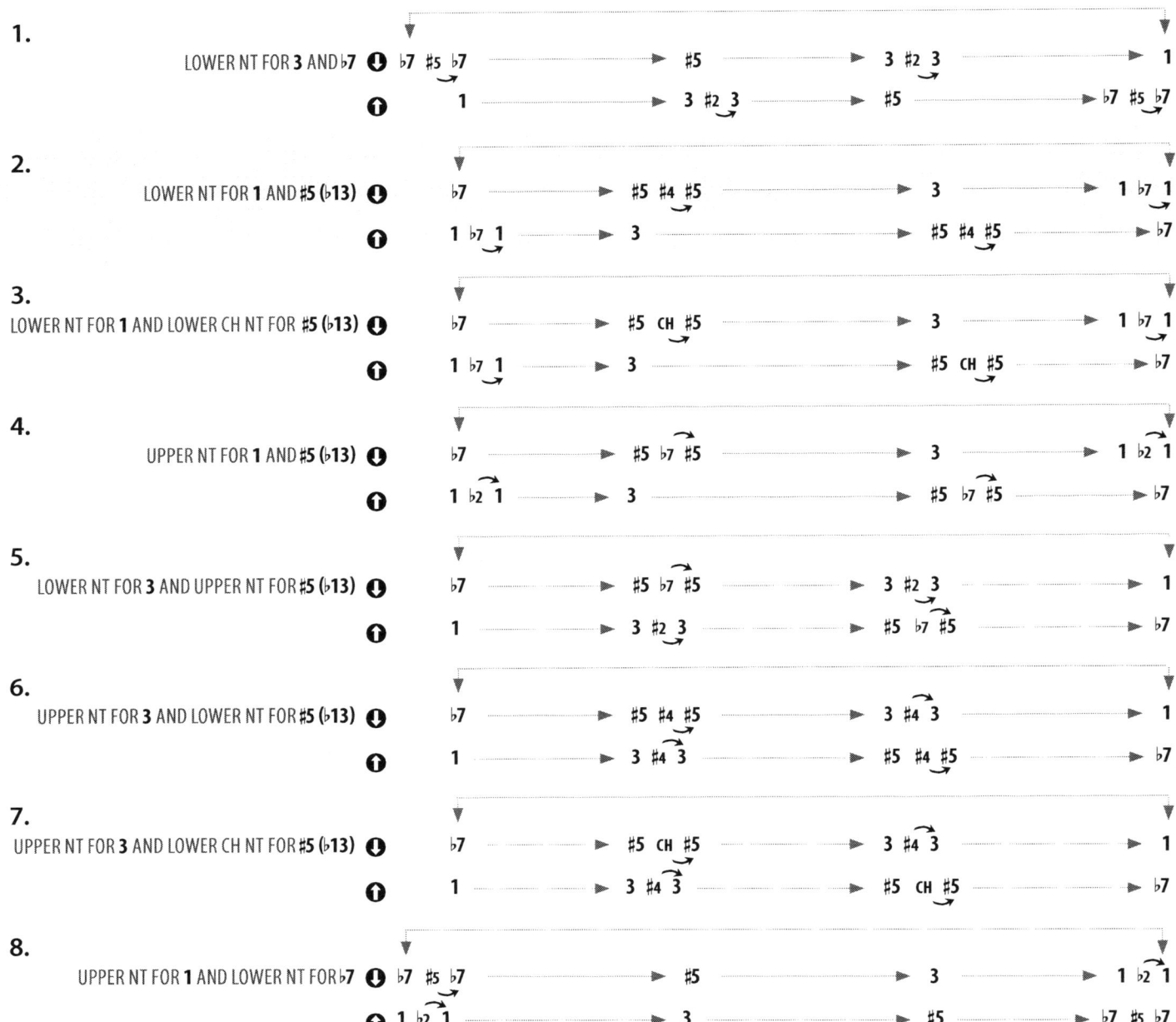

RHYTHM LAB 2 : INTRODUCING SYNCOPATION

If you want your lines to swing, understanding the concept of syncopation is of the essence! In jazz, *syncopation occurs whenever we place an accent on an upbeat, or extend a note starting on an upbeat for more than an 8th note.* Although time is a relative concept and this definition would vary for music at a fast tempo, I believe it is accurate enough for slow to medium swing which is the tempo we will be dealing with throughout this series.

In order to have a good grasp of syncopated rhythms, it is crucial to keep track of downbeats and upbeats. The following exercise was conceived with the purpose of getting you accustomed to feel and keep track of where the 8th note downbeats and upbeats lie within a measure of 4/4 time. Please spend as much time as needed to get comfortable at it, as it will help you acquire a foundation for all the rhythms that follow.

PROCEDURE: *Practice the following rhythms using any single note, while simultaneously tapping your foot in sync with the downbeat and upbeat arrows above each rhythmic value. Be sure to use «alternate picking» which in turn should mimic the downward and upward motion of your foot. During the rests, if necessary you may keep your pick in motion without touching the string—again, always staying in sync with your foot! This will help initially in keeping track of when you are on a downbeat or upbeat.*

SUBDIVIDING IN 8TH NOTES: «DOWNBEATS & UPBEATS»

The following exercise, «Syncopated Rhythms 1», consists of 2 beat patterns. They can be viewed as the rhythmic cells that form the essence of numerous 4 beat phrases containing syncopation in the bebop idiom. This should become evident when you play the etudes in the main lesson book, as well as «Syncopated Rhythms 2» in the upcoming pages.

Each rhythm below (except #6), appears twice, notated in 2 different ways. Although «Notation B» will be employed throughout this series, it is recommended that you learn to sight-read and recognize both forms as they will alternatively come up in written music.

 As customary, practice these rhythms using any single note, while simultaneously tapping your foot in sync with each downbeat and upbeat. Remember to use «alternate picking» which in turn should mimic the downward and upward motion of your foot. Initially you may need to subdivide in eighth notes by counting: «1 and 2 and» etc. to know precisely where each note starts. Your goal however, should be to internally preconceive how each rhythm sounds at just a quick glance—as if it were a familiar written word!

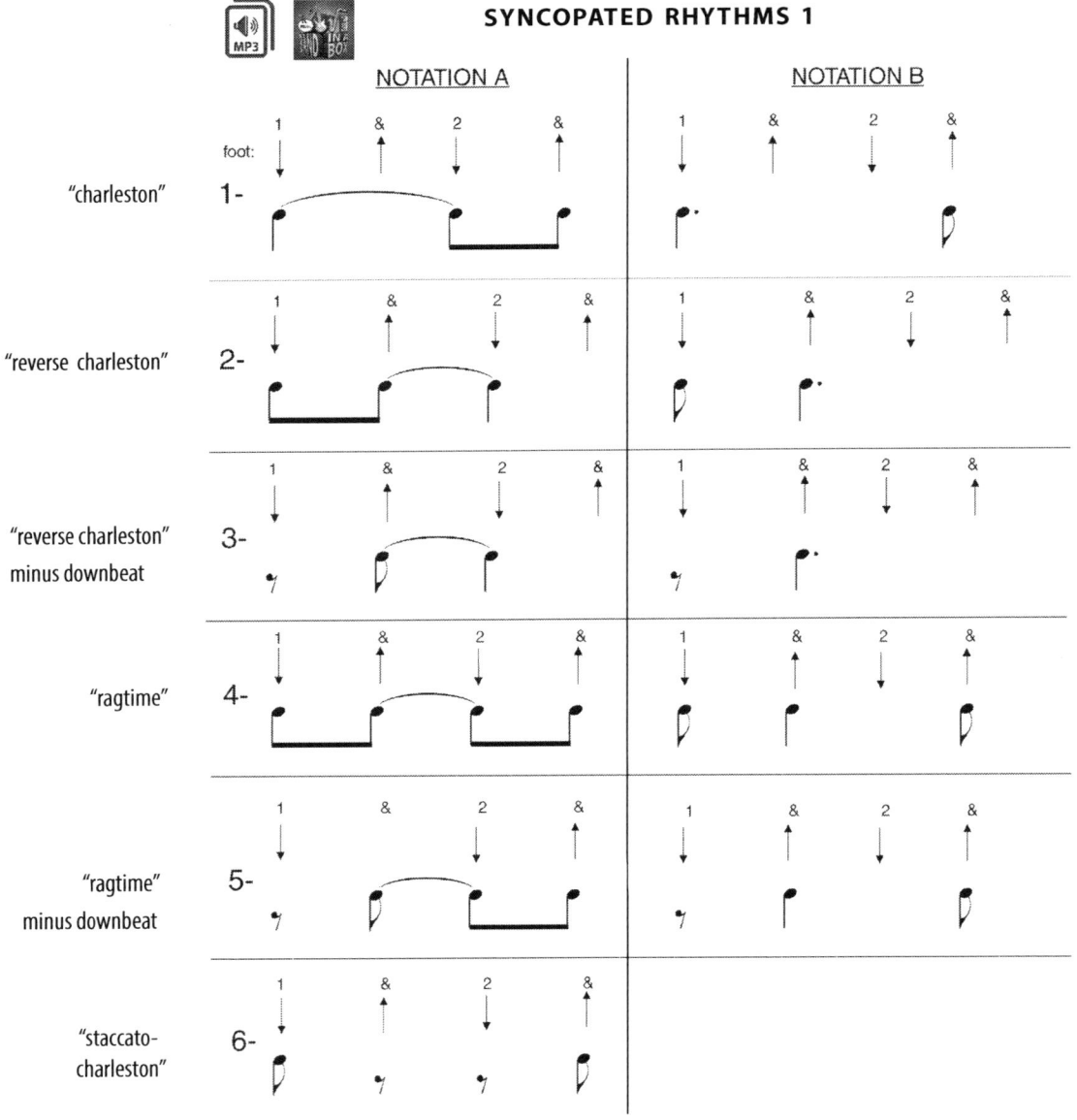

COMBINING EIGHTH NOTE TRIPLETS AND SWING EIGHTH NOTES

In «Syncopated Rhythms 2» we will explore 4/4 phrases featuring several of the 2 beat rhythm cells introduced in the previous study, frequently in combination with eighth note triplets. Because I have found that many new improvisors are not initially comfortable transitioning between swing eighth notes and eighth note triplets, I am including this preparatory exercise.

One way to grasp the concept of eighth note triplets is to view any beat of the measure in which they are present, as a «micro measure» of 3/4 time in itself. Correctly speaking, when doing so, we are actually feeling said measure in 3/8 time. Because we are subdividing in 3, we count: «1-2-3» or «1-and-a» during the course of that beat. If you are comfortable feeling swing eighth notes you are already doing this, knowingly or not. As previously noted, 2 swing eighth notes consist of playing the first 2 figures of the triplet tied together, followed by the 3rd figure:

Here is a measure alternating eighth note triplets with swing eighth notes. Notice how the triplet feel constitutes the foundation to properly play the swing eighth notes:

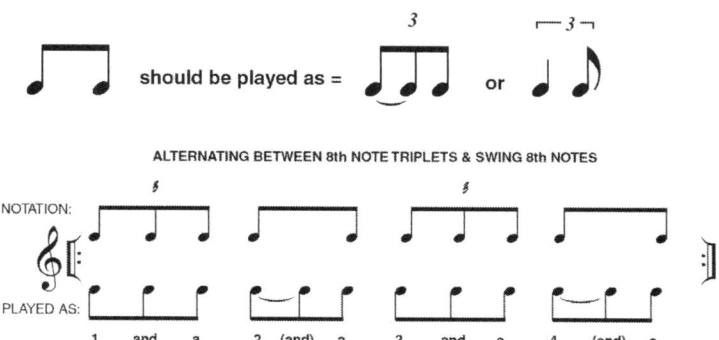

I have previously advised beginners to sync & mimic with their picking, the downward and upward motion of their foot in order to better keep track of downbeats and upbeats. However, when playing eighth note triplets this is not possible due to the 3 pick strokes. This is an instance where the motion of the pick is independent of the foot. When performing the following exercise, try as best as you can to keep the downbeats and upbeats independently with your foot when playing eighth note triplets. Be sure to listen to the related audio files to make sure you are interpreting them correctly.

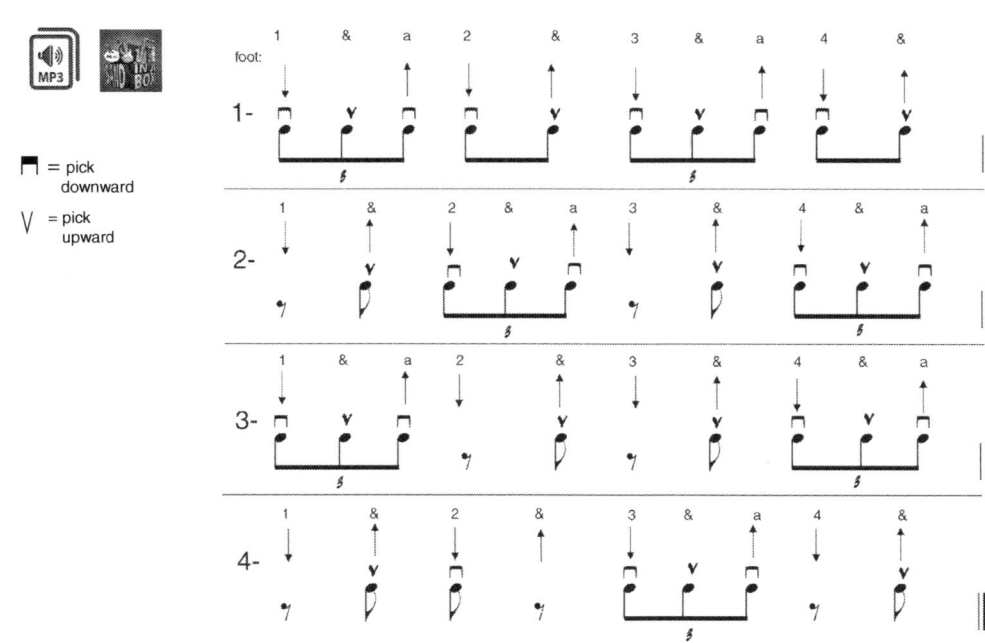

43

THE IMAGINARY BAR LINE

When a rhythmic figure straddles beats 2 & 3, it is preferable to notate the equivalent value using two tied figures. In doing so, we delineate a visual space that denotes the midpoint of the measure. This «imaginary bar line» helps us keep track of what beat of the measure we are currently on, especially when subdividing a syncopated figure that starts on the upbeat of 2. In the examples that follow, the first one is written ignoring the «imaginary bar line» principle. Notice how much harder it is to read than the second one which features the same phrase properly notated.

Please follow this procedure with the following exercises:

(1) Try to visualize the «imaginary bar line» between beats 2 and 3. (2) Identify any of the 2 beat rhythmic cells you learned in «Syncopated Rhythms 1» within either the first or second half of the upcoming 4 beat phrases. This will simplify the process of learning various syncopated rhythms in 4/4 by breaking them down into 2 components. (3) Play each phrase on any single note and be sure to synchronize it with the clocklike motion of your foot on each downbeat and upbeat.

SYNCOPATED RHYTHMS 2

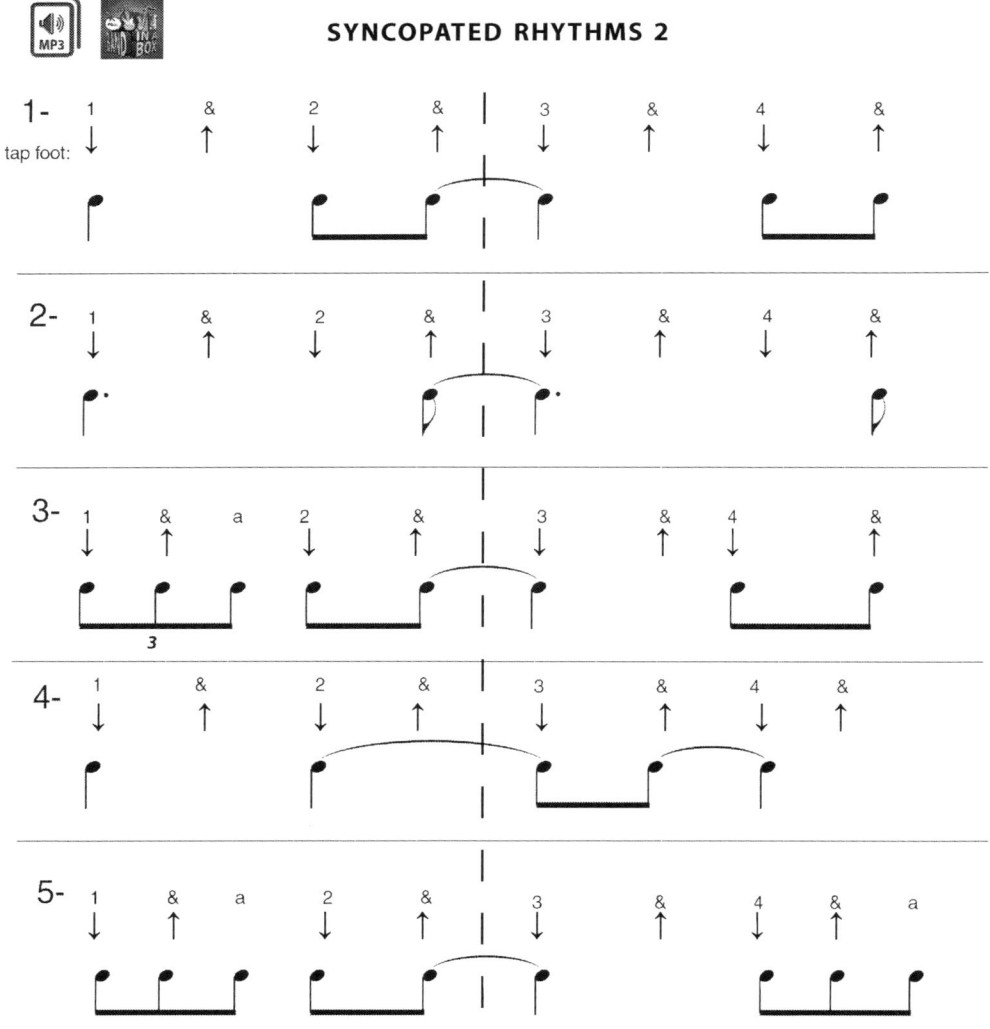

(SYNCOPATED RHYTHMS 2)

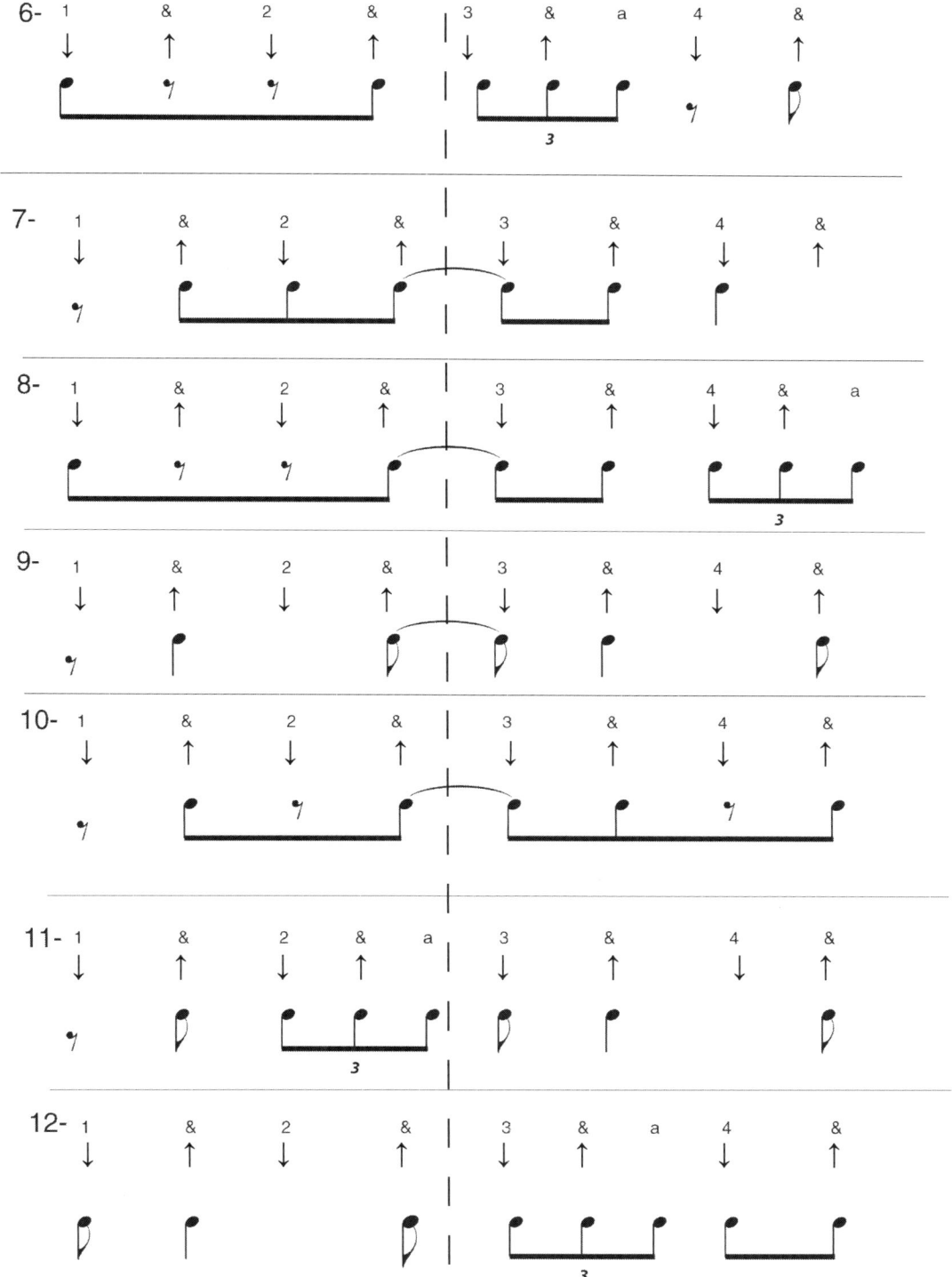

45

BEBOP
CALISTHENICS 2
ARPEGGIOS with UNPREPARED APPROACHES

MIXOLYDIAN PAT 1 / PAT 4 / PAT 5

**Summary for Mixolydian / Dorian /
Ionian / Locrian / Super Locrian**

PAT. 1 MIXOLYDIAN ARPEGGIO w/ UNPREPARED APPROACHES

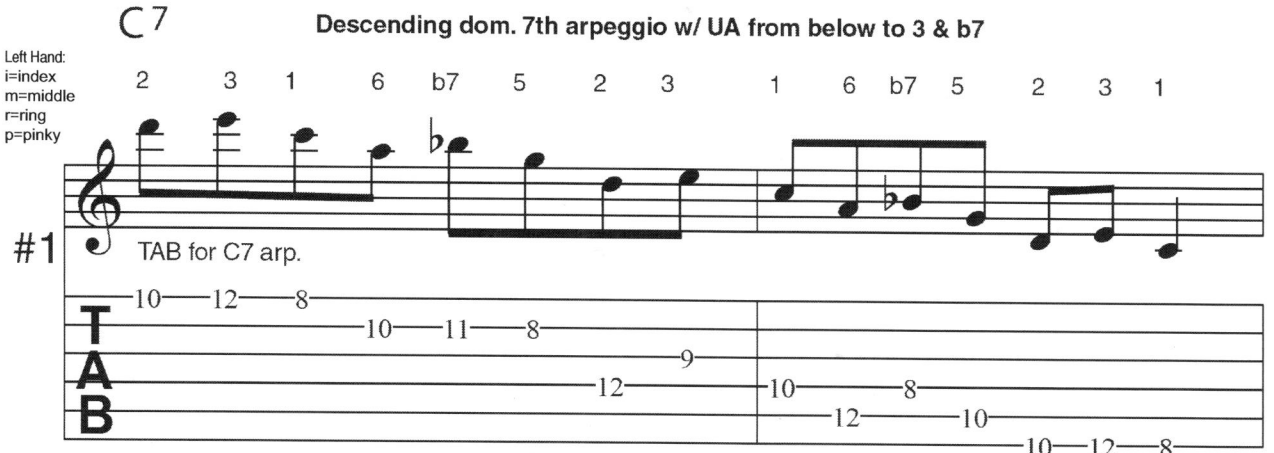

Repeat exercise #1 using lower chromatic UA to 3 instead of "2"

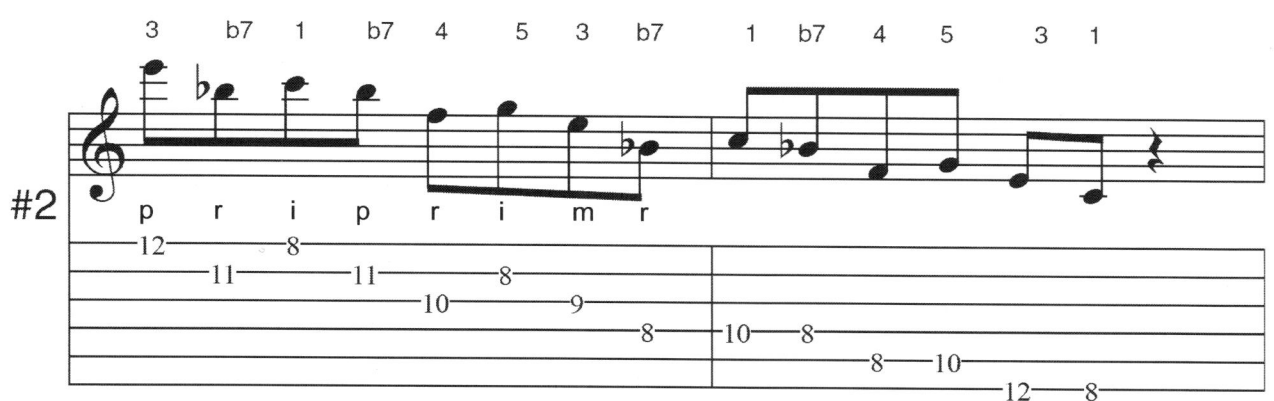

Repeat exercise #2 using lower chromatic UA of 5 instead of "4"

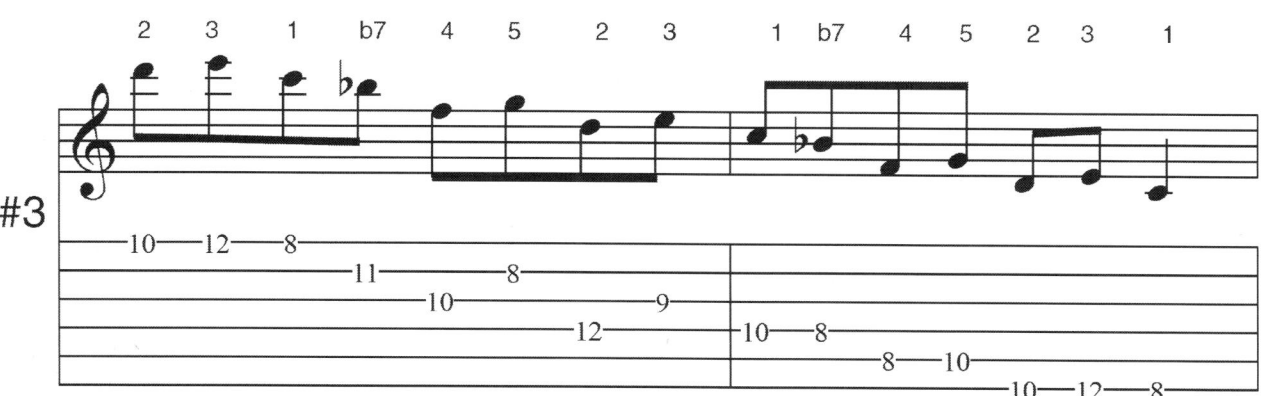

Repeat exercise #3 using lower chromatic UA of 3 instead of "2" and lower chromatic UA of 5 instead of "4"

PAT. 1 MIXOLYDIAN ARPEGGIO w/ UNPREPARED APPROACHES

Ascending dom. 7th arpeggio w/ UA from above to 3 & b7

Ascending dom. 7th arpeggio w/ UA from above to 5 & 1

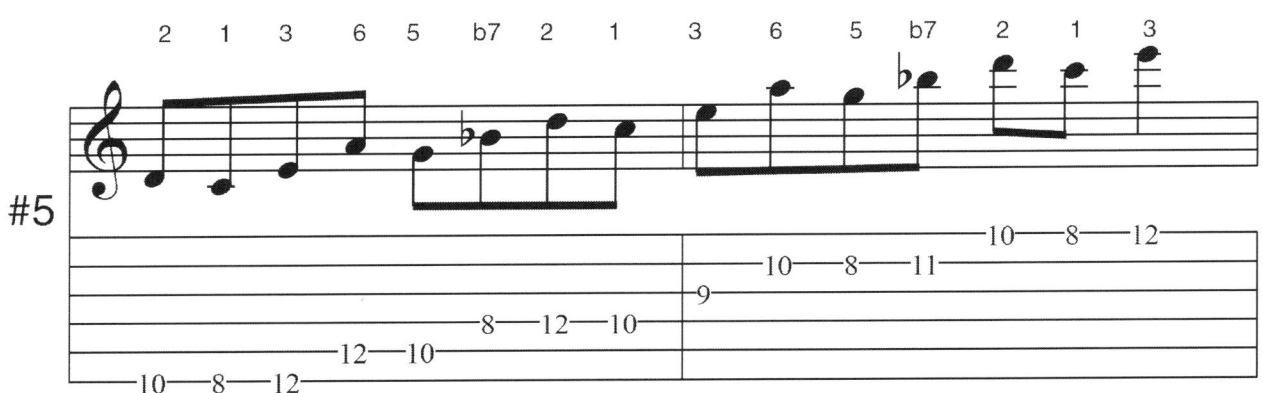

Ascending dom. 7th arpeggio w/ UA from above to 3 & 5

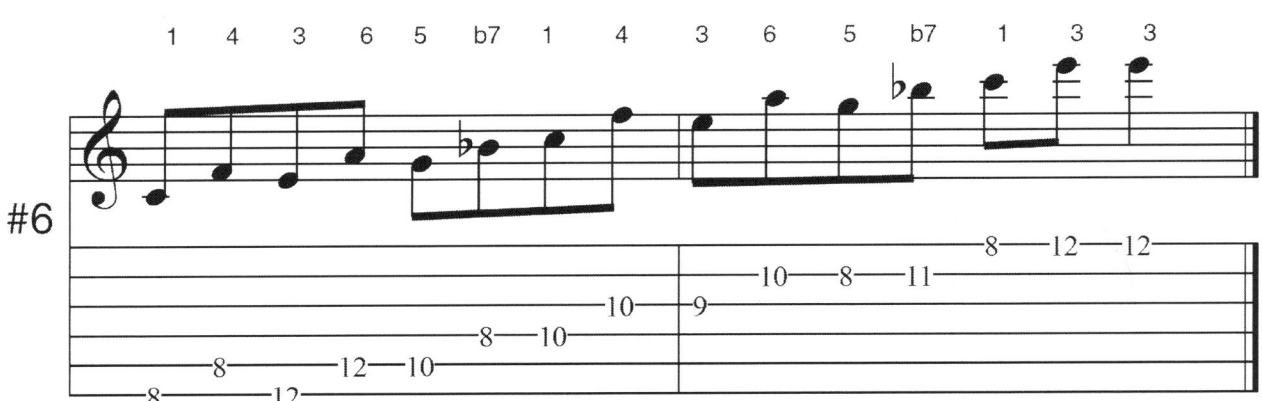

PAT. 4 MIXOLYDIAN ARPEGGIO w/ UNPREPARED APPROACHES

F7   **Descending dom. 7th arpeggio w/ UA from below to 3 & b7**

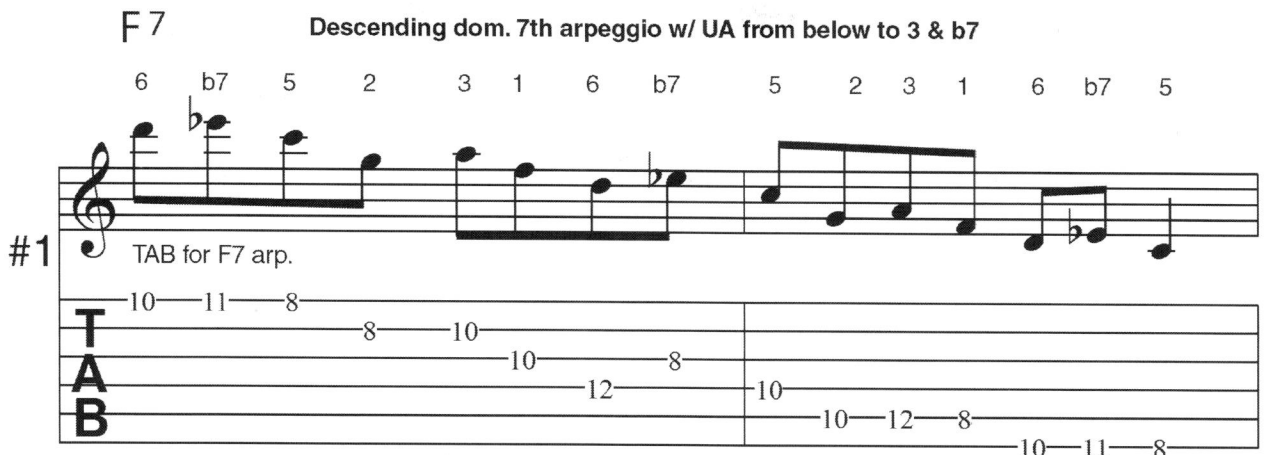

Repeat exercise #1 using lower chromatic UA to 3 instead of "2"

Descending dom. 7th arpeggio w/ w/ UA from below to 1 & 5

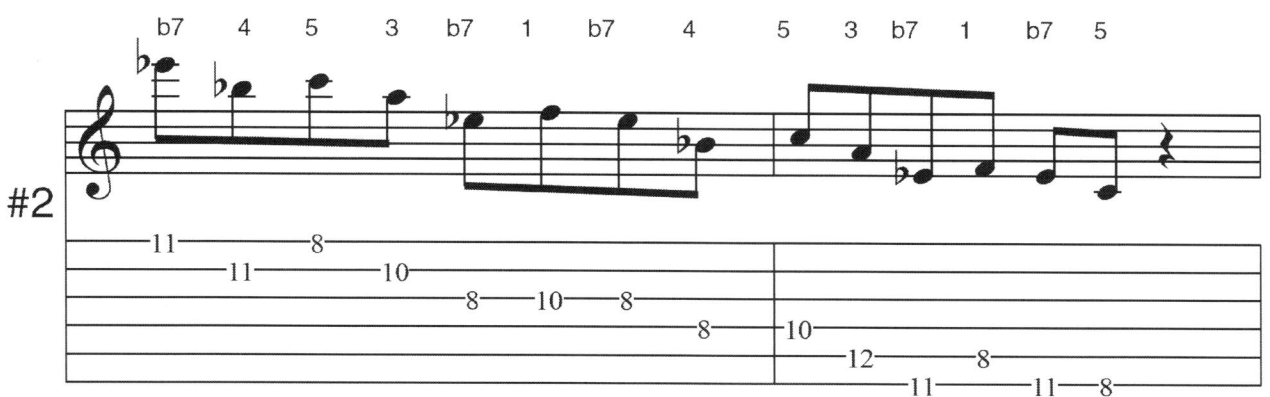

Repeat exercise #2 using lower chromatic UA of 5 instead of "4"

Descending dom. 7th arpeggio w/ UA from below to 3 & 5

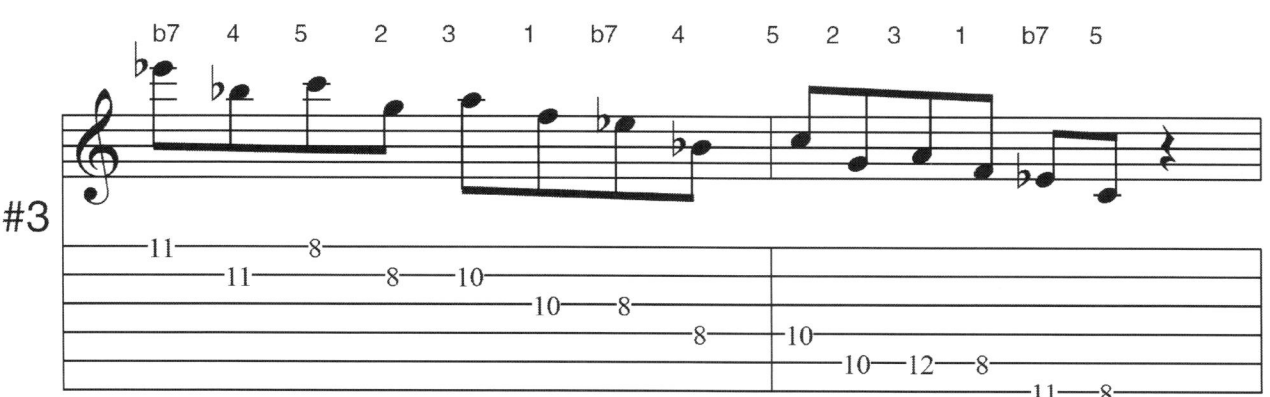

Repeat exercise #3 using lower chromatic UA of 3 instead of "2" and lower chromatic UA of 5 instead of "4"

49

PAT. 4 MIXOLYDIAN ARPEGGIO w/ UNPREPARED APPROACHES

Ascending dom. 7th arpeggio w/ UA from above to 3 & b7

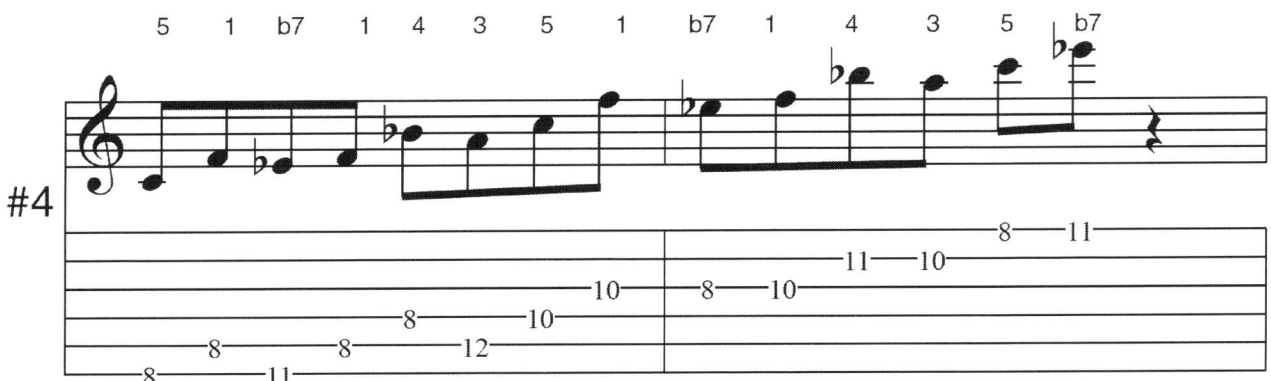

Ascending dom. 7th arpeggio w/ UA from above to 5 & 1

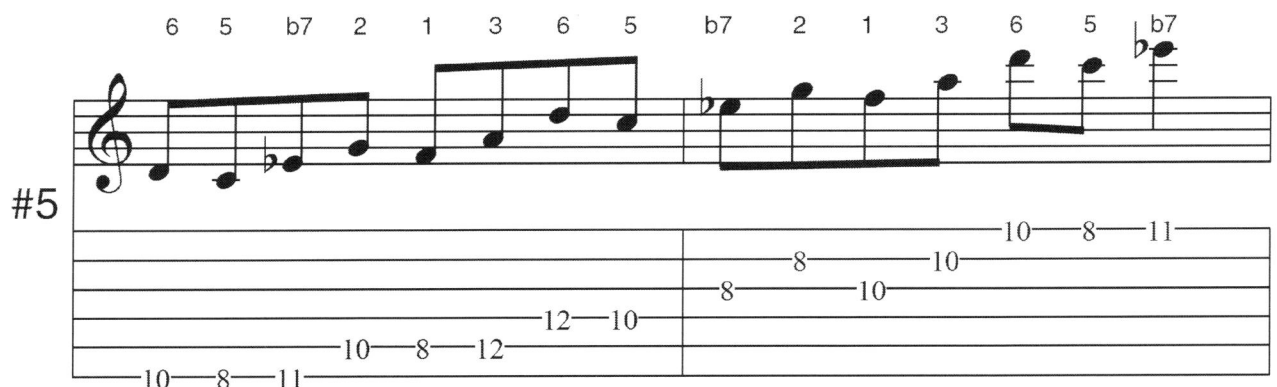

Ascending dom. 7th arpeggio w/ UA from above to 3 & 5

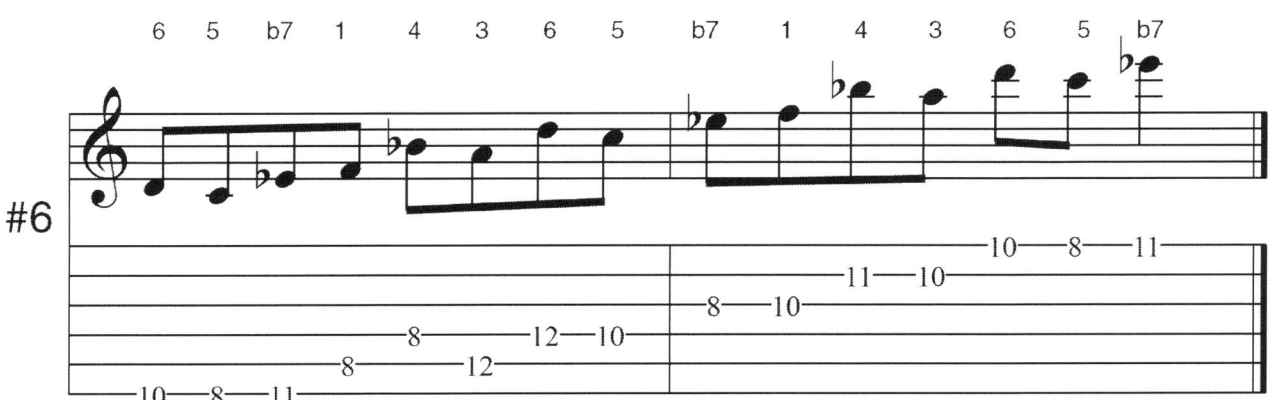

PAT. 5 MIXOLYDIAN ARPEGGIO w/ UNPREPARED APPROACHES

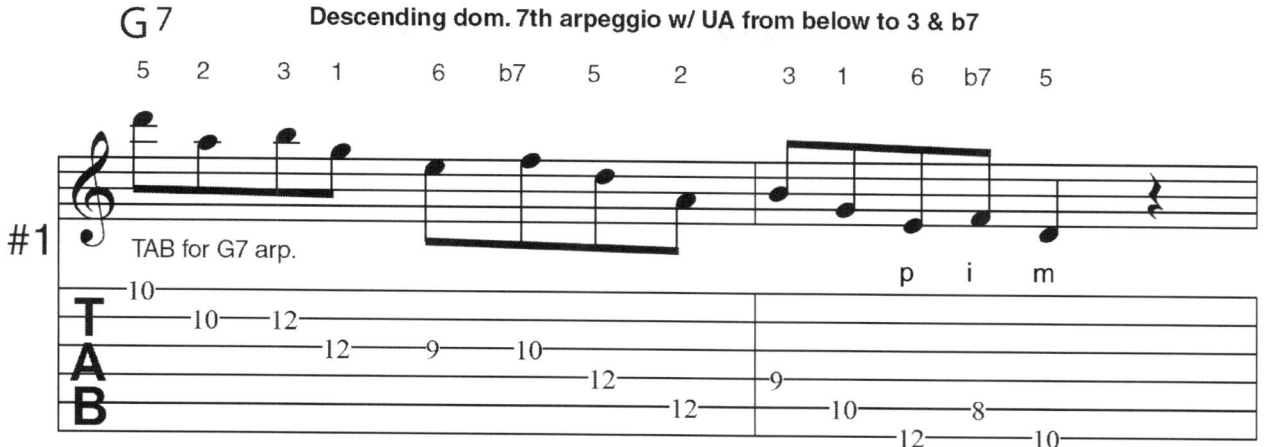

Repeat exercise #1 using lower chromatic UA to 3 instead of "2"

Repeat exercise #2 using lower chromatic UA of 5 instead of "4"

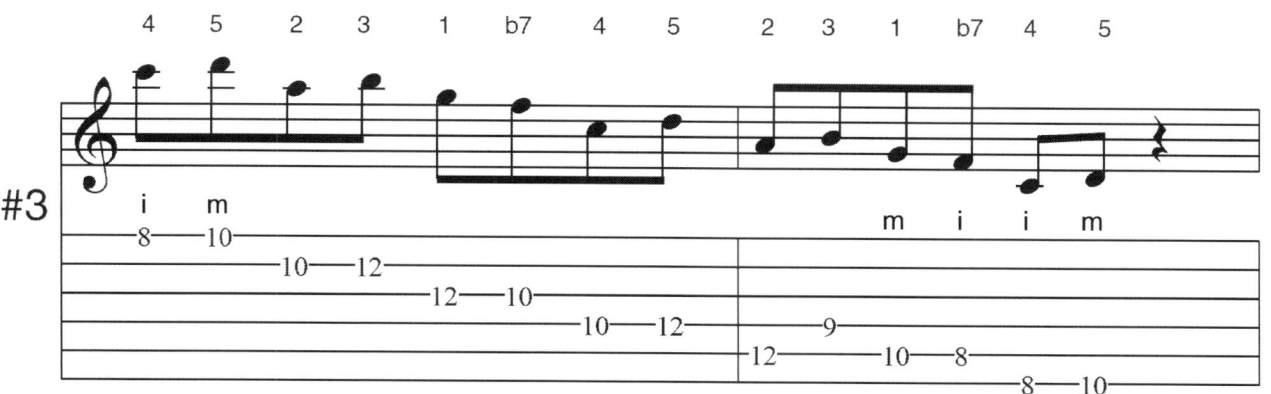

Repeat exercise #3 using lower chromatic UA of 3 instead of "2" and lower chromatic UA of 5 instead of "4"

PAT. 5 MIXOLYDIAN ARPEGGIO w/ UNPREPARED APPROACHES

Ascending dom. 7th arpeggio w/ UA from above to 3 & b7

Ascending dom. 7th arpeggio w/ UA from above to 5 & 1

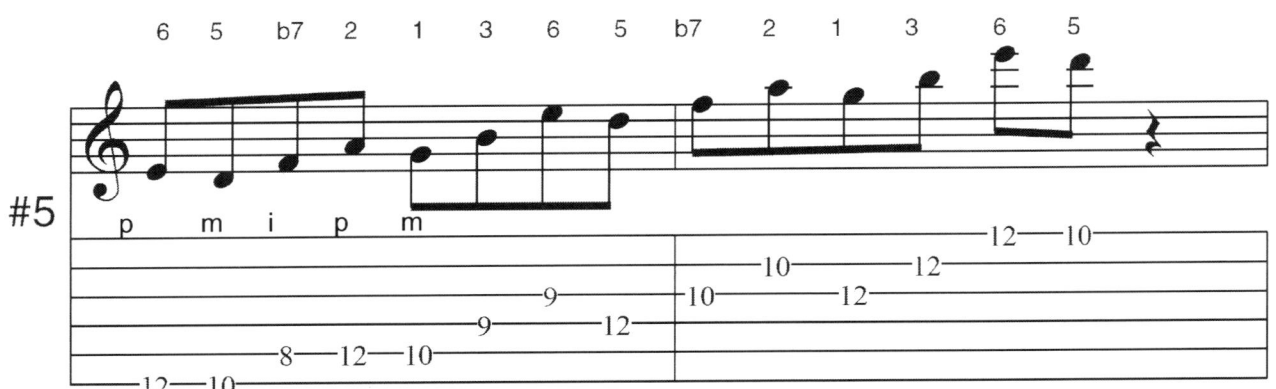

Ascending dom. 7th arpeggio w/ UA from above to 3 & 5

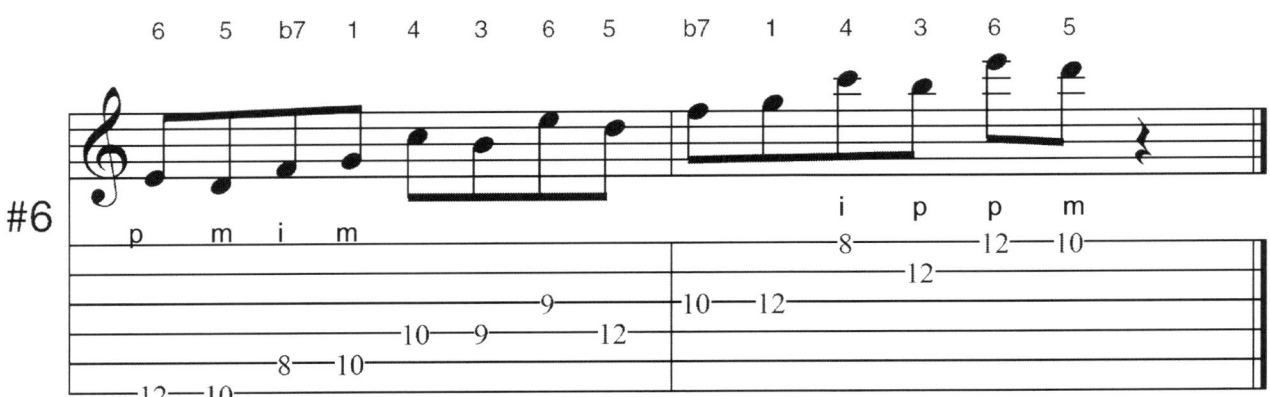

SUMMARY OF BEBOP CALISTHENICS 2A

ARPEGGIOS WITH UNPREPARED APPROACHES

Mixolydian (1 - 2 - 3 - 4 - 5 - 6 - ♭7)

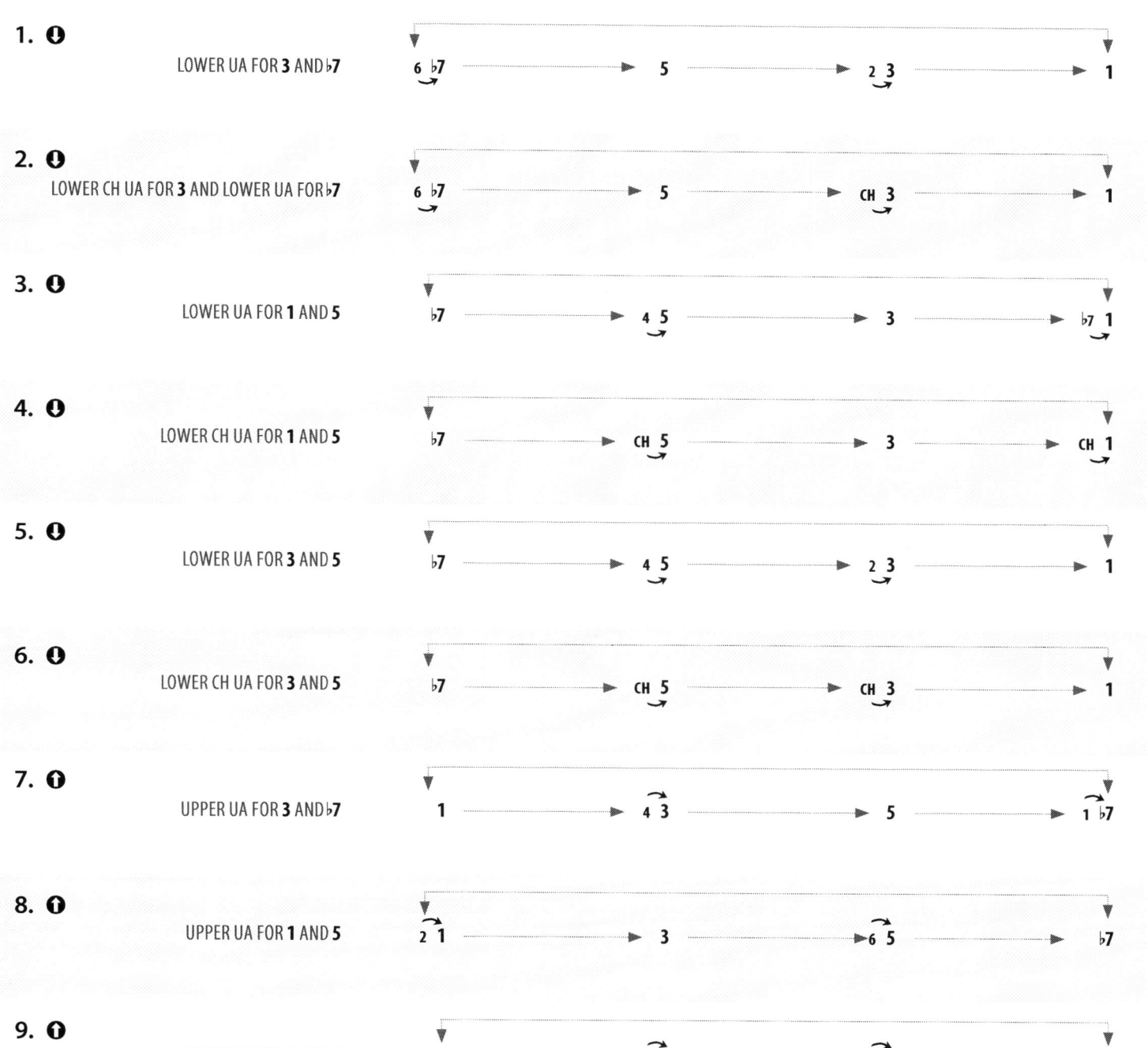

SUMMARY OF BEBOP CALISTHENICS 2B

ARPEGGIOS WITH UNPREPARED APPROACHES

Dorian (1 - 2 - ♭3 - 4 - 5 - 6 - ♭7)

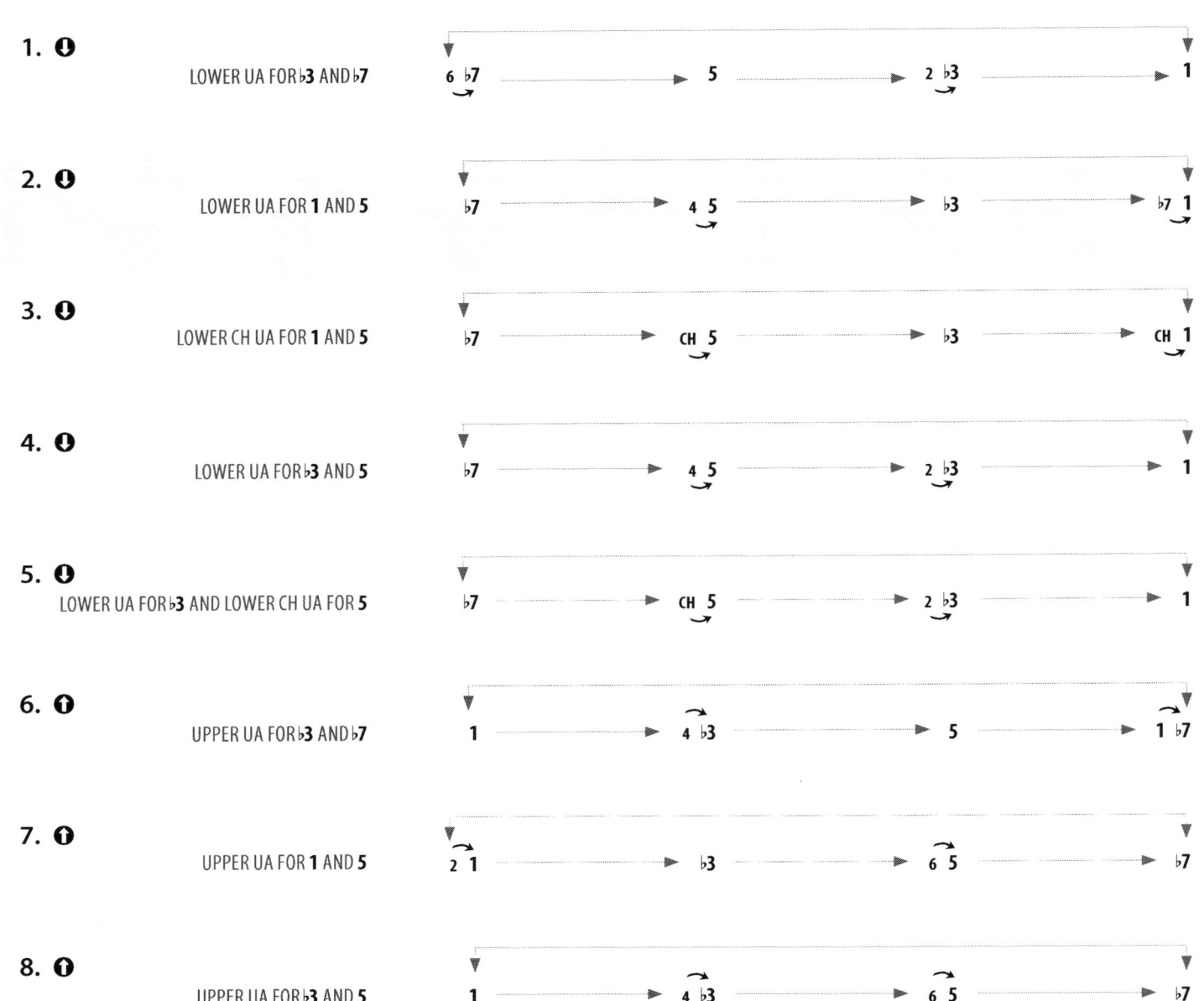

1. ↓
LOWER UA FOR ♭3 AND ♭7

2. ↓
LOWER UA FOR 1 AND 5

3. ↓
LOWER CH UA FOR 1 AND 5

4. ↓
LOWER UA FOR ♭3 AND 5

5. ↓
LOWER UA FOR ♭3 AND LOWER CH UA FOR 5

6. ↑
UPPER UA FOR ♭3 AND ♭7

7. ↑
UPPER UA FOR 1 AND 5

8. ↑
UPPER UA FOR ♭3 AND 5

SUMMARY OF BEBOP CALISTHENICS 2C

ARPEGGIOS WITH UNPREPARED APPROACHES

Ionian (1 - 2 - 3 - 4 - 5 - 6 - 7)

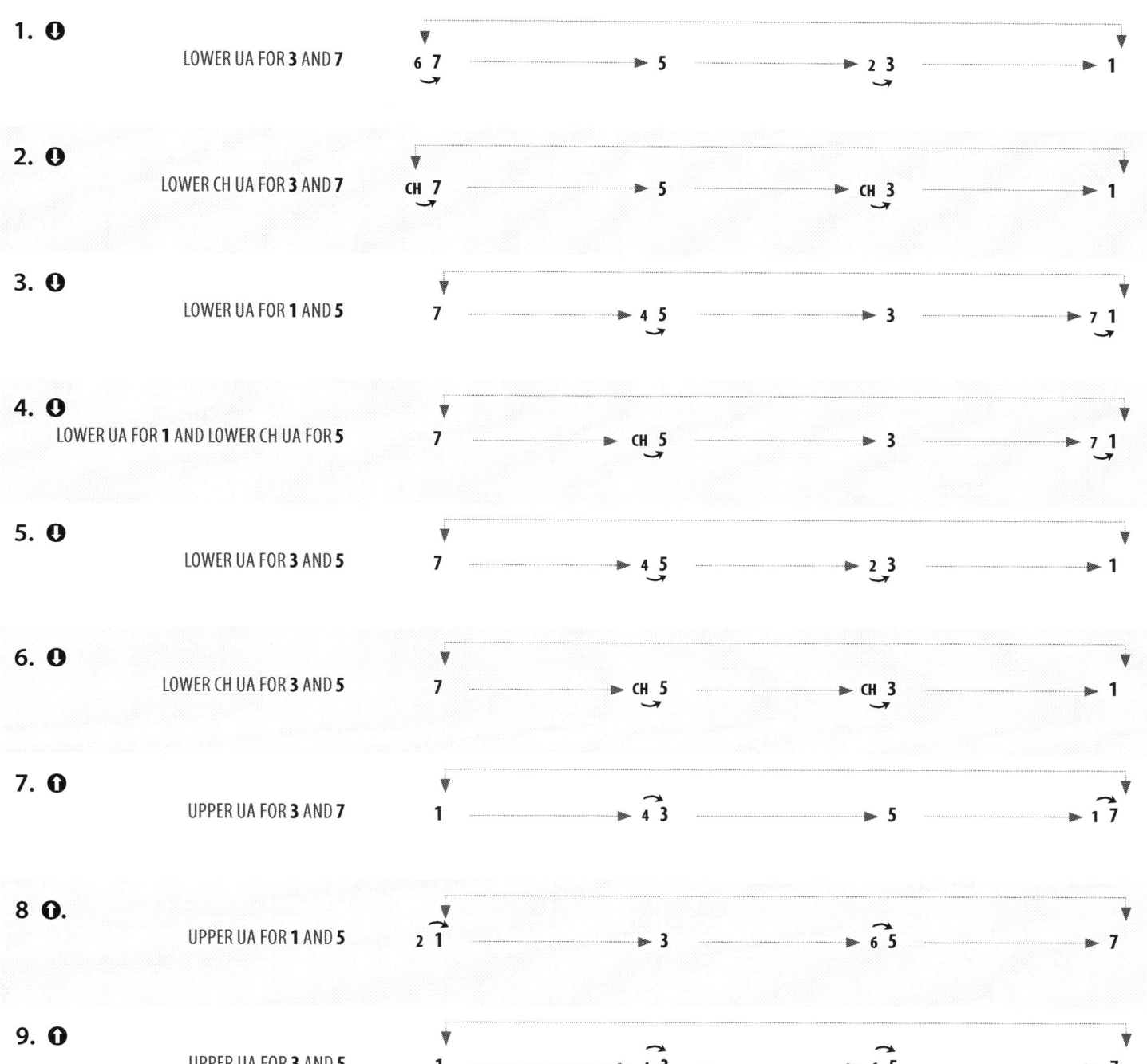

SUMMARY OF BEBOP CALISTHENICS 2D & 2E

ARPEGGIOS WITH UNPREPARED APPROACHES

Locrian (1 - ♭2 - ♭3 - 4 - ♭5 - ♭6 - ♭7)

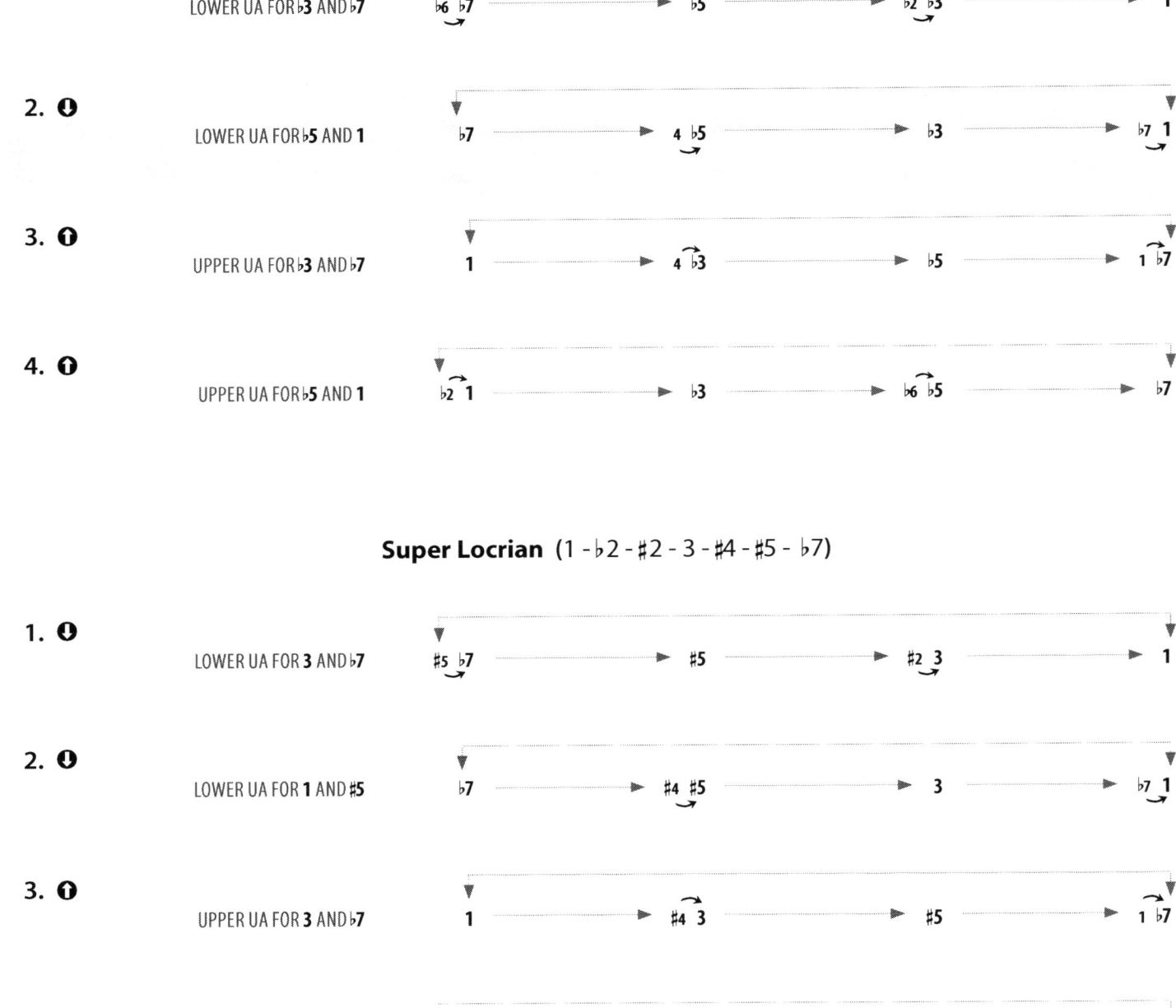

BEBOP
CALISTHENICS 3
ARPEGGIOS with 2 NOTE ENCLOSURES

MIXOLYDIAN PAT 1 / PAT 4 / PAT 5

**Summary for Mixolydian / Dorian /
Ionian / Locrian / Super Locrian**

PAT. 1 MIXOLYDIAN ARPEGGIO w/ 2 NOTE ENCLOSURES

C7 Descending dom. 7th arpeggio w/ enclosure from below and above to 3 & b7

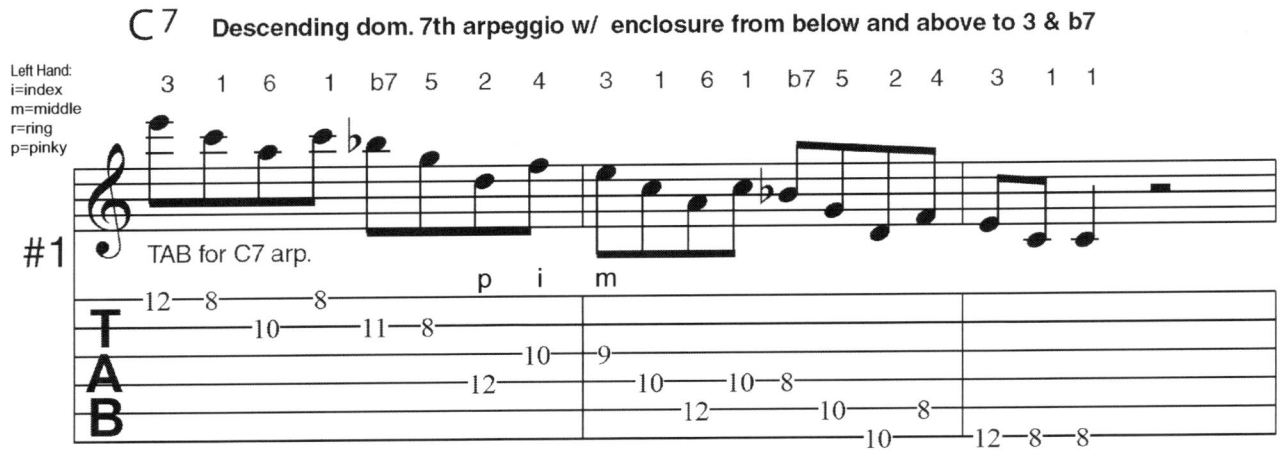

* Repeat exercise #1 using lower chromatic of 3 instead of "2" and upper chromatic of b7 instead of "1"

Descending dom. 7th arpeggio w/ enclosure from below and above to 1 & 5

* Repeat exercise #2 using lower chromatic of 1 instead of "b7" and lower chromatic of 5 instead of "4"

* Repeat exercise #2 using only chromatic enclosures from below and above to 1 and 5

Descending dom. 7th arpeggio w/ enclosure from above and below to 3 & b7

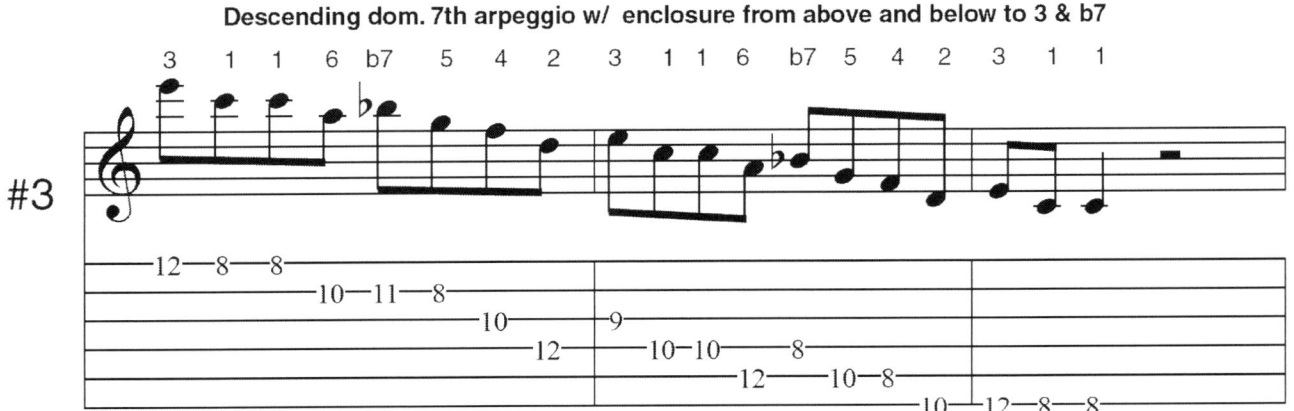

* Repeat exercise #3 using lower chromatic of 3 instead of "2" and upper chromatic of b7 instead of "1"

PAT. 1 MIXOLYDIAN ARPEGGIO w/ 2 NOTE ENCLOSURES

Descending dom. 7th arpeggio w/ enclosure from above and below to 1 & 5

* Repeat exercise #4 using lower chromatic of 1 instead of "b7" and lower chromatic of 5 instead of "4"

* Repeat exercise #4 using only chromatic enclosures from above and below to 1 and 5

Ascending dom. 7th arpeggio w/ enclosure from below and above to 3 & b7

* Repeat exercise #5 using lower chromatic of 3 instead of "2"

Ascending dom. 7th arpeggio w/ enclosure from below and above to 1 & 5

* Repeat exercise #6 using lower chromatic of 1 instead of "b7" and lower chromatic of 5 instead of "4"

* Repeat exercise #6 using only chromatic approaches from below and above to 1 and 5

PAT. 1 MIXOLYDIAN ARPEGGIO w/ 2 NOTE ENCLOSURES

Ascending dom. 7th arpeggio w/ enclosure from above and below to 3 & b7

#7

* Repeat exercise #7 using lower chromatic of 3 instead of "2"

Ascending dom. 7th arpeggio w/ enclosure from above and below to 1 & 5

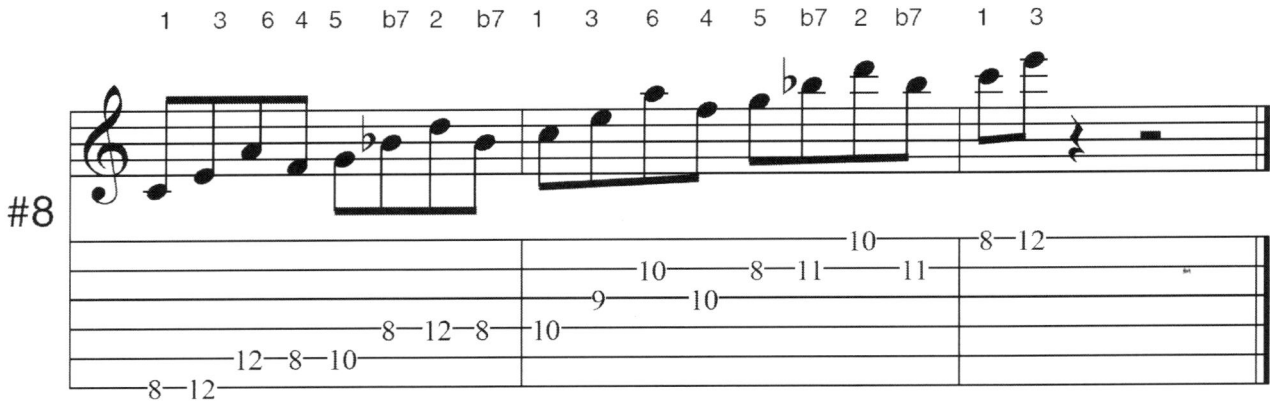

#8

* Repeat exercise #8 using lower chromatic of 1 instead of "b7" and lower chromatic of 5 instead of "4"

* Repeat exercise #8 using only chromatic approaches from above and below to 1 and 5

PAT. 4 MIXOLYDIAN ARPEGGIO w/ 2 NOTE ENCLOSURES

F 7   **Descending dom. 7th arpeggio w/ enclosure from below and above to 3 & b7**

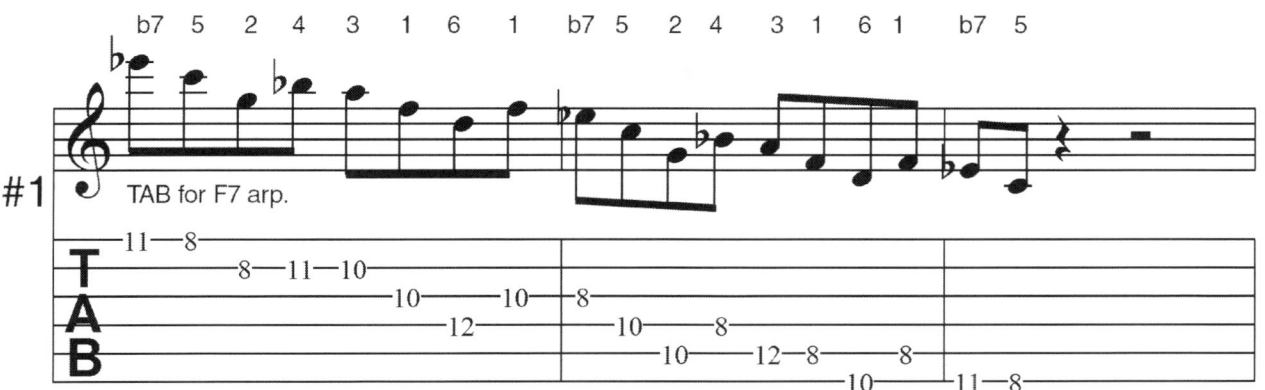

* Repeat exercise #1 using lower chromatic of 3 instead of "2" and upper chromatic of b7 instead of "1"

Descending dom. 7th arpeggio w/ enclosure from below and above to 1 & 5

* Repeat exercise #2 using lower chromatic of 1 instead of "b7" and lower chromatic of 5 instead of "4"

* Repeat exercise #2 using only chromatic approaches from below and above to 1 and 5

Descending dom. 7th arpeggio w/ enclosure from above and below to 3 & b7

* Repeat exercise #3 using lower chromatic of 3 instead of "2" and upper chromatic of b7 instead of "1"

PAT. 4 MIXOLYDIAN ARPEGGIO w/ 2 NOTE ENCLOSURES

Descending dom. 7th arpeggio w/ enclosure from above and below to 1 & 5

* Repeat exercise #4 using lower chromatic of 1 instead of "b7" and lower chromatic of 5 instead of "4"

* Repeat exercise #4 using using only chromatic approaches from above and below to 1 and 5

Ascending dom. 7th arpeggio w/ enclosure from below and above to 3 & b7

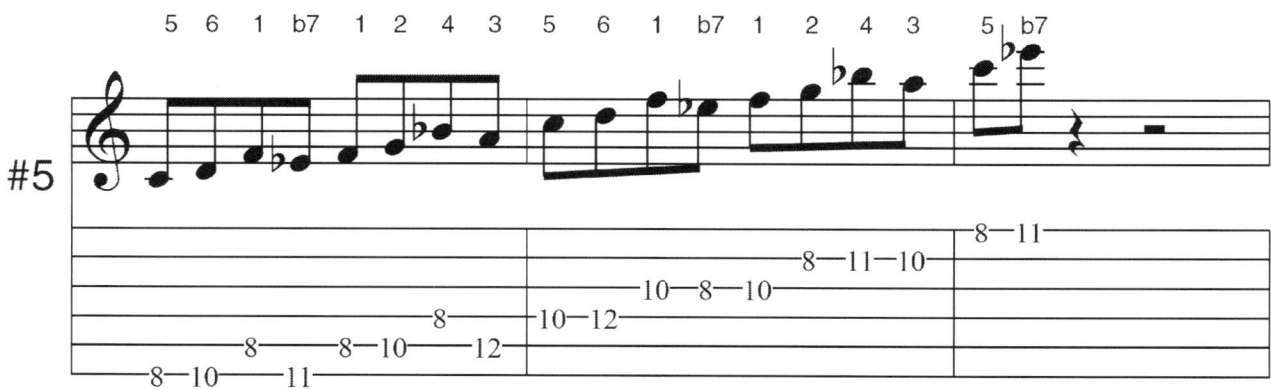

* Repeat exercise #5 using lower chromatic of 3 instead of "2"

Ascending dom. 7th arpeggio w/ enclosure from below and above to 1 & 5

* Repeat exercise #6 using lower chromatic of 1 instead of "b7" and lower chromatic of 5 instead of "4"

* Repeat exercise #6 using only chromatic approaches from below and above to 1 and 5

PAT. 4 MIXOLYDIAN ARPEGGIO w/ 2 NOTE ENCLOSURES

Ascending dom. 7th arpeggio w/ enclosure from above and below to 3 & b7

* Repeat exercise #7 using lower chromatic of 3 instead of "2"

Ascending dom. 7th arpeggio w/ enclosure from above and below to 1 & 5

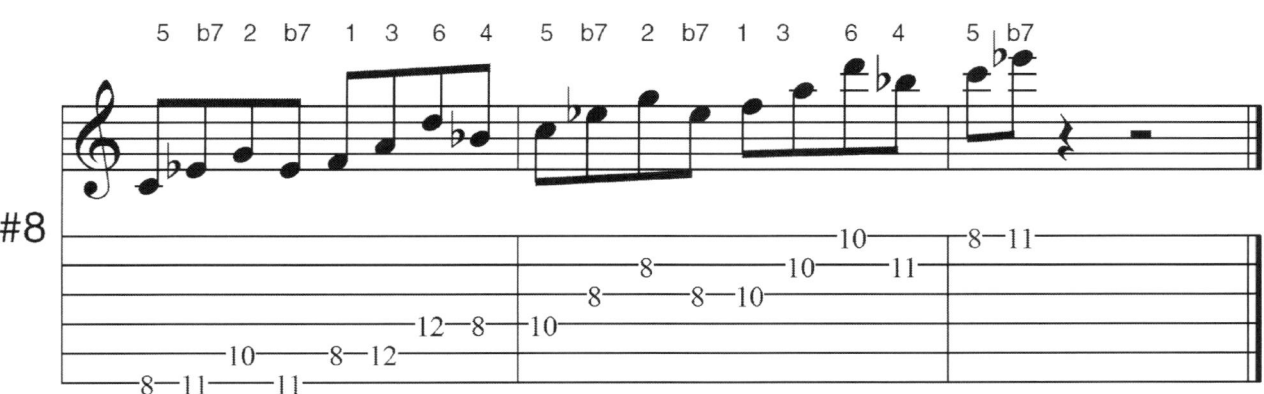

* Repeat exercise #8 using lower chromatic of 1 instead of "b7" and lower chromatic of 5 instead of "4"

* Repeat exercise #8 using only chromatic approaches from above and below to 1 and 5

PAT. 5 MIXOLYDIAN ARPEGGIO w/ 2 NOTE ENCLOSURES

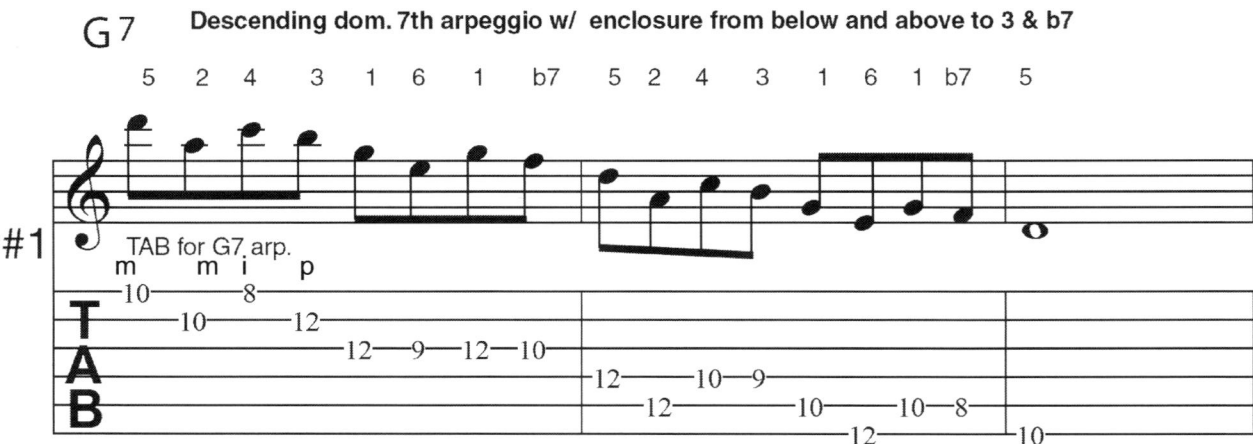

* Repeat exercise #1 using lower chromatic of 3 instead of "2" and upper chromatic of b7 instead of "1"

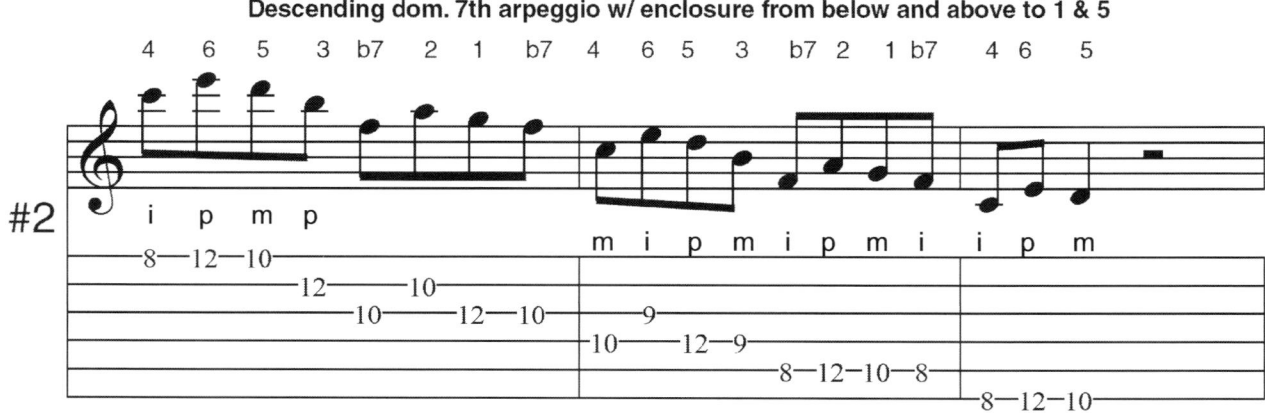

* Repeat exercise #2 using lower chromatic of 1 instead of "b7" and lower chromatic of 5 instead of "4"

* Repeat exercise #2 using only chromatic approaches from below and above to 1 and 5

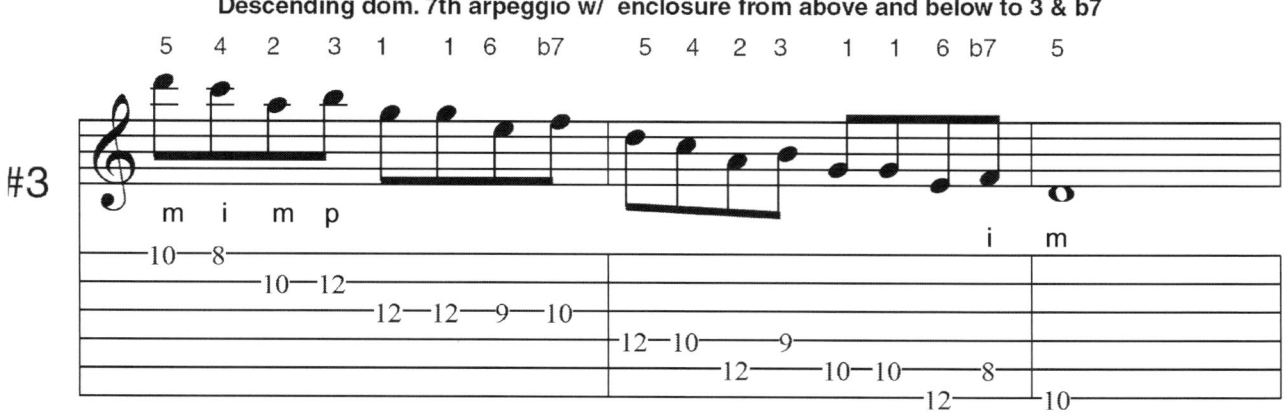

* Repeat exercise #3 using lower chromatic of 3 instead of "2" and upper chromatic of b7 instead of "1"

PAT. 5 MIXOLYDIAN ARPEGGIO w/ 2 NOTE ENCLOSURES

Descending dom. 7th arpeggio w/ enclosure from above and below to 1 & 5

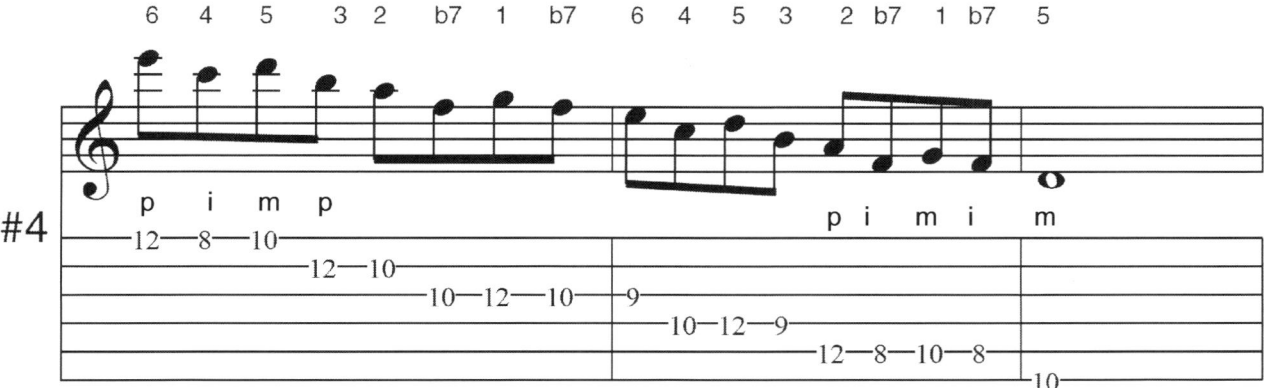

* Repeat exercise #4 using lower chromatic of 1 instead of "b7" and lower chromatic of 5 instead of "4"

* Repeat exercise #4 using only chromatic approaches from above and below to 1 and 5

Ascending dom. 7th arpeggio w/ enclosure from below and above to 3 & b7

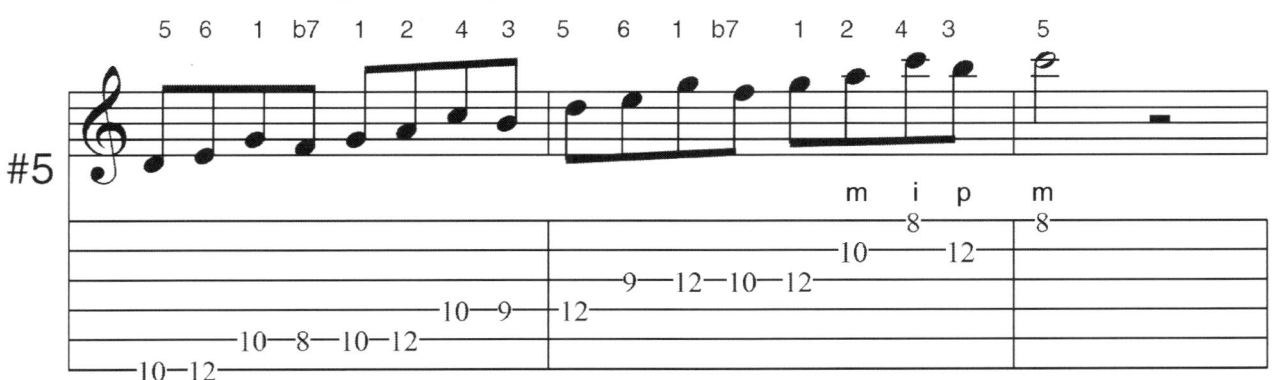

* Repeat exercise #5 using lower chromatic of 3 instead of "2"

Ascending dom. 7th arpeggio w/ enclosure from below and above to 1 & 5

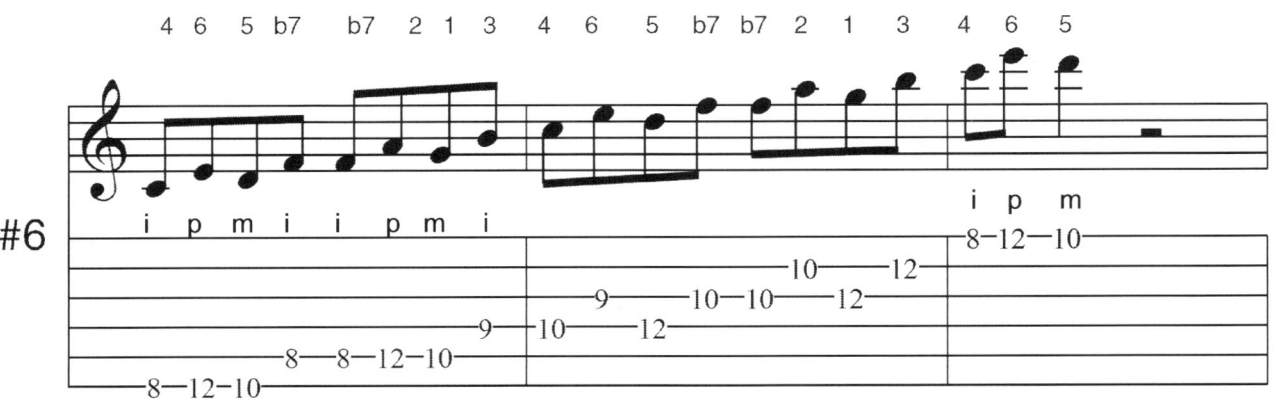

* Repeat exercise #6 using lower chromatic of 1 instead of "b7" and lower chromatic of 5 instead of "4"

* Repeat exercise #6 using only chromatic approaches from below and above to 1 and 5

PAT. 5 MIXOLYDIAN ARPEGGIO w/ 2 NOTE ENCLOSURES

Ascending dom. 7th arpeggio w/ enclosure from above and below to 3 & b7

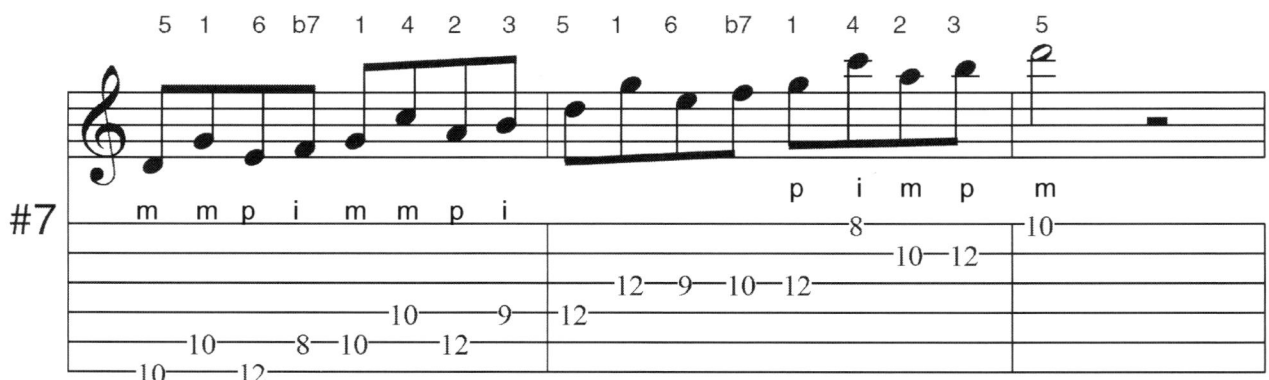

* Repeat exercise #7 using lower chromatic of 3 instead of "2"

Ascending dom. 7th arpeggio w/ enclosure from above and below to 1 & 5

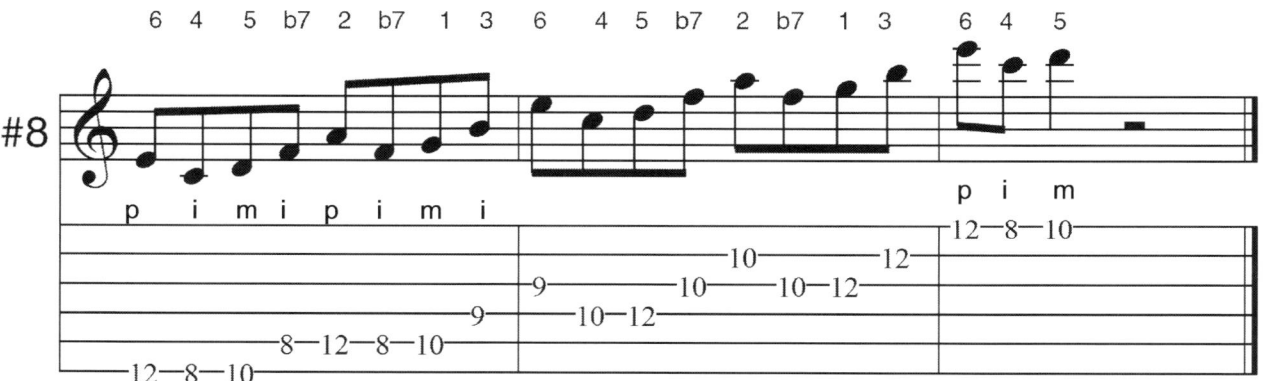

* Repeat exercise #8 using lower chromatic of 1 instead of "b7" and lower chromatic of 5 instead of "4"

* Repeat exercise #8 using only chromatic approaches from above and below to 1 and 5

SUMMARY OF BEBOP CALISTHENICS 3A

ARPEGGIOS WITH 2 NOTE ENCLOSURES

Mixolydian (1 - 2 - 3 - 4 - 5 - 6 - ♭7)

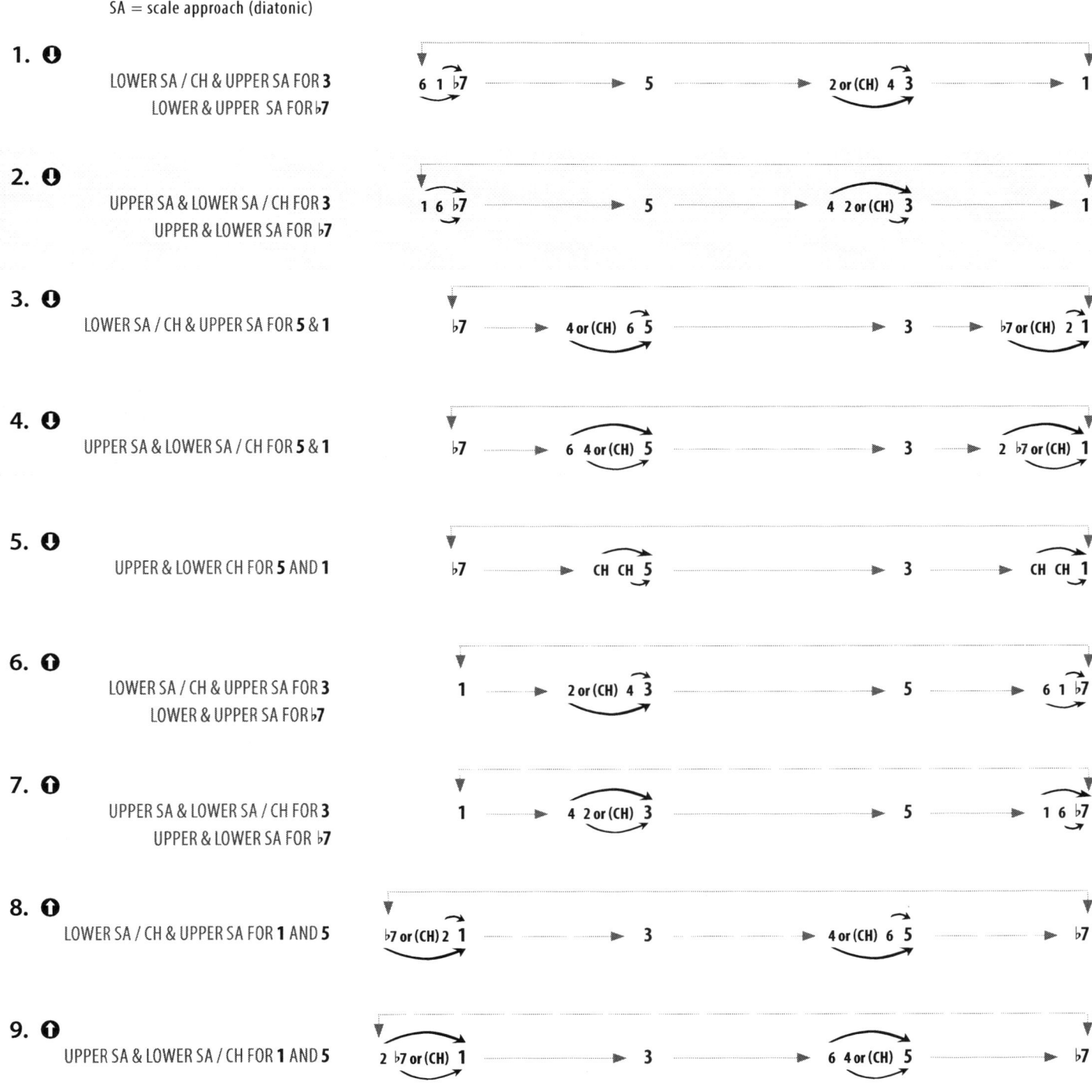

SUMMARY OF BEBOP CALISTHENICS 3B

ARPEGGIOS WITH 2 NOTE ENCLOSURES

Dorian (1 - 2 - ♭3 - 4 - 5 - 6 - ♭7)

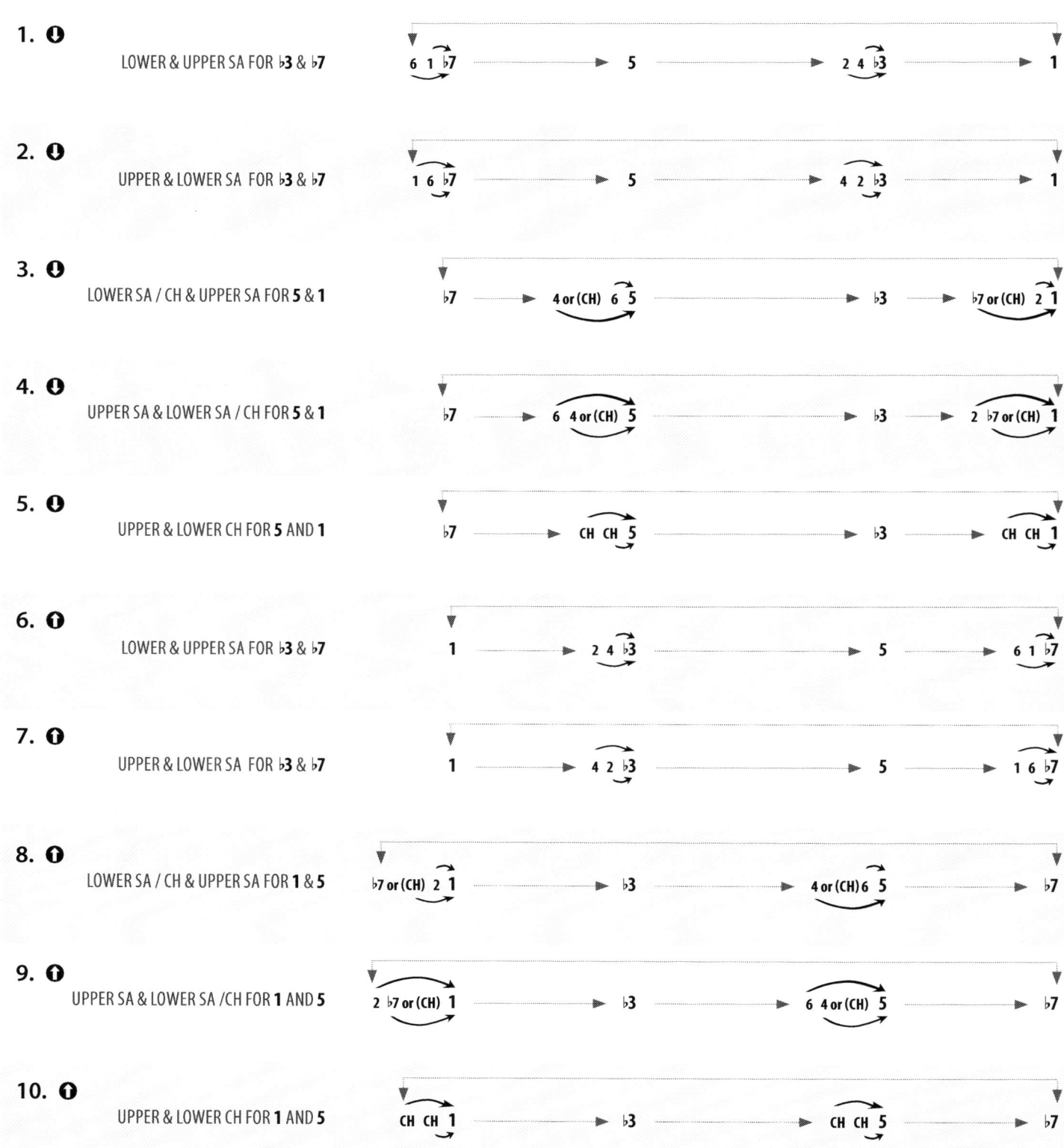

1. ❶ LOWER & UPPER SA FOR ♭3 & ♭7

2. ❶ UPPER & LOWER SA FOR ♭3 & ♭7

3. ❶ LOWER SA / CH & UPPER SA FOR **5** & **1**

4. ❶ UPPER SA & LOWER SA / CH FOR **5** & **1**

5. ❶ UPPER & LOWER CH FOR **5** AND **1**

6. ❶ LOWER & UPPER SA FOR ♭3 & ♭7

7. ❶ UPPER & LOWER SA FOR ♭3 & ♭7

8. ❶ LOWER SA / CH & UPPER SA FOR **1** & **5**

9. ❶ UPPER SA & LOWER SA / CH FOR **1** AND **5**

10. ❶ UPPER & LOWER CH FOR **1** AND **5**

SUMMARY OF BEBOP CALISTHENICS 3C

ARPEGGIOS WITH 2 NOTE ENCLOSURES

Ionian (1 - 2 - 3 - 4 - 5 - 6 - 7)

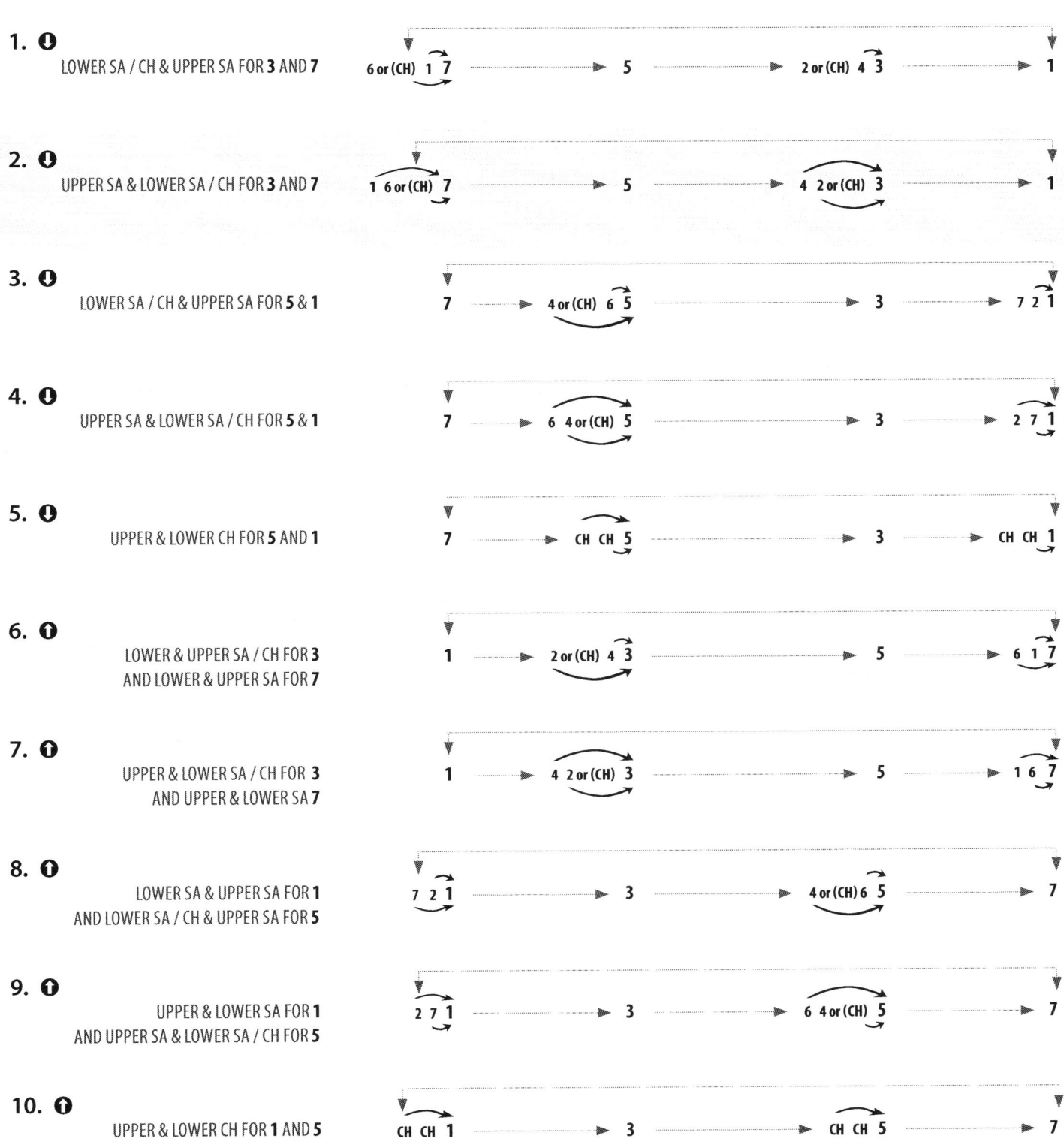

1. ⬇ LOWER SA / CH & UPPER SA FOR **3** AND **7**

2. ⬇ UPPER SA & LOWER SA / CH FOR **3** AND **7**

3. ⬇ LOWER SA / CH & UPPER SA FOR **5** & **1**

4. ⬇ UPPER SA & LOWER SA / CH FOR **5** & **1**

5. ⬇ UPPER & LOWER CH FOR **5** AND **1**

6. ⬆ LOWER & UPPER SA / CH FOR **3** AND LOWER & UPPER SA FOR **7**

7. ⬆ UPPER & LOWER SA / CH FOR **3** AND UPPER & LOWER SA **7**

8. ⬆ LOWER SA & UPPER SA FOR **1** AND LOWER SA / CH & UPPER SA FOR **5**

9. ⬆ UPPER & LOWER SA FOR **1** AND UPPER SA & LOWER SA / CH FOR **5**

10. ⬆ UPPER & LOWER CH FOR **1** AND **5**

SUMMARY OF BEBOP CALISTHENICS 3D & E

ARPEGGIOS WITH 2 NOTE ENCLOSURES

Locrian (1 - ♭2 - ♭3 - 4 - ♭5 - ♭6 - ♭7) Play each exercise descending and ascending ⬇ ⬆

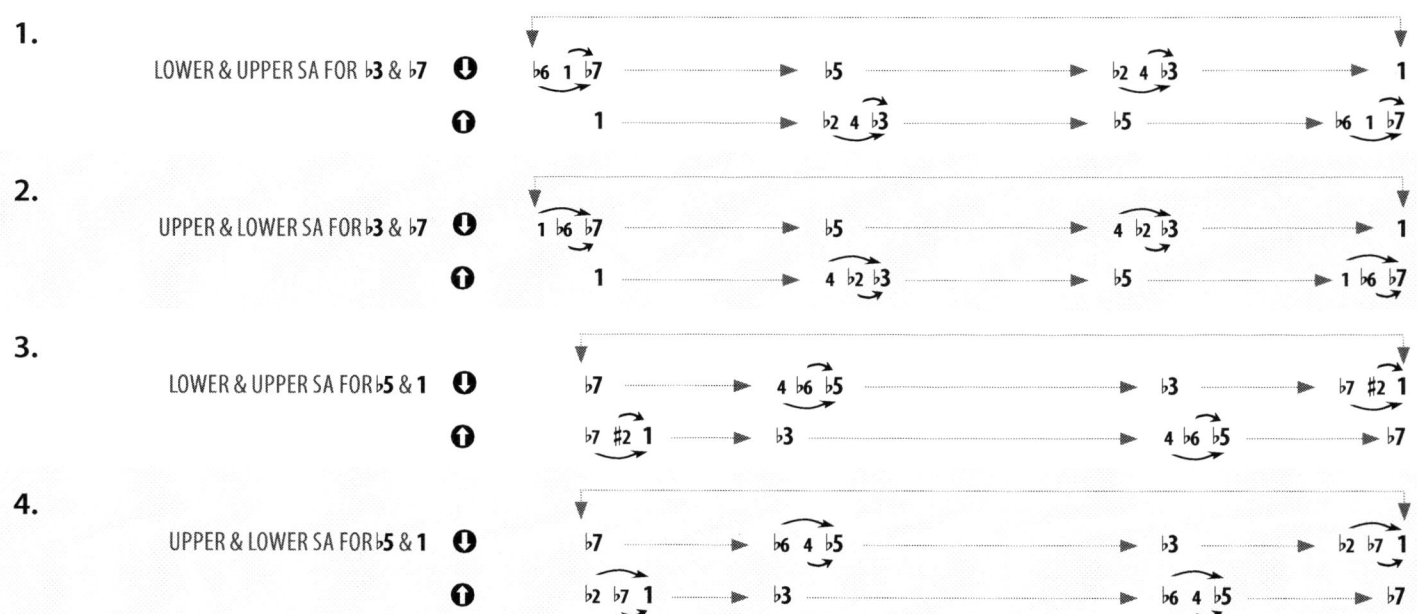

Super Locrian (1 - ♭2 - ♯2 - 3 - ♯4 - ♯5 - ♭7) Play each exercise descending and ascending ⬇ ⬆

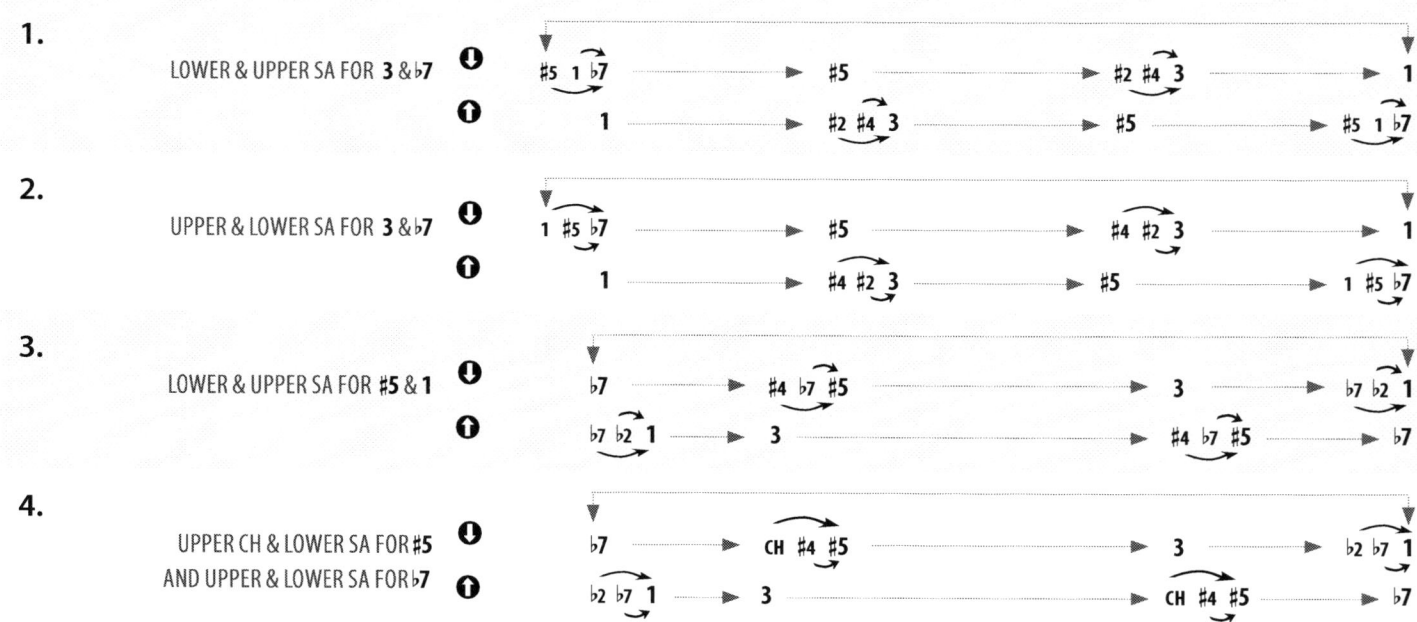

BEBOP
CALISTHENICS 4
ARPEGGIOS with DOUBLE CHROMATIC APPROACHES

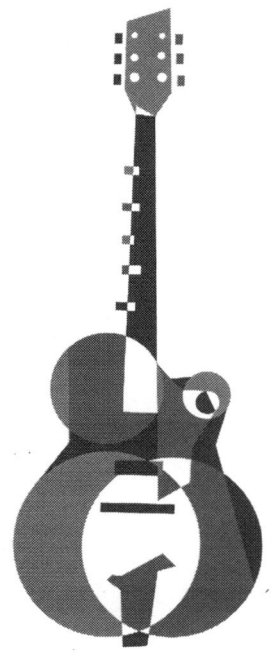

DORIAN PAT 4 / PAT 2

**Summary for Mixolydian / Dorian /
Ionian / Locrian / Super Locrian**

PAT. 4 DORIAN ARPEGGIO w/ DOUBLE CHROMATIC APPROACHES

Descending min. 7th arpeggio w/ lower double chromatic app. to b3 & b7

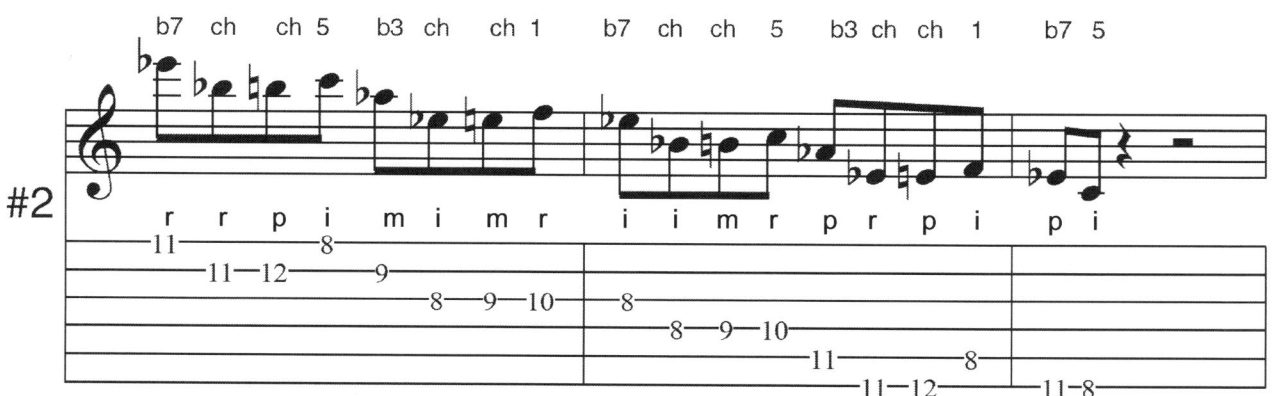

Descending min. 7th arpeggio w/ lower double chromatic app. to 1 & 5

Descending min. 7th arpeggio w/ upper double chromatic app. to 1 & 5

PAT. 4 DORIAN ARPEGGIO w/ DOUBLE CHROMATIC APPROACHES

Ascending min. 7th arpeggio w/ lower double chromatic app. to b3 & b7

Ascending min. 7th arpeggio w/ lower double chromatic app. to 1 & 5

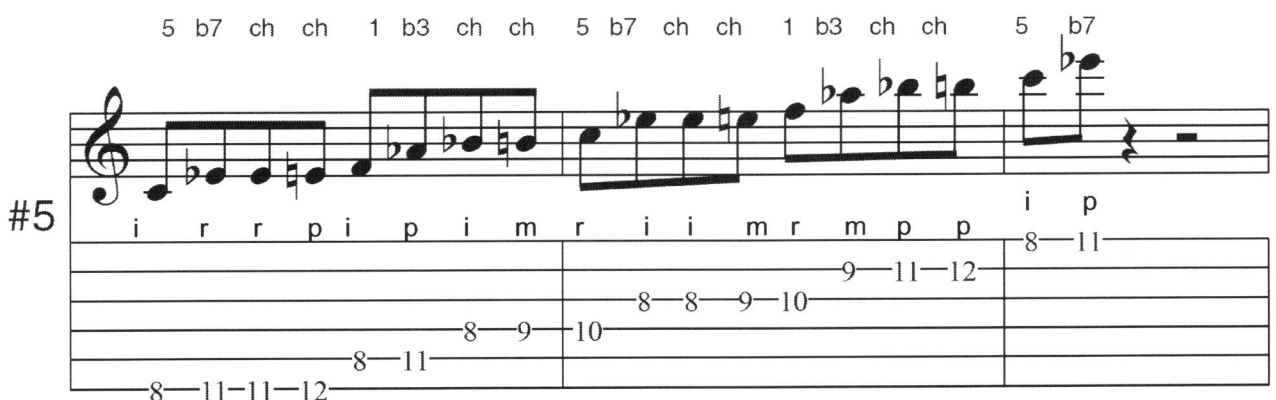

Ascending min. 7th arpeggio w/ upper double chromatic app. to 1 & 5

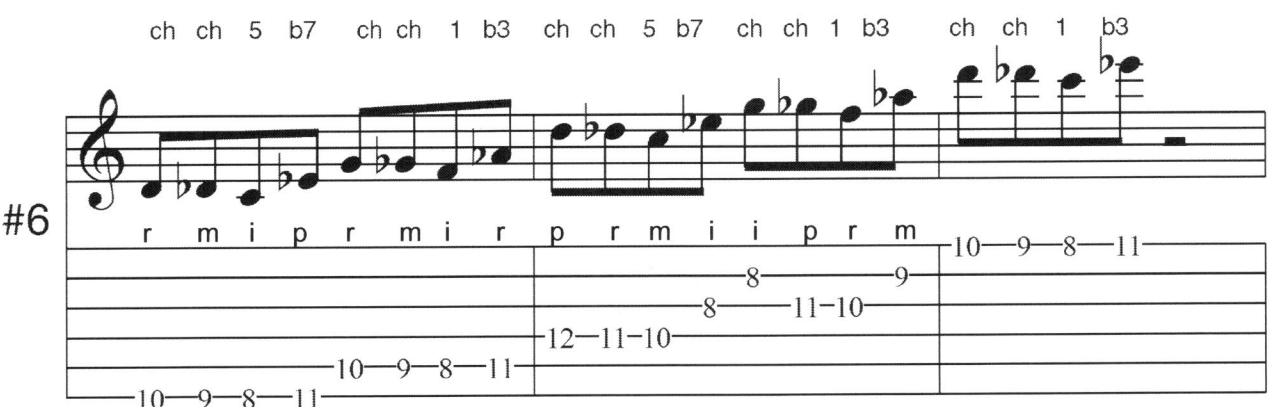

PAT. 4 DORIAN ARPEGGIO w/ DOUBLE CHROMATIC APPROACHES

Ascending min. 7th arpeggio w/ upper double chromatic app. to b3 & b7

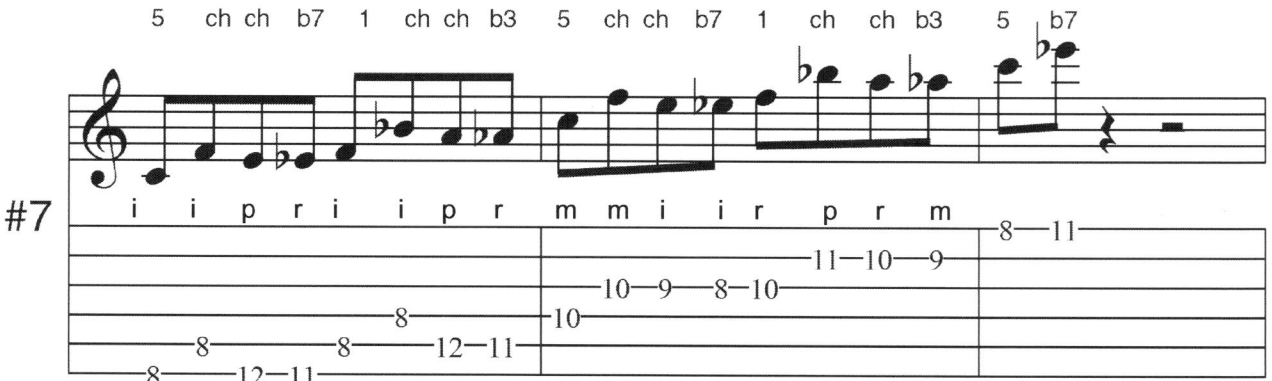

Ascending min. 7th arpeggio w/ lower dbl. ch. to b3 & upper dbl. ch. to 5

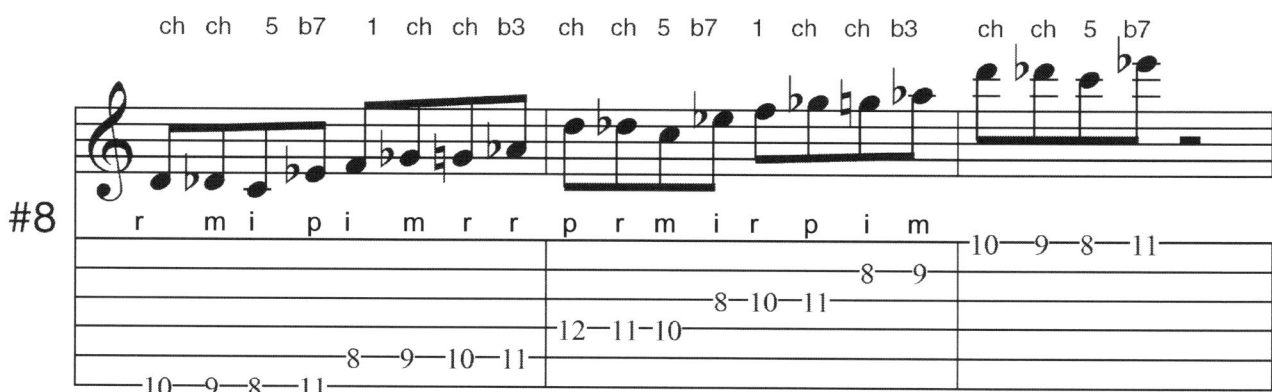

Ascending min. 7th arpeggio w/ upper dbl. ch. for b3 & lower dbl. ch. to 5

PAT. 4 DORIAN ARPEGGIO w/ DOUBLE CHROMATIC APPROACHES

Descending min. 7th arpeggio w/ lower dbl. ch.to b3 & upper dbl. ch. to 5

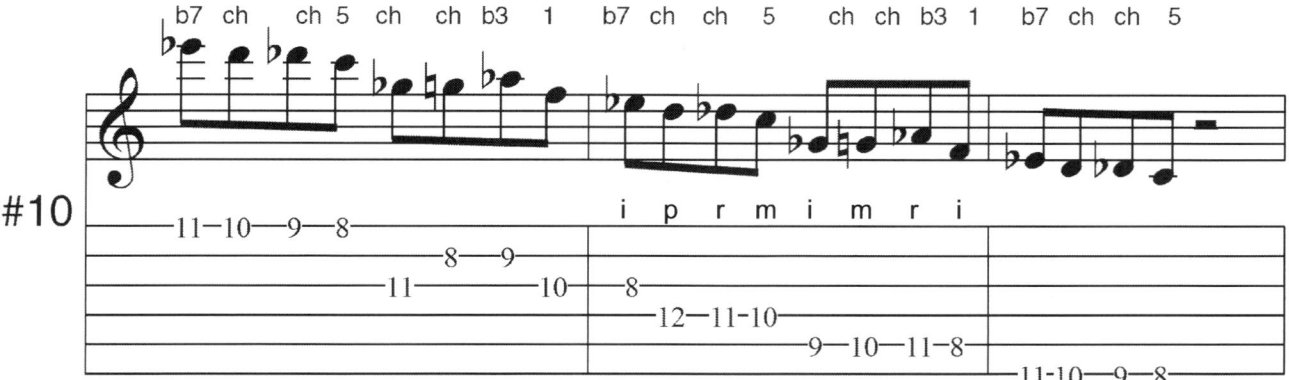

Descending min. 7th arpeggio w/ upper dbl. ch. to b3 & lower dbl. ch. to 5

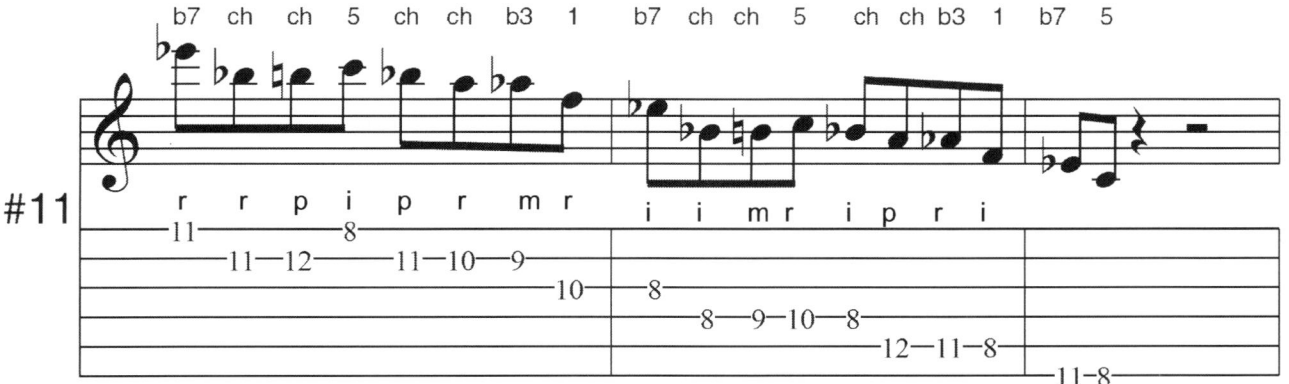

Descending min.7th arpeggio w/ upper dbl. ch. to 1 & lower dbl. ch. to b7

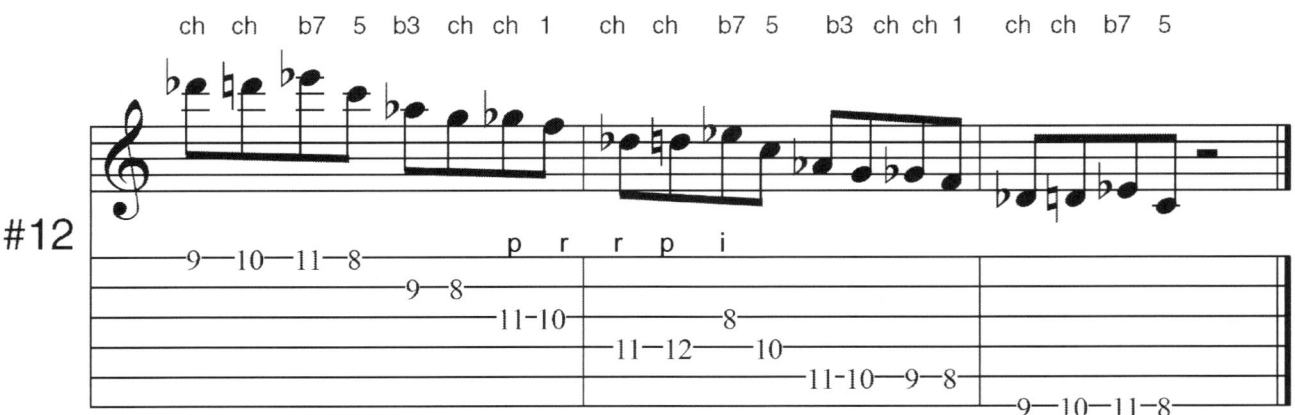

PAT. 2 DORIAN ARPEGGIO w/ DOUBLE CHROMATIC APPROACHES

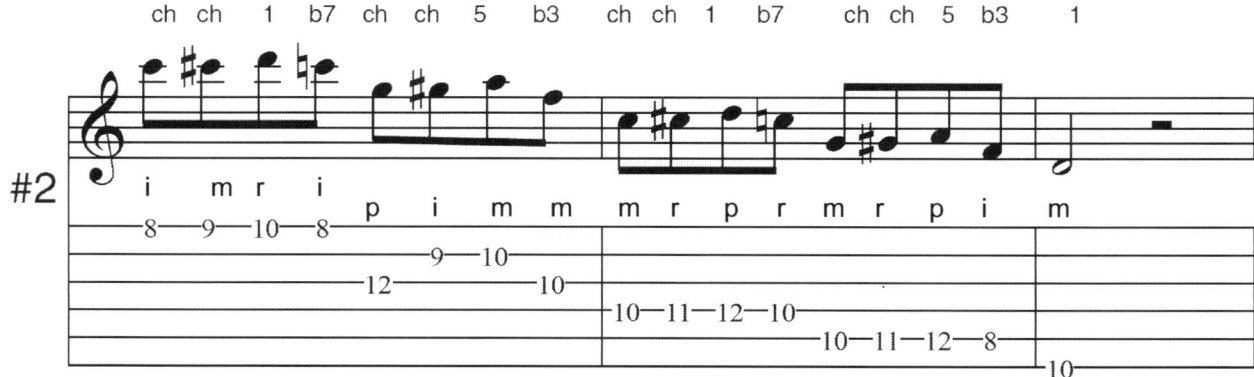

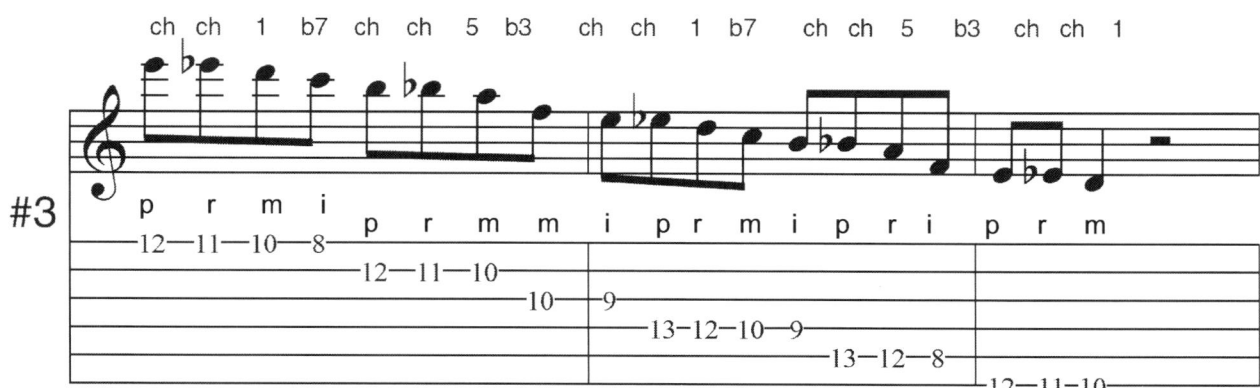

PAT. 2 DORIAN ARPEGGIO w/ DOUBLE CHROMATIC APPROACHES

Ascending min. 7th arpeggio w/ lower double chromatic app. to b3 & b7

Ascending min. 7th arpeggio w/ lower double chromatic app. to 1 & 5

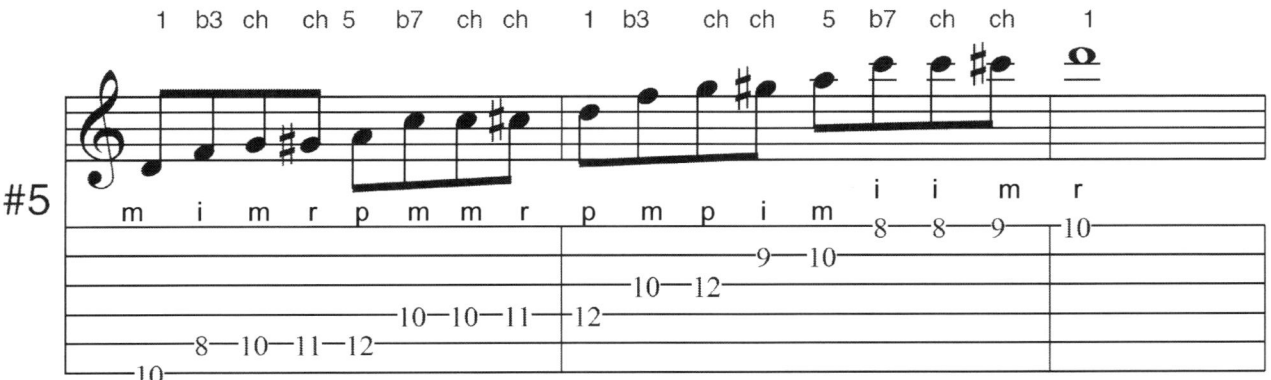

Ascending min. 7th arpeggio w/ upper double chromatic app. to 1 & 5

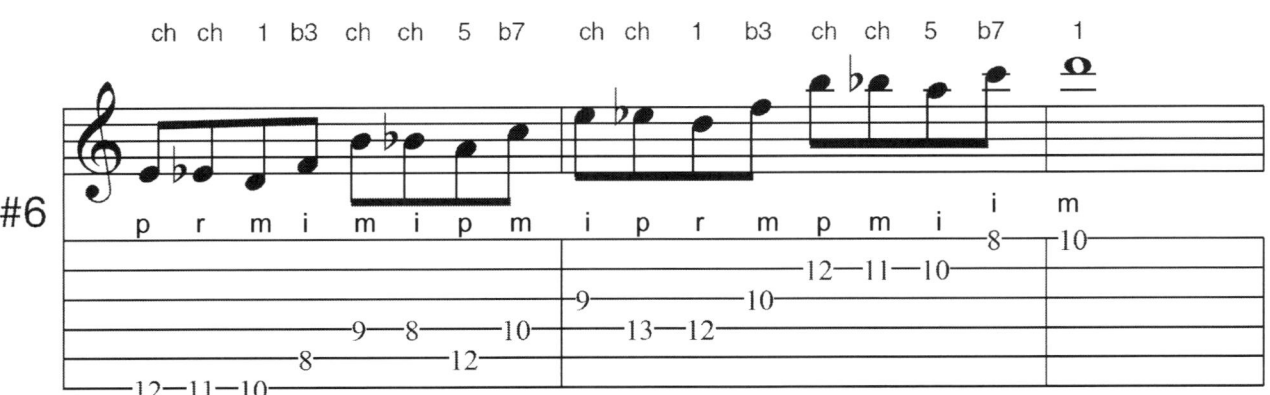

PAT. 2 DORIAN ARPEGGIO w/ DOUBLE CHROMATIC APPROACHES

Ascending min. 7th arpeggio w/ upper double chromatic app. to b3 & b7

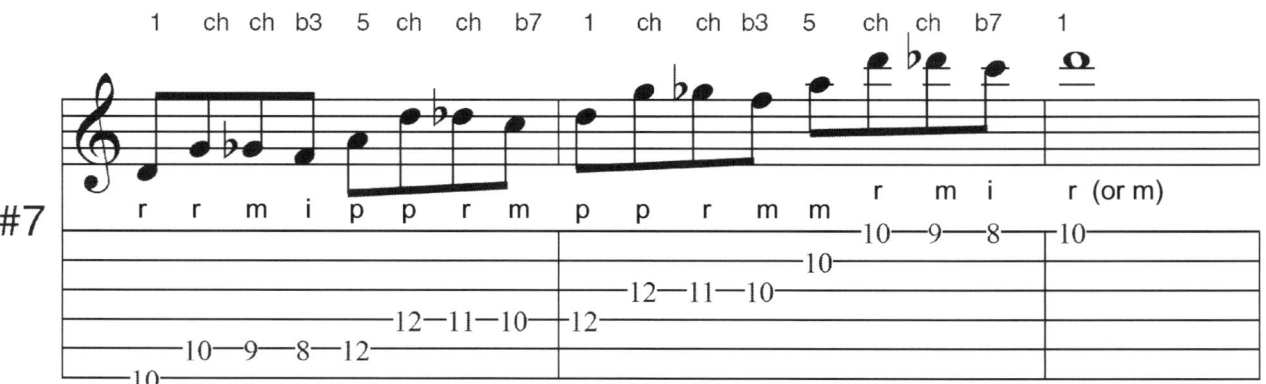

Ascending min. 7th arpeggio w/ lower dbl. ch. to b3 & upper dbl. ch. to 5

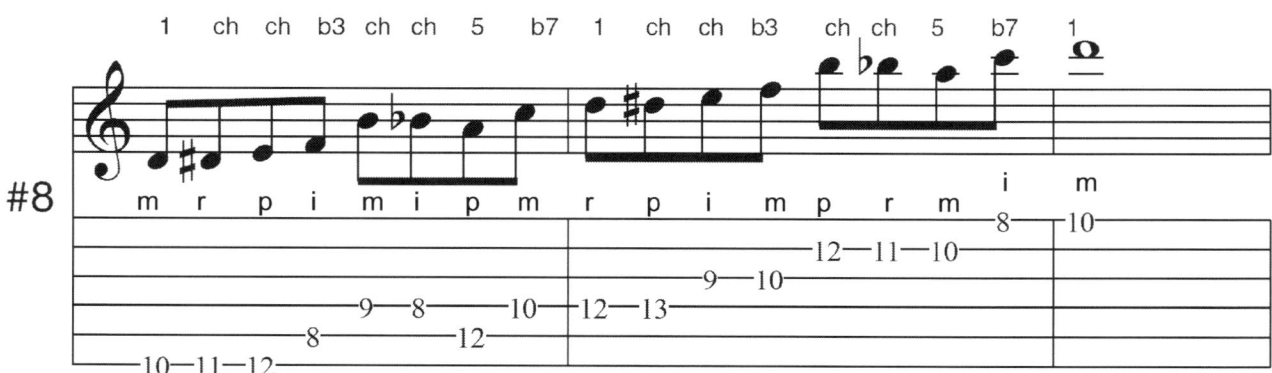

Ascending min. 7th arpeggio w/ upper dbl. ch. for b3 & lower dbl. ch. to 5

PAT. 2 DORIAN ARPEGGIO w/ DOUBLE CHROMATIC APPROACHES

Descending min. 7th arpeggio w/ lower dbl. ch. to b3 & upper dbl. ch. to 5

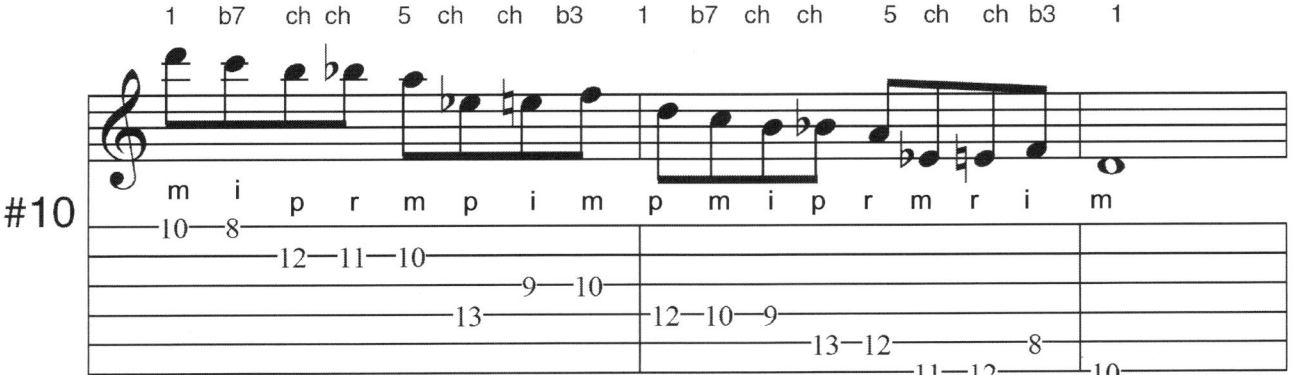

Descending min. 7th arpeggio w/ upper dbl. ch. to b3 & lower dbl. ch. to 5

Descending min. 7th arpeggio w/ upper dbl. ch. to 1 & lower dbl. ch. to b7

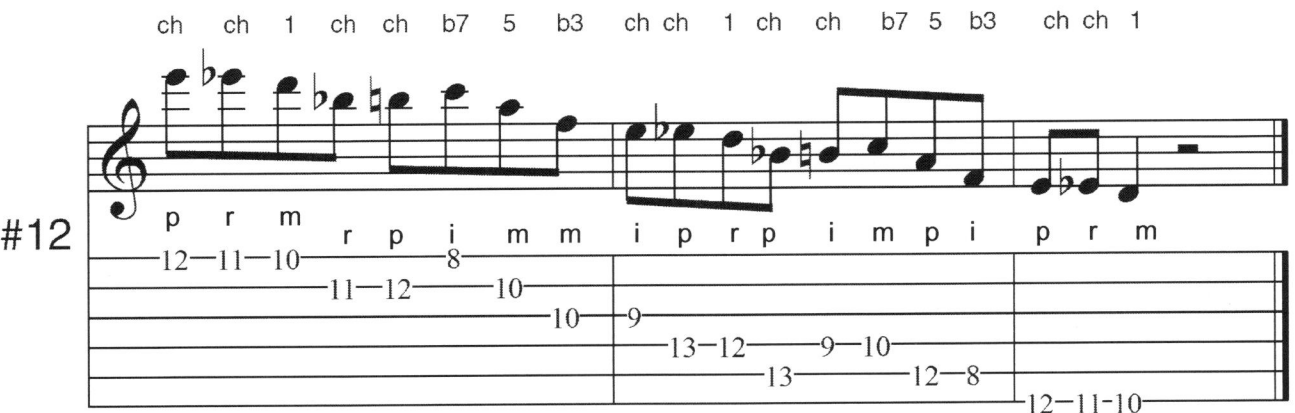

SUMMARY OF BEBOP CALISTHENICS 4A

ARPEGGIOS WITH DOUBLE CHROMATIC APPROACHES

Dorian (1 - 2 - ♭3 - 4 - 5 - 6 - ♭7) Play each exercise descending and ascending ⬇ ⬆

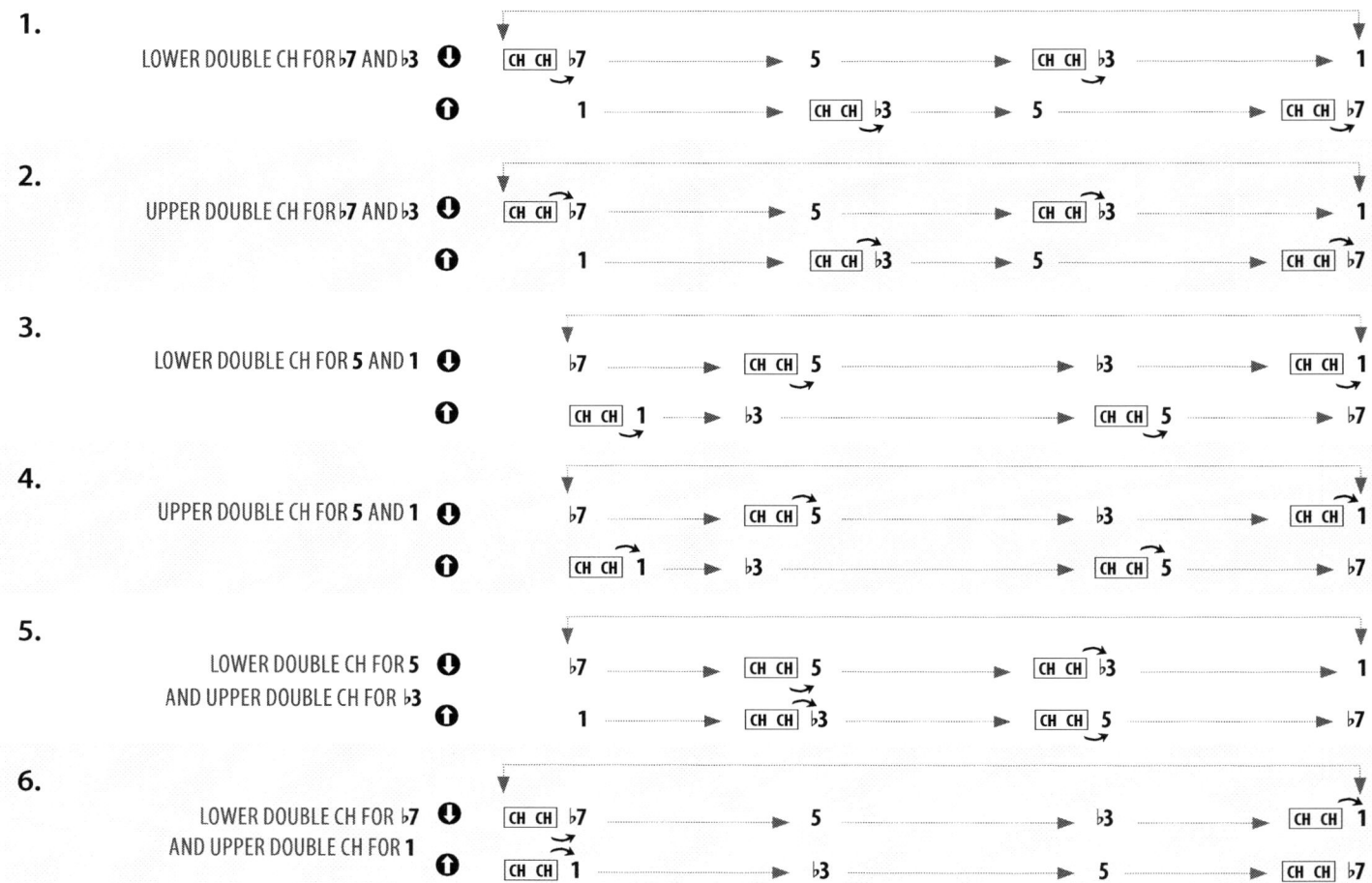

1.

LOWER DOUBLE CH FOR ♭7 AND ♭3 ⬇ | CH CH | ♭7 ⟶ 5 ⟶ | CH CH | ♭3 ⟶ 1

⬆   1 ⟶ | CH CH | ♭3 ⟶ 5 ⟶ | CH CH | ♭7

2.

UPPER DOUBLE CH FOR ♭7 AND ♭3 ⬇ | CH CH | ♭7 ⟶ 5 ⟶ | CH CH | ♭3 ⟶ 1

⬆   1 ⟶ | CH CH | ♭3 ⟶ 5 ⟶ | CH CH | ♭7

3.

LOWER DOUBLE CH FOR 5 AND 1 ⬇   ♭7 ⟶ | CH CH | 5 ⟶ ♭3 ⟶ | CH CH | 1

⬆ | CH CH | 1 ⟶ ♭3 ⟶ | CH CH | 5 ⟶ ♭7

4.

UPPER DOUBLE CH FOR 5 AND 1 ⬇   ♭7 ⟶ | CH CH | 5 ⟶ ♭3 ⟶ | CH CH | 1

⬆ | CH CH | 1 ⟶ ♭3 ⟶ | CH CH | 5 ⟶ ♭7

5.

LOWER DOUBLE CH FOR 5
AND UPPER DOUBLE CH FOR ♭3 ⬇   ♭7 ⟶ | CH CH | 5 ⟶ | CH CH | ♭3 ⟶ 1

⬆   1 ⟶ | CH CH | ♭3 ⟶ | CH CH | 5 ⟶ ♭7

6.

LOWER DOUBLE CH FOR ♭7
AND UPPER DOUBLE CH FOR 1 ⬇ | CH CH | ♭7 ⟶ 5 ⟶ ♭3 ⟶ | CH CH | 1

⬆ | CH CH | 1 ⟶ ♭3 ⟶ 5 ⟶ | CH CH | ♭7

SUMMARY OF BEBOP CALISTHENICS 4B

ARPEGGIOS WITH DOUBLE CHROMATIC APPROACHES

Mixolydian (1 - 2 - 3 - 4 - 5 - 6 - ♭7) Play each exercise descending and ascending ⓿ ⓿

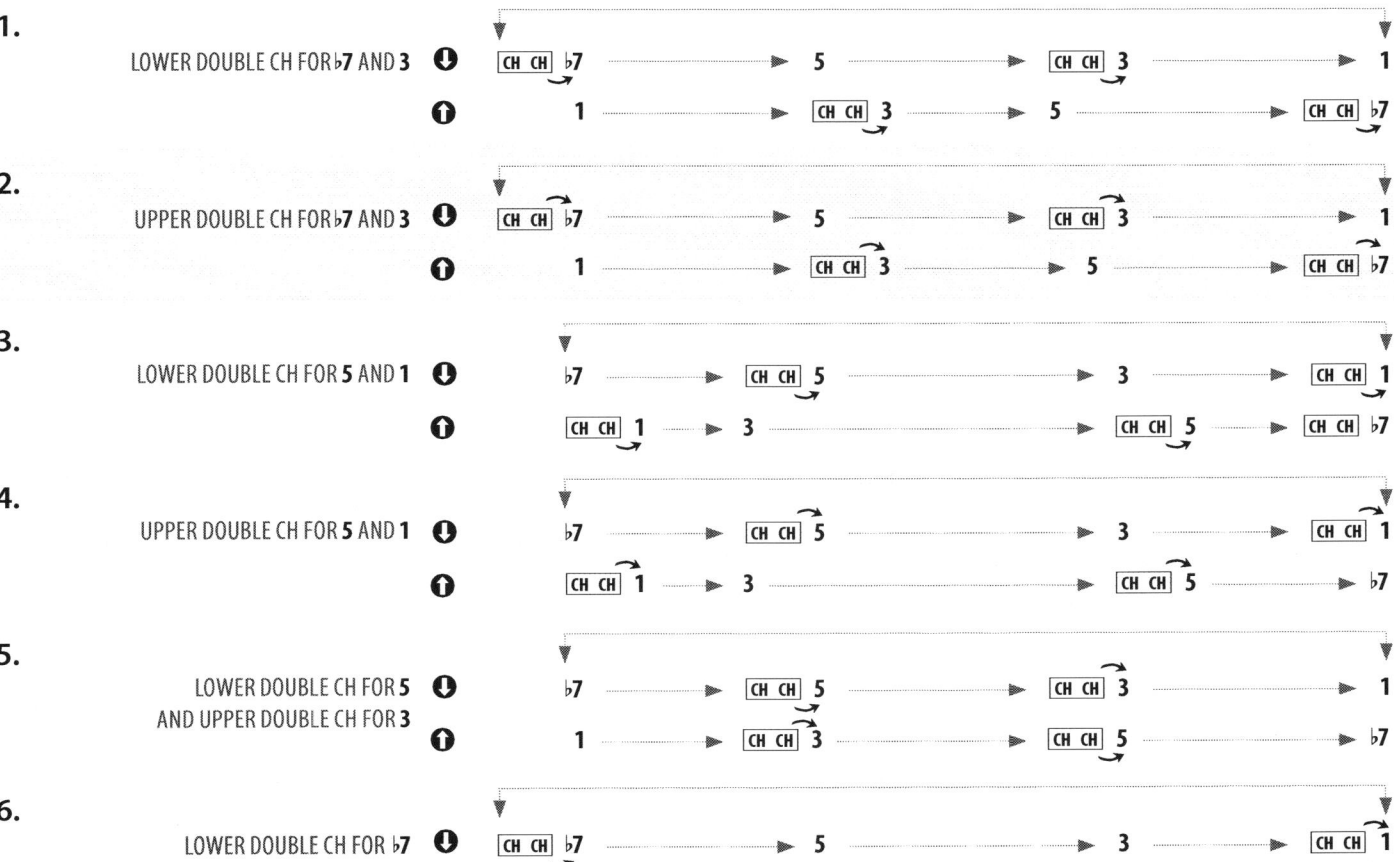

1. LOWER DOUBLE CH FOR ♭7 AND 3
2. UPPER DOUBLE CH FOR ♭7 AND 3
3. LOWER DOUBLE CH FOR 5 AND 1
4. UPPER DOUBLE CH FOR 5 AND 1
5. LOWER DOUBLE CH FOR 5 AND UPPER DOUBLE CH FOR 3
6. LOWER DOUBLE CH FOR ♭7 AND UPPER DOUBLE CH FOR 1

SUMMARY OF BEBOP CALISTHENICS 4C

ARPEGGIOS WITH DOUBLE CHROMATIC APPROACHES

Ionian (1 - 2 - 3 - 4 - 5 - 6 - 7) Play each exercise descending and ascending ↓ ↑

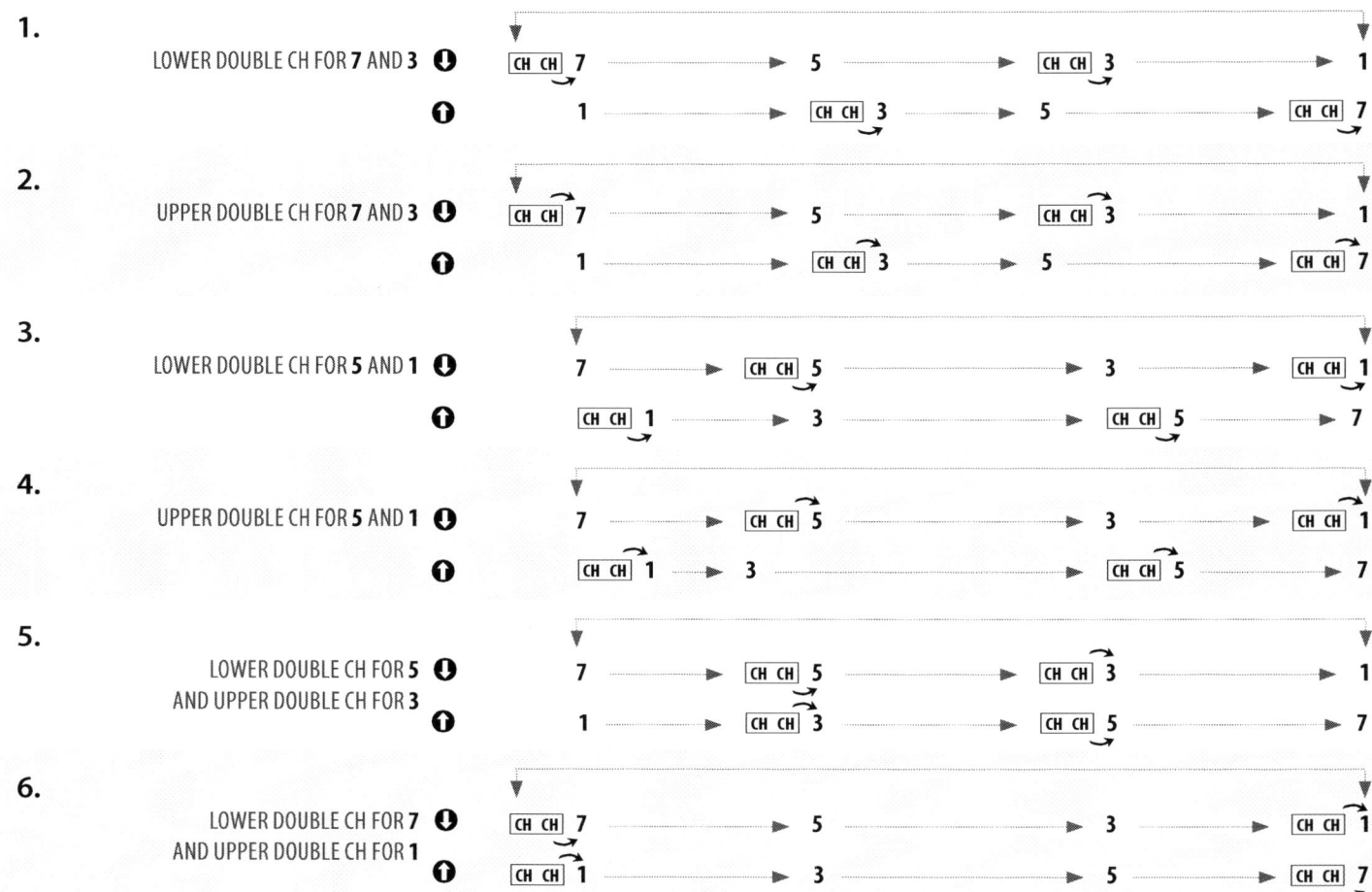

1.

LOWER DOUBLE CH FOR **7** AND **3** ↓   CH CH 7 → 5 → CH CH 3 → 1

↑   1 → CH CH 3 → 5 → CH CH 7

2.

UPPER DOUBLE CH FOR **7** AND **3** ↓   CH CH 7 → 5 → CH CH 3 → 1

↑   1 → CH CH 3 → 5 → CH CH 7

3.

LOWER DOUBLE CH FOR **5** AND **1** ↓   7 → CH CH 5 → 3 → CH CH 1

↑   CH CH 1 → 3 → CH CH 5 → 7

4.

UPPER DOUBLE CH FOR **5** AND **1** ↓   7 → CH CH 5 → 3 → CH CH 1

↑   CH CH 1 → 3 → CH CH 5 → 7

5.

LOWER DOUBLE CH FOR **5** ↓   7 → CH CH 5 → CH CH 3 → 1
AND UPPER DOUBLE CH FOR **3**

↑   1 → CH CH 3 → CH CH 5 → 7

6.

LOWER DOUBLE CH FOR **7** ↓   CH CH 7 → 5 → 3 → CH CH 1
AND UPPER DOUBLE CH FOR **1**

↑   CH CH 1 → 3 → 5 → CH CH 7

SUMMARY OF BEBOP CALISTHENICS 4D

ARPEGGIOS WITH DOUBLE CHROMATIC APPROACHES

Locrian (1 - ♭2 - ♭3 - 4 - ♭5 - ♭6 - ♭7) Play each exercise descending and ascending ⬇ ⬆

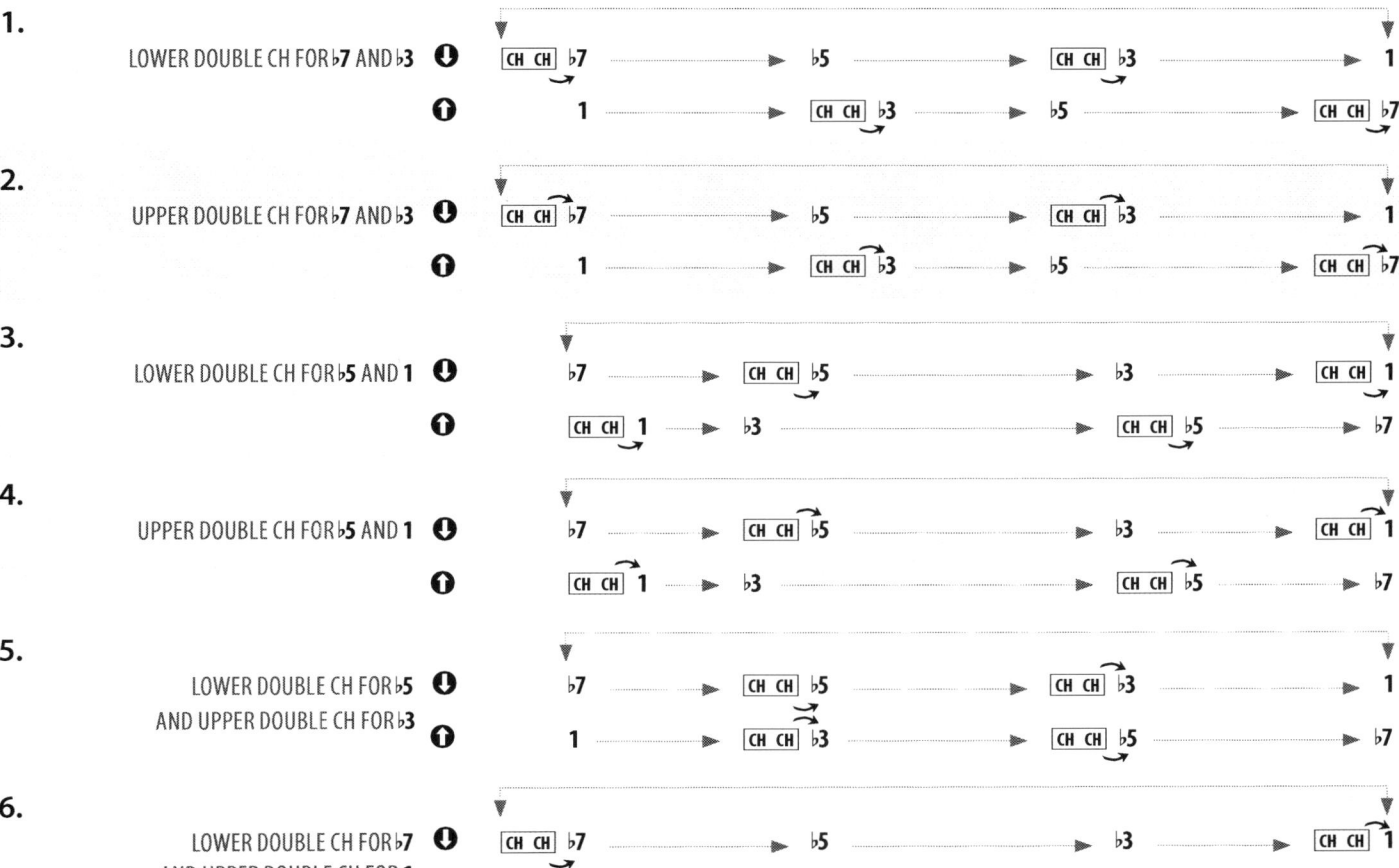

1. LOWER DOUBLE CH FOR ♭7 AND ♭3

2. UPPER DOUBLE CH FOR ♭7 AND ♭3

3. LOWER DOUBLE CH FOR ♭5 AND 1

4. UPPER DOUBLE CH FOR ♭5 AND 1

5. LOWER DOUBLE CH FOR ♭5 AND UPPER DOUBLE CH FOR ♭3

6. LOWER DOUBLE CH FOR ♭7 AND UPPER DOUBLE CH FOR 1

SUMMARY OF BEBOP CALISTHENICS 4E

ARPEGGIOS WITH DOUBLE CHROMATIC APPROACHES

Super Locrian (1 - ♭2 - ♯2 - 3 - ♯4 - ♯5 - ♭7) Play each exercise descending and ascending ⬇ ⬆

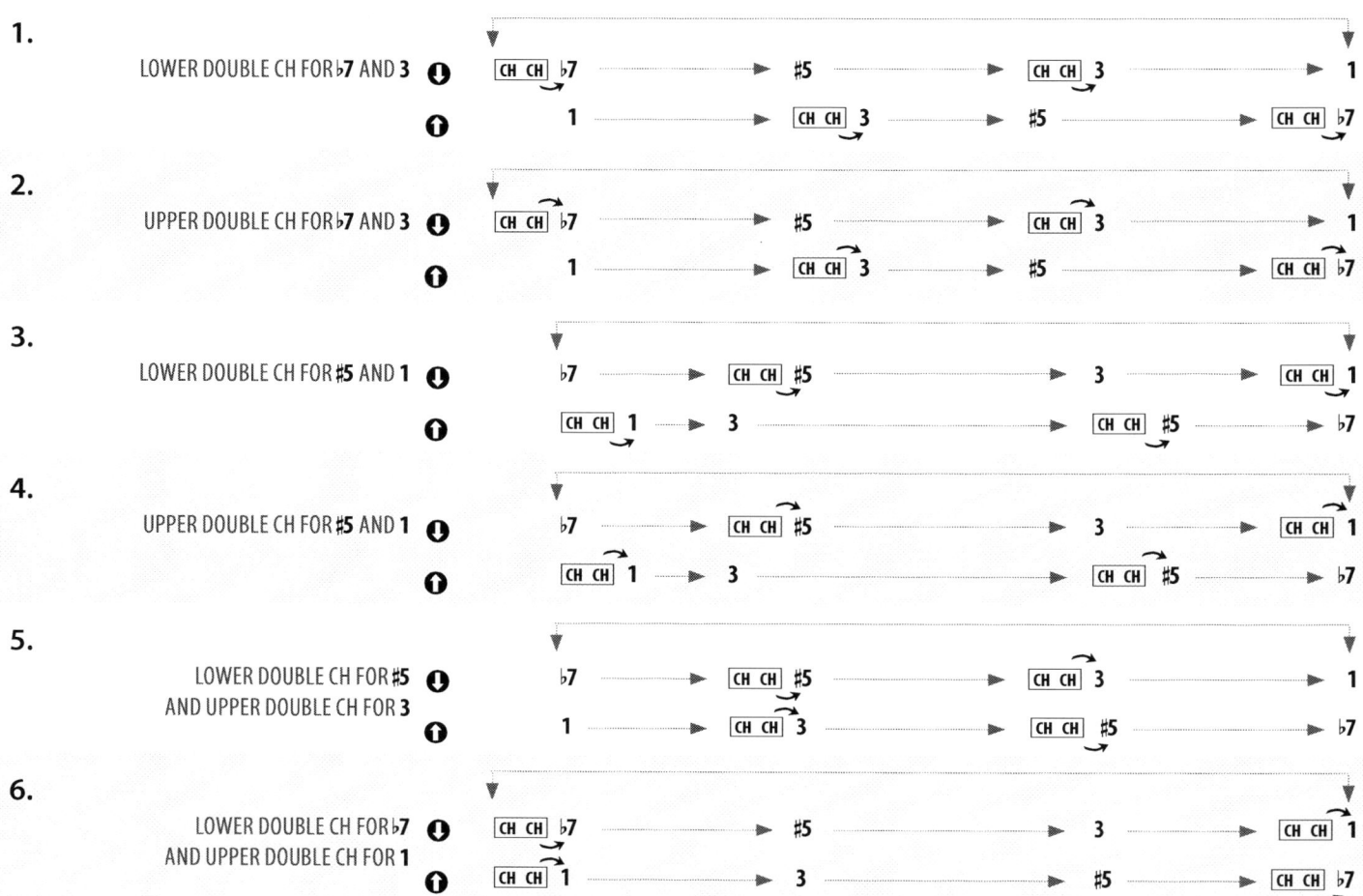

BEBOP
CALISTHENICS 5
ARPEGGIOS with 3 NOTE ENCLOSURES

DORIAN PAT 2 / PAT 4

**Summary for Mixolydian / Dorian /
Ionian / Locrian / Super Locrian**

PAT. 2 DORIAN ARPEGGIO w/ 3 NOTE ENCLOSURES

Descending min. 7th arpeggio w/ lower double and single upper to b3

*Repeat exercise #1 inverting the order of the 3 note enclosure to single upper and lower double to b3

Descending min. 7th arpeggio w/ lower double and single upper to b7

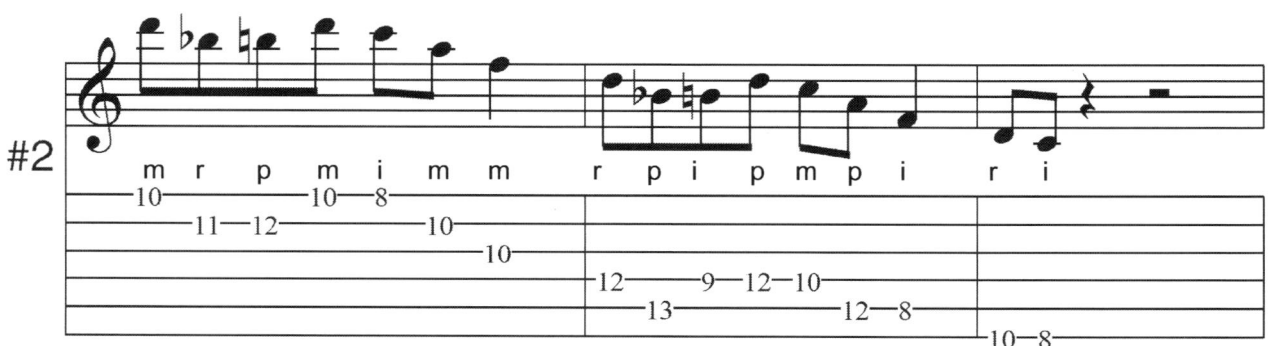

*Repeat exercise #2 inverting the order of the 3 note enclosure to single upper and lower double to b7

Descending min. 7th arpeggio w/ lower double and single upper to 1

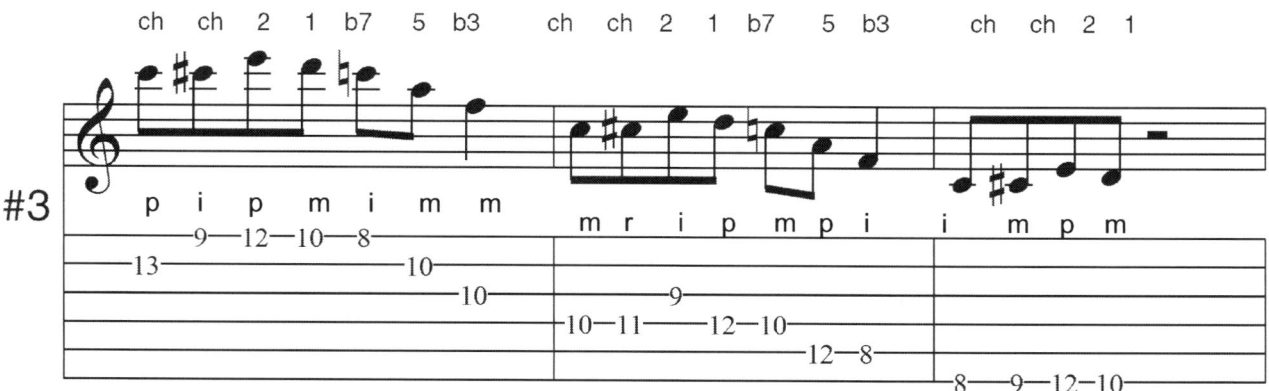

*Repeat exercise #3 inverting the order of the 3 note enclosure to single upper and lower double to 1

PAT. 2 DORIAN ARPEGGIO w/ 3 NOTE ENCLOSURES

Descending min. 7th arpeggio w/ lower double and single upper to 5

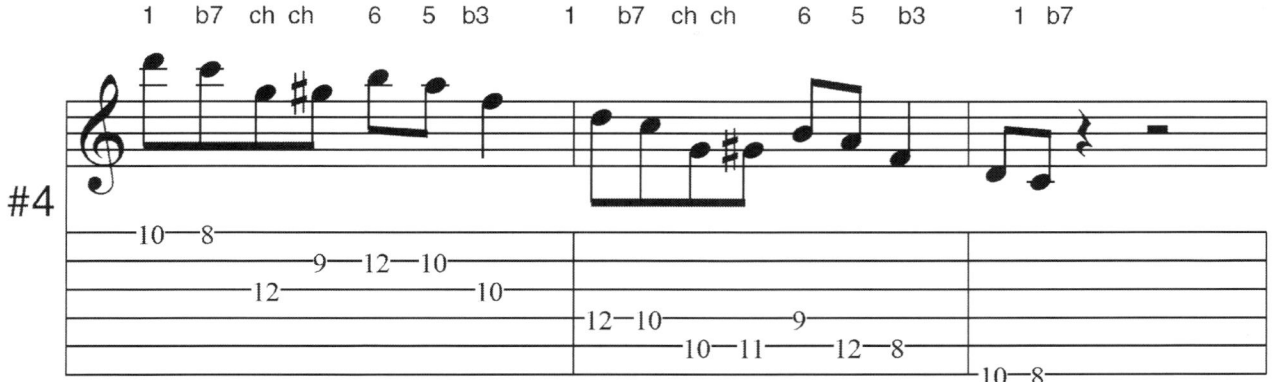

*Repeat exercise #4 inverting the order of the 3 note enclosure to single upper and lower double to 5

Ascending min. 7th arpeggio w/ single upper and lower double to b3

*Repeat exercise #5 inverting the order of the 3 note enclosure to lower double and single upper to b3

Ascending min. 7th arpeggio w/ single upper and lower double to b7

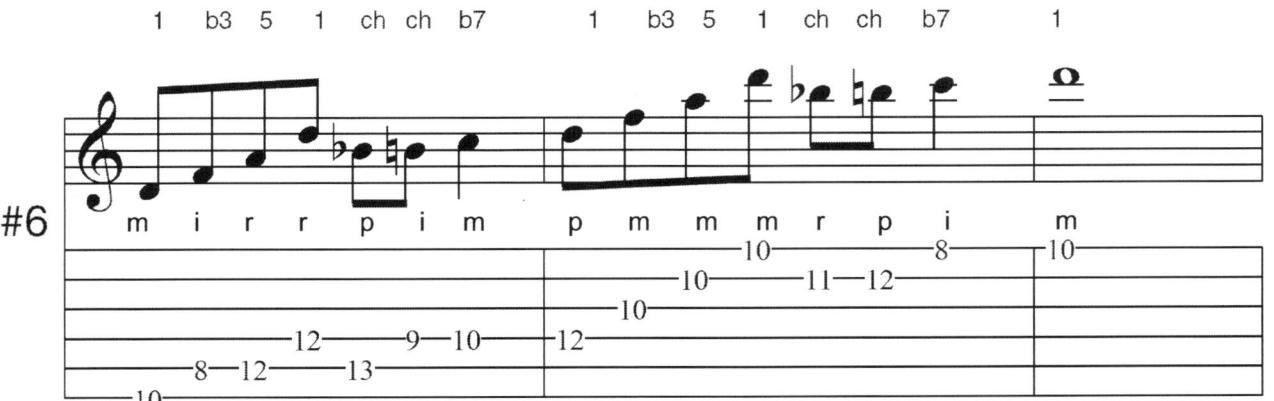

*Repeat exercise #6 inverting the order of the 3 note enclosure to lower double and single upper to b7

PAT. 2 DORIAN ARPEGGIO w/ 3 NOTE ENCLOSURES

Ascending min. 7th arpeggio w/ single upper and lower double to 1

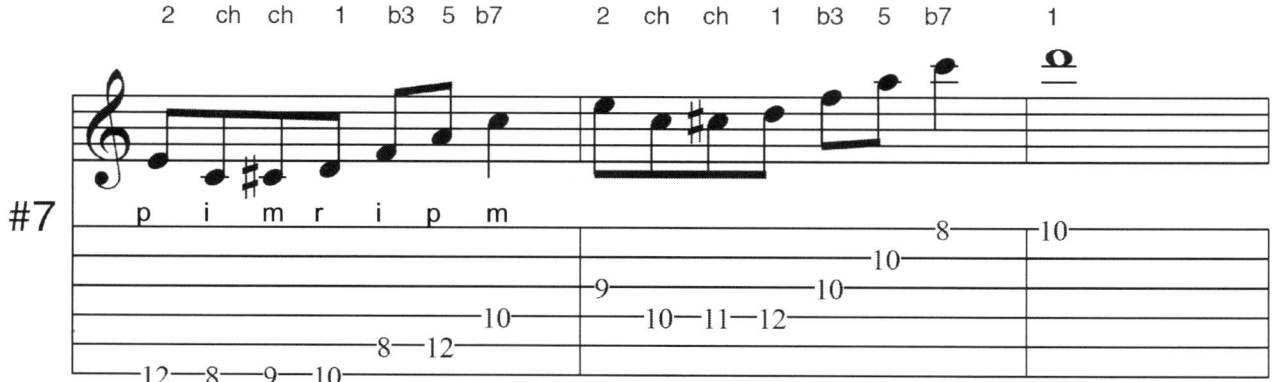

*Repeat exercise #7 inverting the order of the 3 note enclosure to lower double and single upper to 1

Ascending min. 7th arpeggio w/ single upper and lower double to 5

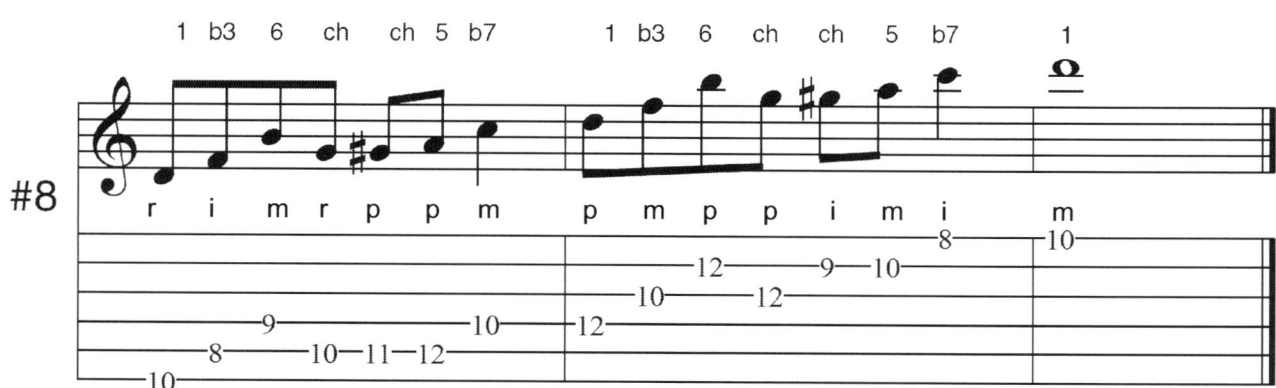

*Repeat exercise #8 inverting the order of the 3 note enclosure to lower double and single upper to 5

PAT. 4 DORIAN ARPEGGIO w/ 3 NOTE ENCLOSURES

*Repeat exercise #1 inverting the order of the 3 note enclosure to single upper and lower double to b3

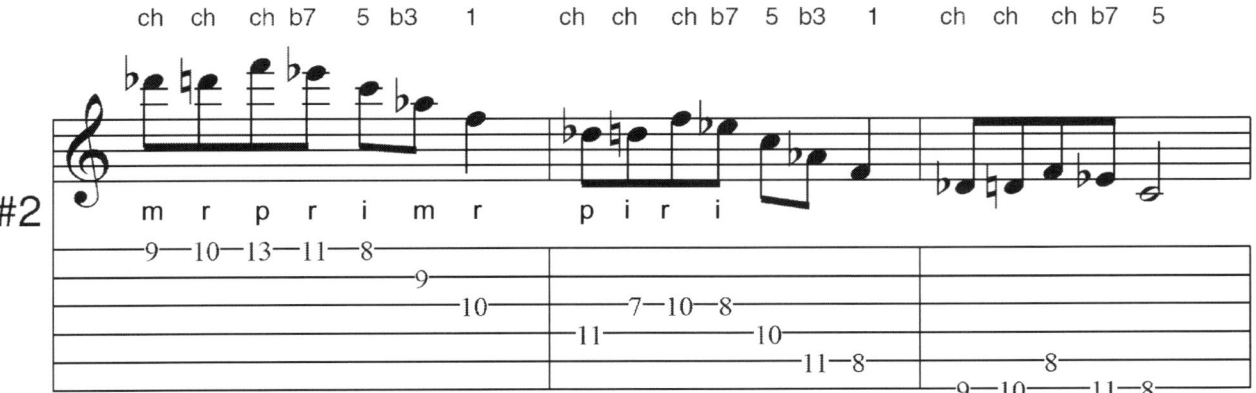

*Repeat exercise #2 inverting the order of the 3 note enclosure to single upper and lower double to b7

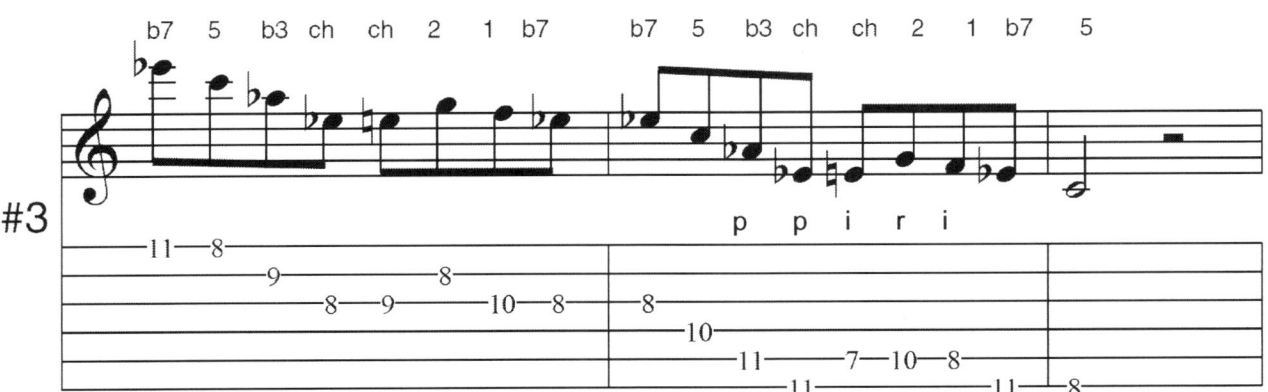

*Repeat exercise #3 inverting the order of the 3 note enclosure to single upper and lower double to 1

PAT. 4 DORIAN ARPEGGIO w/ 3 NOTE ENCLOSURES

Descending min. 7th arpeggio w/ lower double and single upper to 5

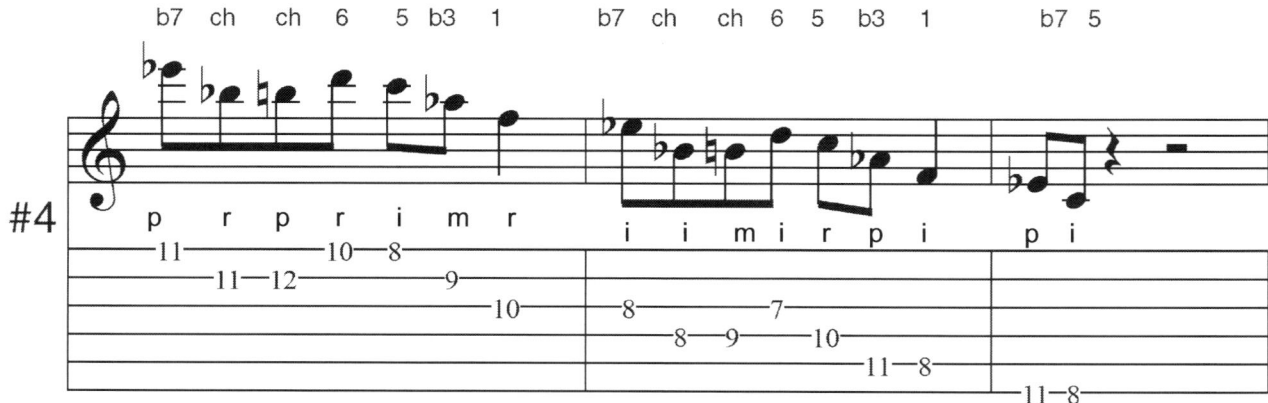

*Repeat exercise #4 inverting the order of the 3 note enclosure to single upper and lower double to 5

Ascending min. 7th arpeggio w/ single lower and upper double to b3

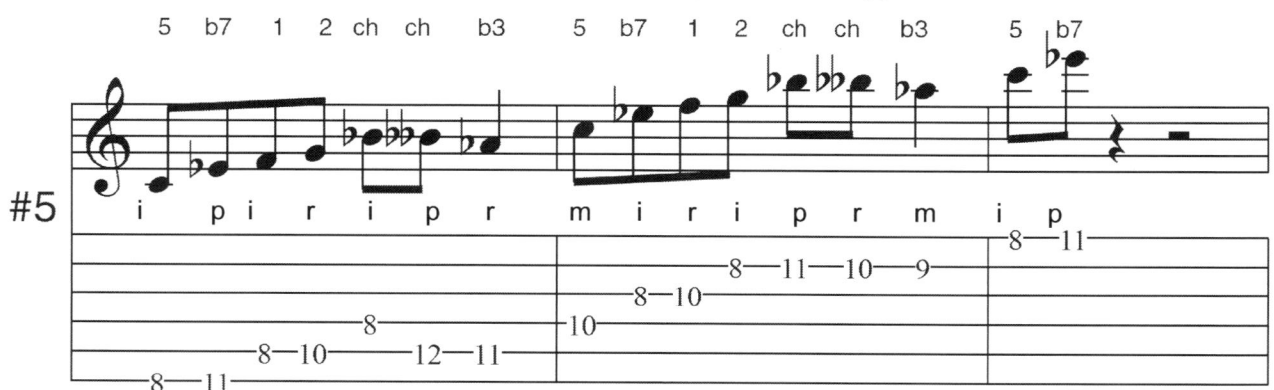

*Repeat exercise #5 inverting the order of the 3 note enclosure to lower double and single upper to b3

Ascending min. 7th arpeggio w/ single upper and lower double to b7

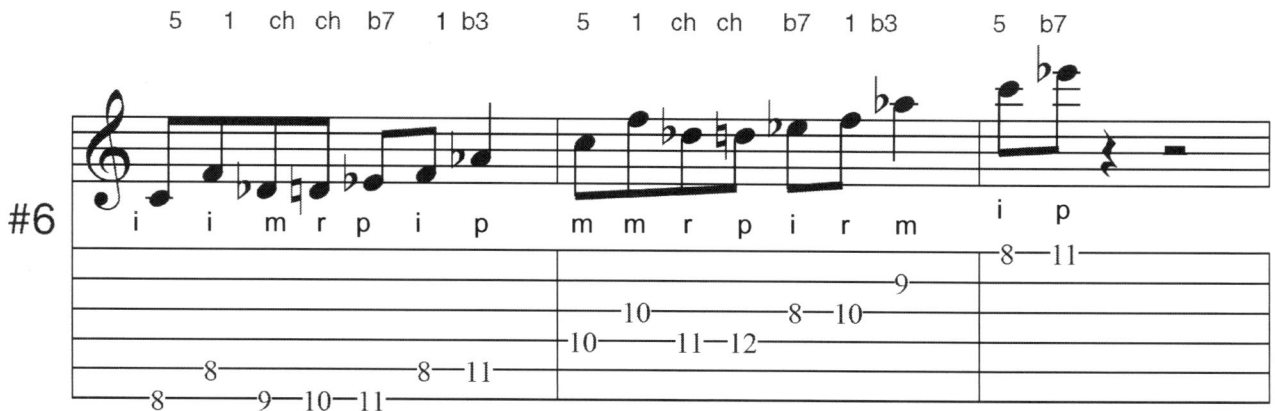

*Repeat exercise #6 inverting the order of the 3 note enclosure to lower double and single upper to b7

PAT. 4 DORIAN ARPEGGIO w/ 3 NOTE ENCLOSURES

Ascending min. 7th arpeggio w/ single upper and lower double to 1

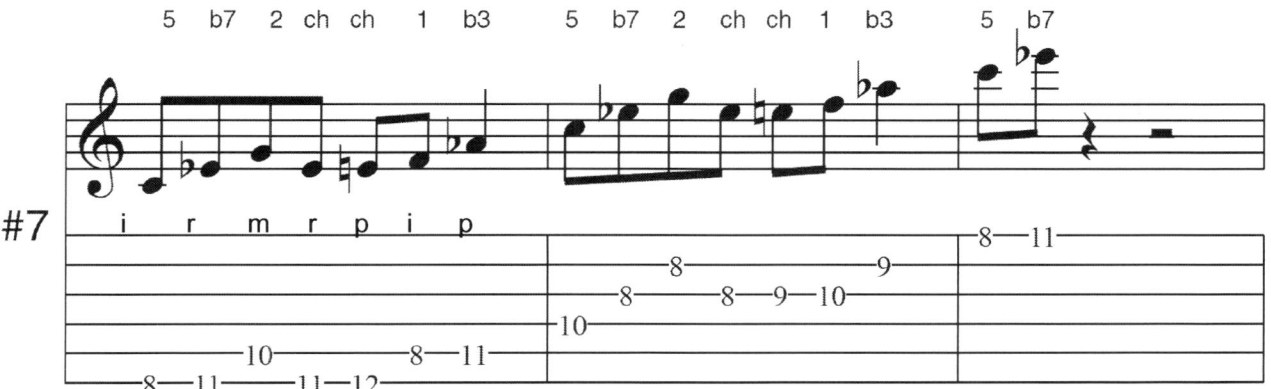

*Repeat exercise #7 inverting the order of the 3 note enclosure to lower double and single upper to 1

Ascending min. 7th arpeggio w/ single upper and lower double to 5

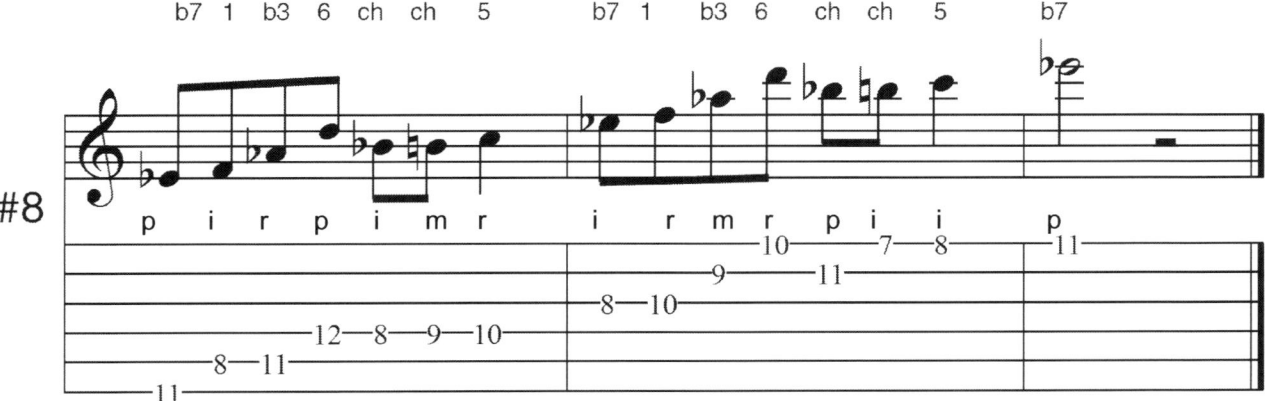

*Repeat exercise #8 inverting the order of the 3 note enclosure to lower double and single upper to 5

SUMMARY OF BEBOP CALISTHENICS 5A

ARPEGGIOS WITH 3 NOTE ENCLOSURES

Dorian (1 - 2 - ♭3 - 4 - 5 - 6 - ♭7) Play each exercise descending and ascending ⊙ ⊙

NOTE: Each exercise consists of 7 notes. For rhythmic symmetry when practicing in eighth notes, please assign a quarter note to every 4th chord tone.

SA = scale approach (diatonic)

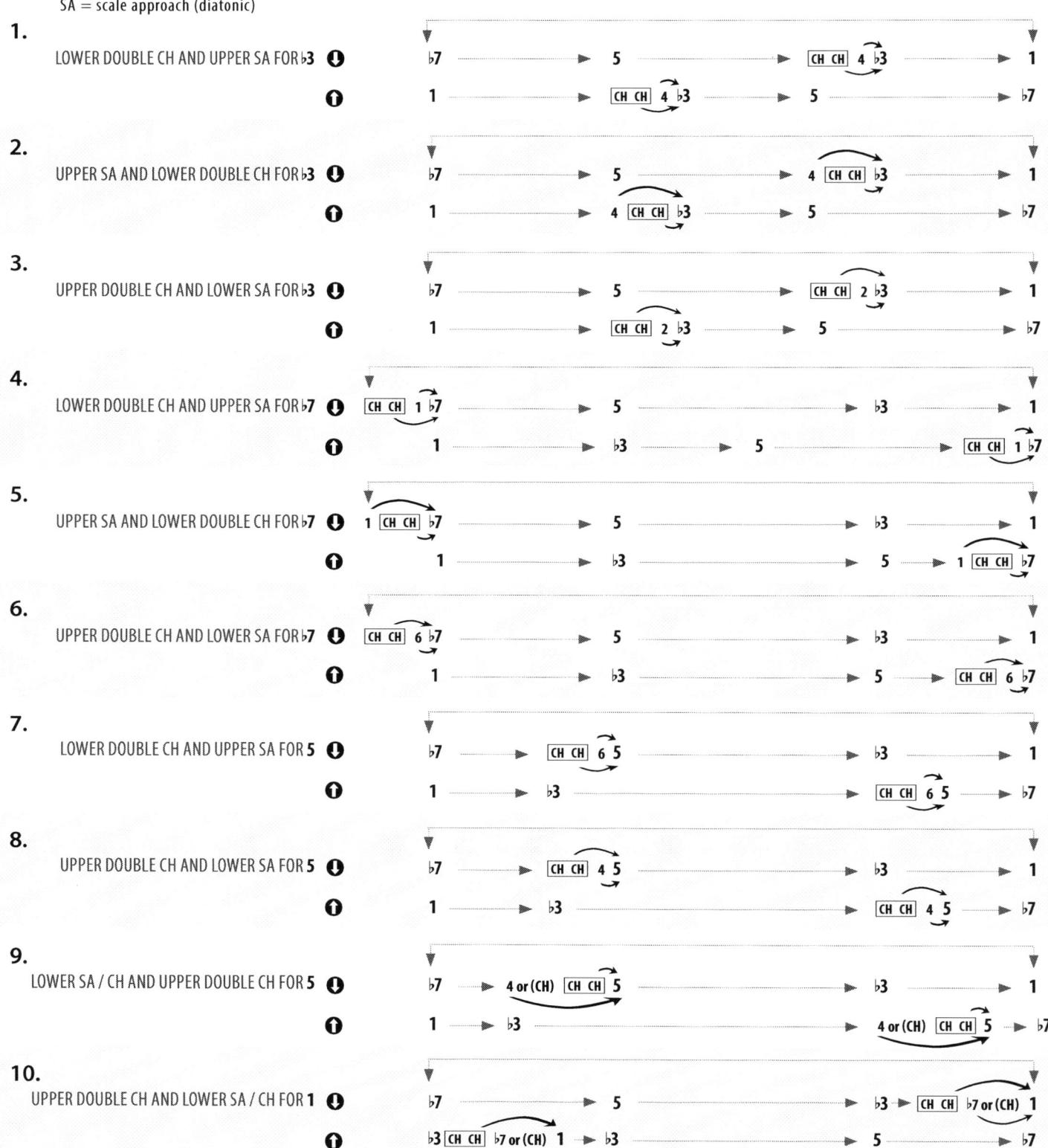

SUMMARY OF BEBOP CALISTHENICS 5B

ARPEGGIOS WITH 3 NOTE ENCLOSURES

Mixolydian (1 - 2 - 3 - 4 - 5 - 6 - ♭7) Play each exercise descending and ascending ⬇ ⬆

1.
LOWER DOUBLE CH AND UPPER SA FOR **3** ⬇   ♭7 ➤ 5 ➤ CH CH 4 3 ➤ 1
⬆   1 ➤ CH CH 4 3 ➤ 5 ➤ ♭7

2.
UPPER SA AND LOWER DOUBLE CH FOR **3** ⬇   ♭7 ➤ 5 ➤ 4 CH CH 3 ➤ 1
⬆   1 ➤ 4 CH CH 3 ➤ 5 ➤ ♭7

3.
UPPER DOUBLE CH AND LOWER SA / CH FOR **3** ⬇   ♭7 ➤ 5 ➤ CH CH 2 or (CH) 3 ➤ 1
⬆   1 ➤ CH CH 2 or (CH) 3 ➤ 5 ➤ ♭7

4.
LOWER SA / CH AND UPPER DOUBLE CH FOR **3** ⬇   ♭7 ➤ 5 ➤ 2 or (CH) CH CH 3 ➤ 1
⬆   1 ➤ 2 or (CH) CH CH 3 ➤ 5 ➤ ♭7

5.
LOWER DOUBLE CH AND UPPER SA FOR **♭7** ⬇   CH CH 1 ♭7 ➤ 5 ➤ 3 ➤ 1
⬆   1 ➤ 3 ➤ 5 ➤ CH CH 1 ♭7

6.
UPPER DOUBLE CH AND LOWER SA FOR **♭7** ⬇   CH CH 6 ♭7 ➤ 5 ➤ 3 ➤ 1
⬆   1 ➤ 3 ➤ 5 ➤ CH CH 6 ♭7

7.
LOWER DOUBLE CH AND UPPER SA FOR **5** ⬇   ♭7 ➤ CH CH 6 5 ➤ 3 ➤ 1
⬆   1 ➤ 3 ➤ CH CH 6 5 ➤ ♭7

8.
UPPER DOUBLE CH AND LOWER SA / CH FOR **5** ⬇   ♭7 ➤ CH CH 4 or (CH) 5 ➤ 3 ➤ 1
⬆   1 ➤ 3 ➤ CH CH 4 or (CH) 5 ➤ ♭7

9.
LOWER SA / CH AND UPPER DOUBLE CH FOR **5** ⬇   ♭7 ➤ 4 or (CH) CH CH 5 ➤ 3 ➤ 1
⬆   1 ➤ 3 ➤ 4 or (CH) CH CH 5 ➤ ♭7

10.
UPPER DOUBLE CH AND LOWER SA / CH FOR **1** ⬇   ♭7 ➤ 5 ➤ 3 ➤ CH CH ♭7 or (CH) 1
⬆   CH CH ♭7 or (CH) 1 ➤ 3 ➤ 5 ➤ ♭7

SUMMARY OF BEBOP CALISTHENICS 5C

ARPEGGIOS WITH 3 NOTE ENCLOSURES

Ionian (1 - 2 - 3 - 4 - 5 - 6 - 7) Play each exercise descending and ascending ⬇ ⬆

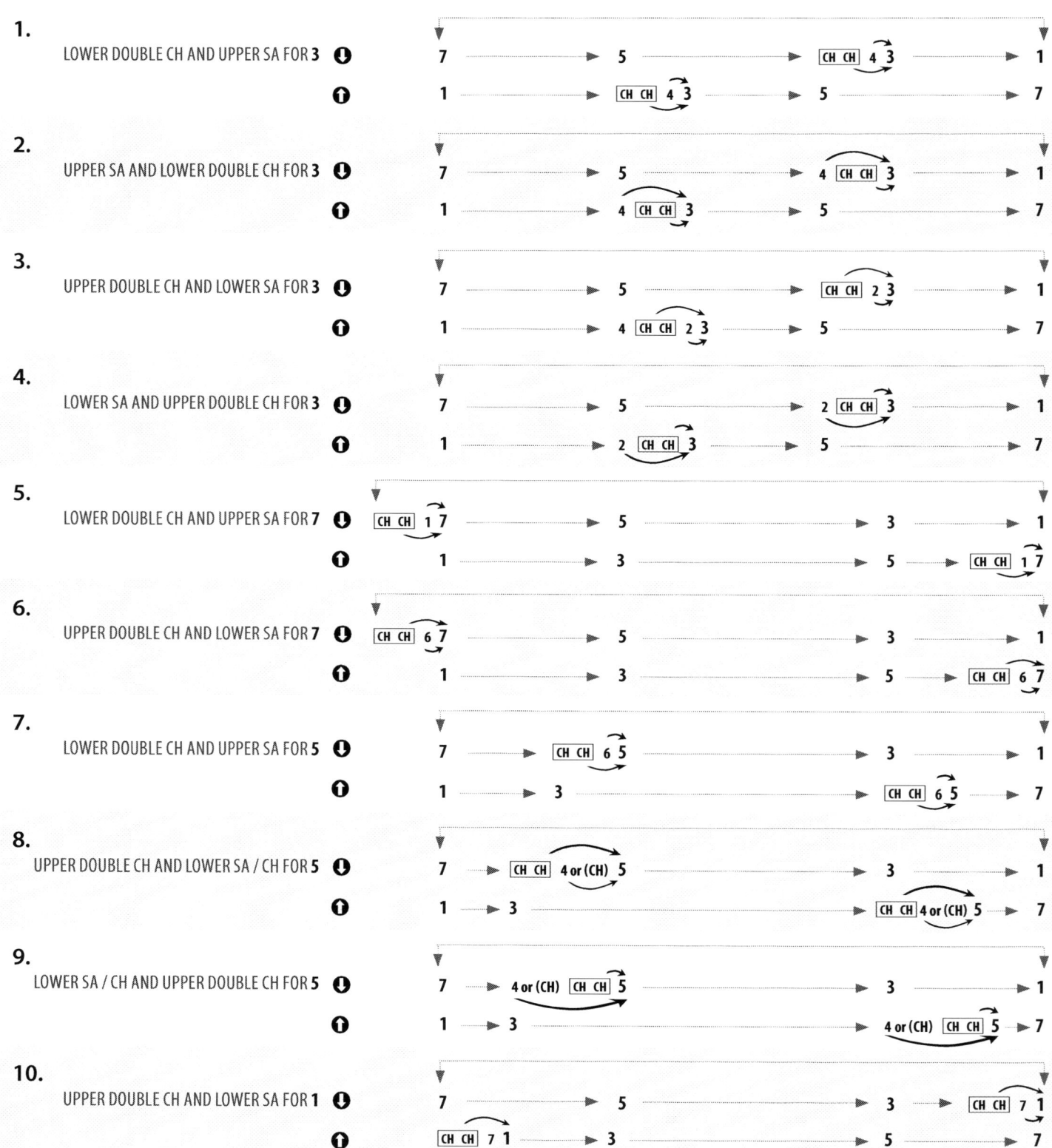

SUMMARY OF BEBOP CALISTHENICS 5D

ARPEGGIOS WITH 3 NOTE ENCLOSURES

Locrian (1 - ♭2 - ♭3 - 4 - ♭5 - ♭6 - ♭7) Play each exercise descending and ascending ⬇ ⬆

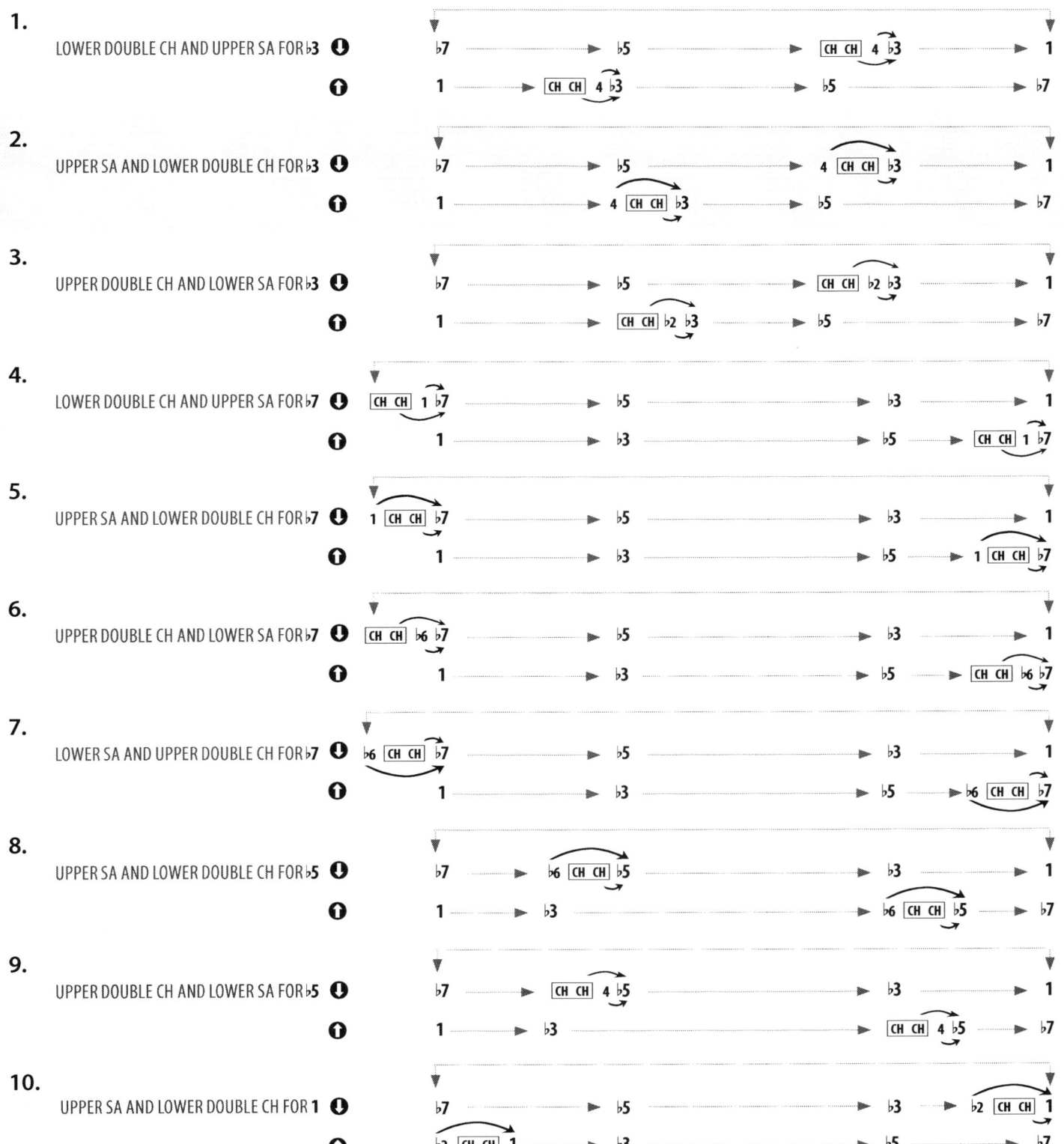

95

SUMMARY OF BEBOP CALISTHENICS 5E

ARPEGGIOS WITH 3 NOTE ENCLOSURES

Super Locrian (1 - ♭2 - #2 - 3 - #4 - #5 - ♭7) Play each exercise descending and ascending ⬇ ⬆

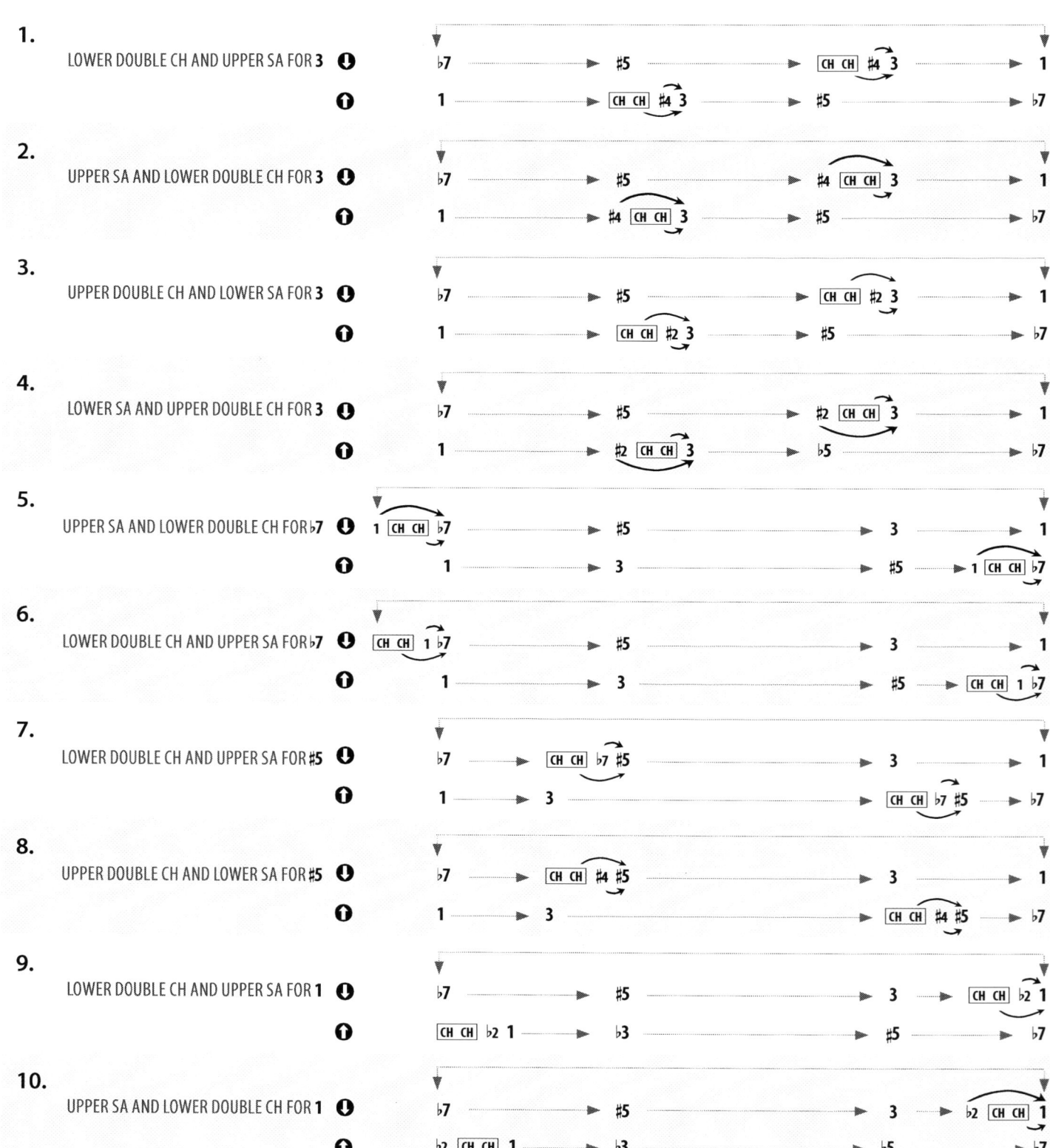

BEBOP
CALISTHENICS 6
ARPEGGIOS with 4 NOTE ENCLOSURES

DORIAN PAT 1 / PAT 4 / PAT 5

**Summary for Mixolydian / Dorian /
Ionian / Locrian / Super Locrian**

PAT. 1 DORIAN ARPEGGIO w/ 4 NOTE ENCLOSURES

l dch = lower double chromatic
u dch = upper double chromatic

Left Hand:
i=index
m=middle
r=ring
p=pinky

Descending min. 7th arpeggio w/ lower double chrom. & upper double chrom. to b7

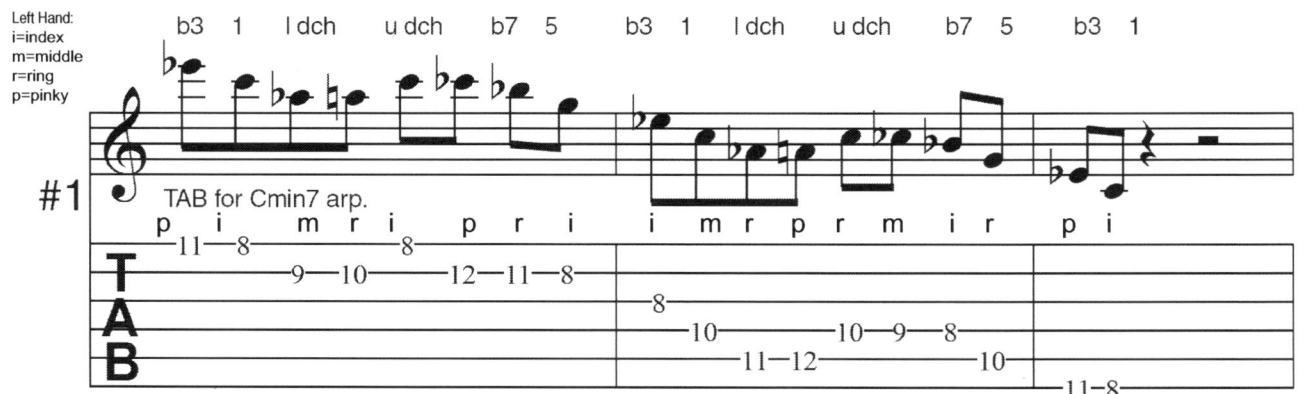

*Repeat Exercise #1 using upper double chrom. & lower double chrom. to b7

Descending min. 7th arpeggio w/ lower double chrom. & upper double chrom. to 5

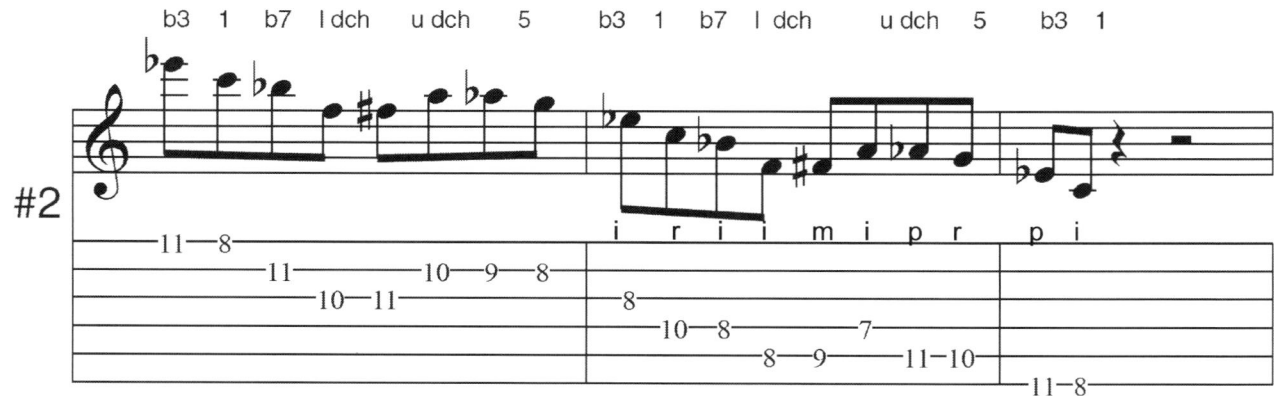

*Repeat Exercise #2 using upper double chrom. & lower double chrom. to 5

Descending min. 7th arpeggio w/ lower double chrom. & upper double chrom. to b3

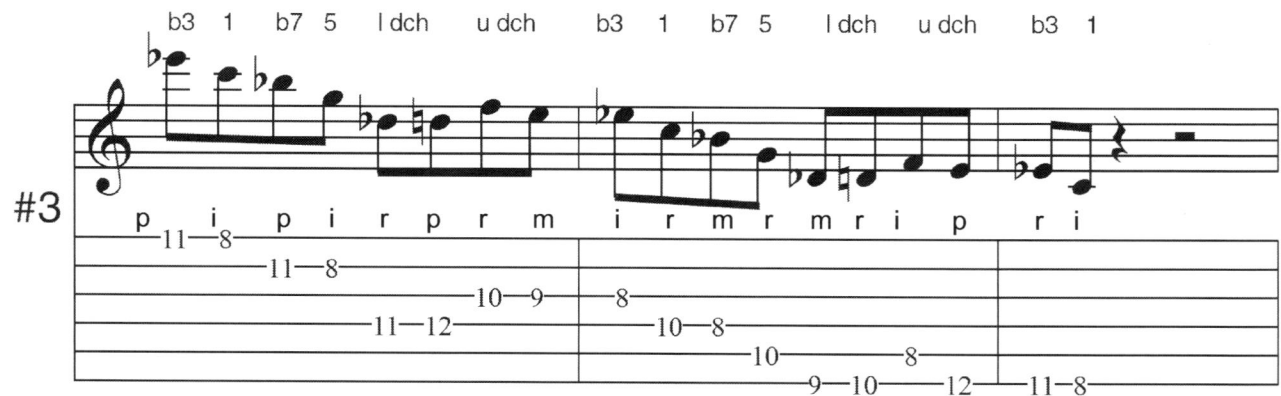

*Repeat Exercise #3 using upper double chrom. & lower double chrom. to b3

98

PAT. 1 DORIAN ARPEGGIO w/ 4 NOTE ENCLOSURES

Descending min. 7th arpeggio w/ lower double chrom. & upper double chrom. to 1

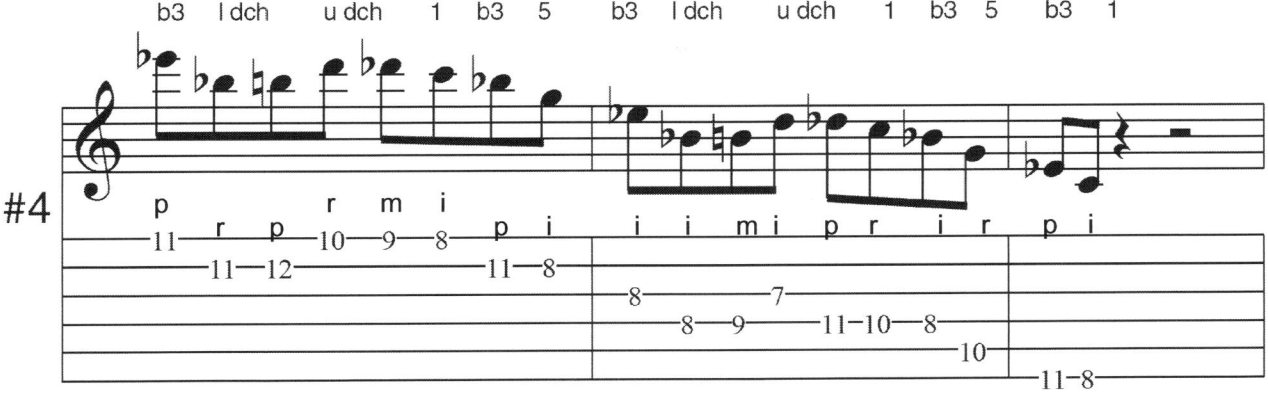

*Repeat Exercise #4 using upper double chrom. & lower double chrom. to 1

Ascending min. 7th arpeggio w/ upper double chrom. & lower double chrom. to b7

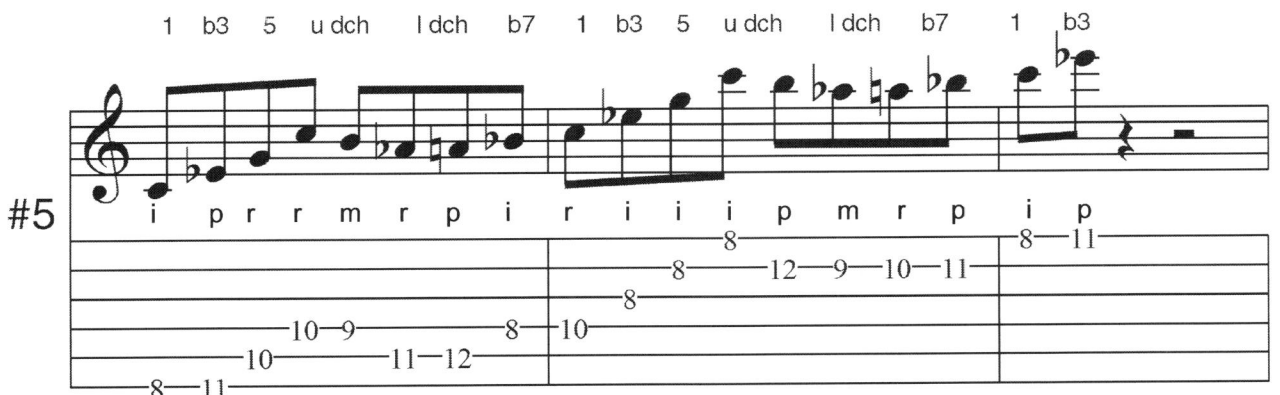

*Repeat Exercise #5 using lower double chrom. & upper double chrom. to b7

Ascending min. 7th arpeggio w/ upper double chrom. & lower double chrom. to 5

*Repeat Exercise #6 using lower double chrom. & upper double chrom. to 5

PAT. 1 DORIAN ARPEGGIO w/ 4 NOTE ENCLOSURES

Ascending min. 7th arpeggio w/ upper double chrom. & lower double chrom. to b3

*Repeat Exercise #7 using lower double chrom. & upper double chrom. to b3

Ascending min. 7th arpeggio w/ upper double chrom. & lower double chrom. to 1

*Repeat Exercise #8 using lower double chrom. & upper double chrom. to 1

l dch = lower double chromatic

u dch = upper double chromatic

PAT. 4 DORIAN ARPEGGIO w/ 4 NOTE ENCLOSURES

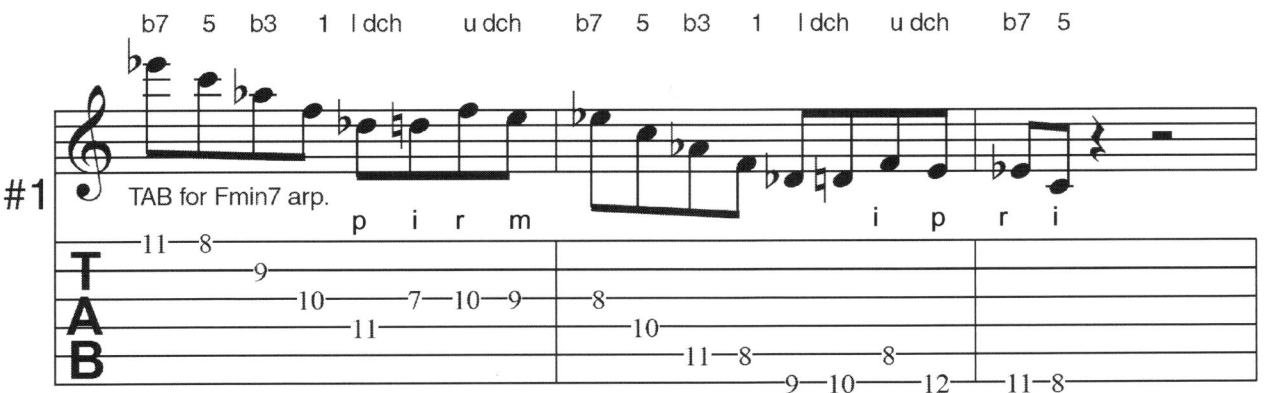

#1

TAB for Fmin7 arp.

*Repeat Exercise #1 using upper double chrom. & lower double chrom. to b7

Descending min. 7th arpeggio w/ lower double chrom. & upper double chrom. to 5

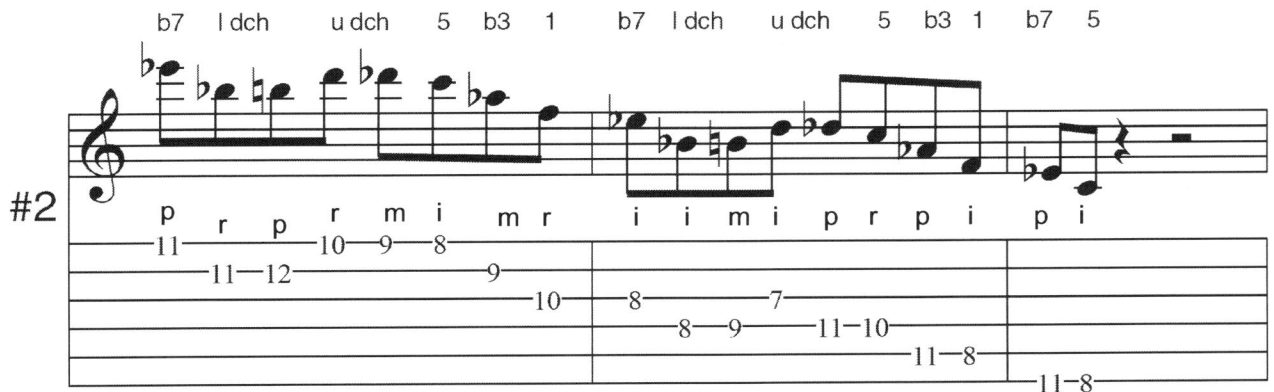

#2

*Repeat Exercise #2 using upper double chrom. & lower double chrom. to 5

Descending min. 7th arpeggio w/ lower double chrom. & upper double chrom. to b3

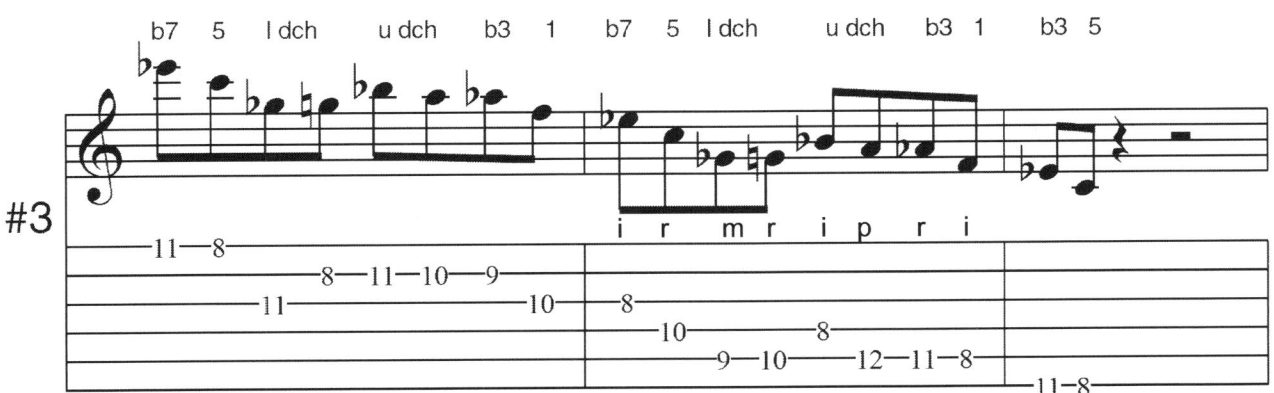

#3

*Repeat Exercise #3 using upper double chrom. & lower double chrom. to b3

101

PAT. 4 DORIAN ARPEGGIO w/ 4 NOTE ENCLOSURES

Descending min. 7th arpeggio w/ lower double chrom. & upper double chrom. to 1

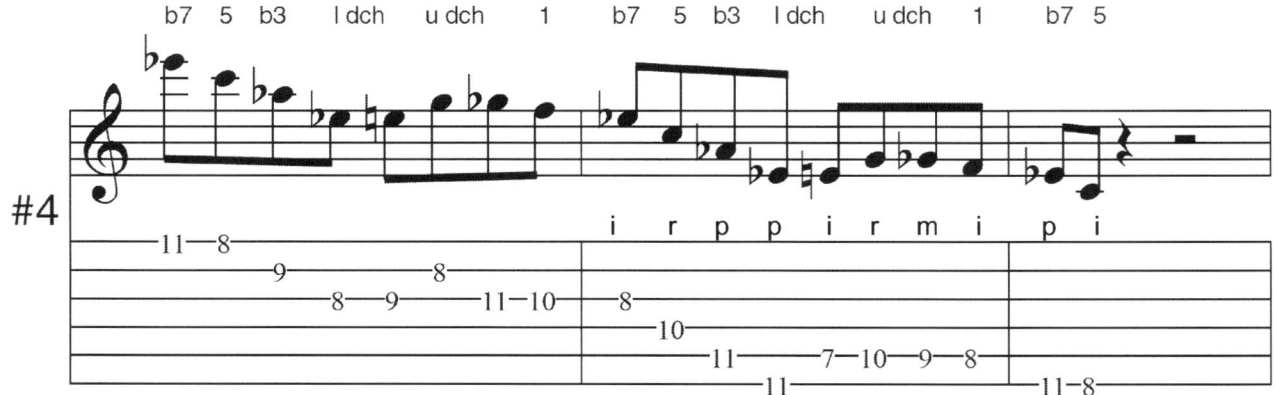

*Repeat Exercise #4 using upper double chrom. & lower double chrom. to 1

Ascending min. 7th arpeggio w/ upper double chrom. & lower double chrom. to b7

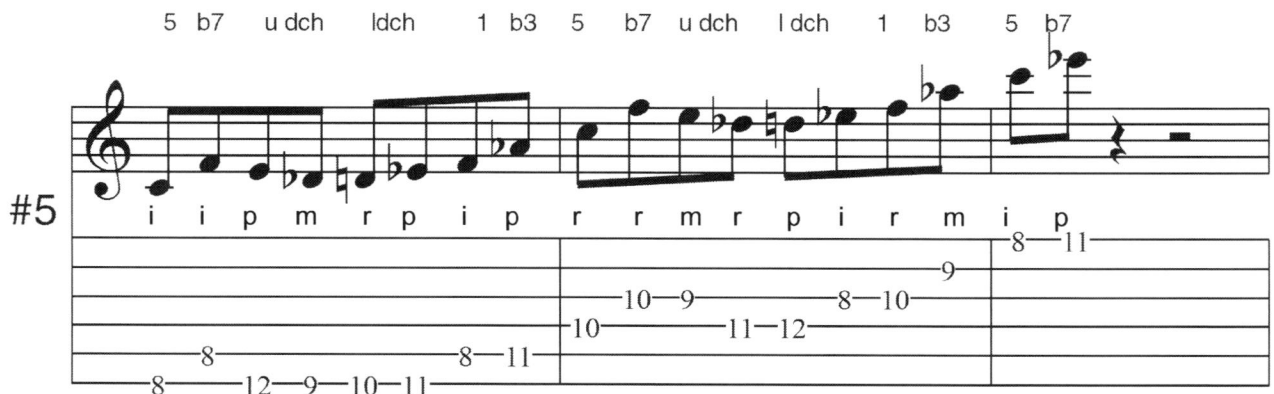

*Repeat Exercise #5 using lower double chrom. & upper double chrom. to b7

Ascending min. 7th arpeggio w/ upper double chrom. & lower double chrom. to 5

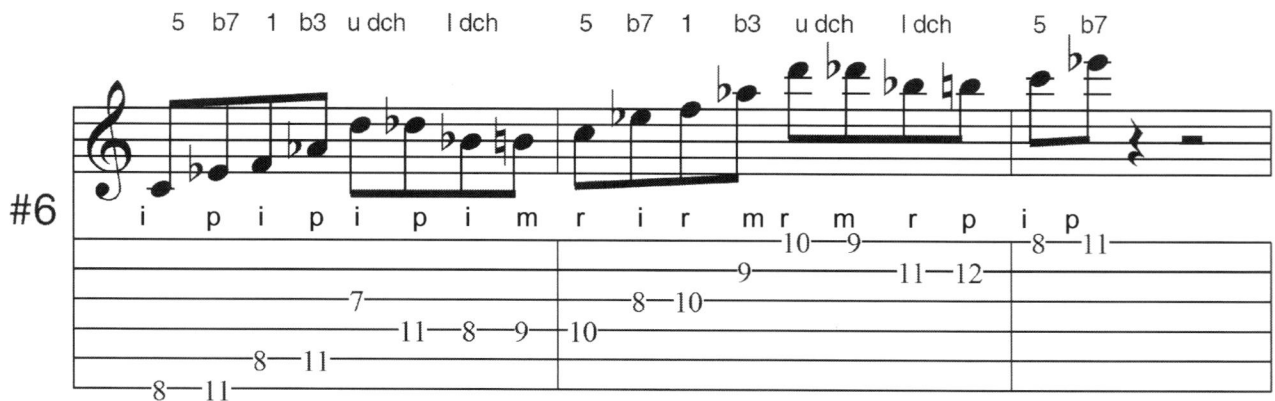

*Repeat Exercise #6 using lower double chrom. & upper double chrom. to 5

PAT. 4 DORIAN ARPEGGIO w/ 4 NOTE ENCLOSURES

Ascending min. 7th arpeggio w/ upper double chrom. & lower double chrom. to b3

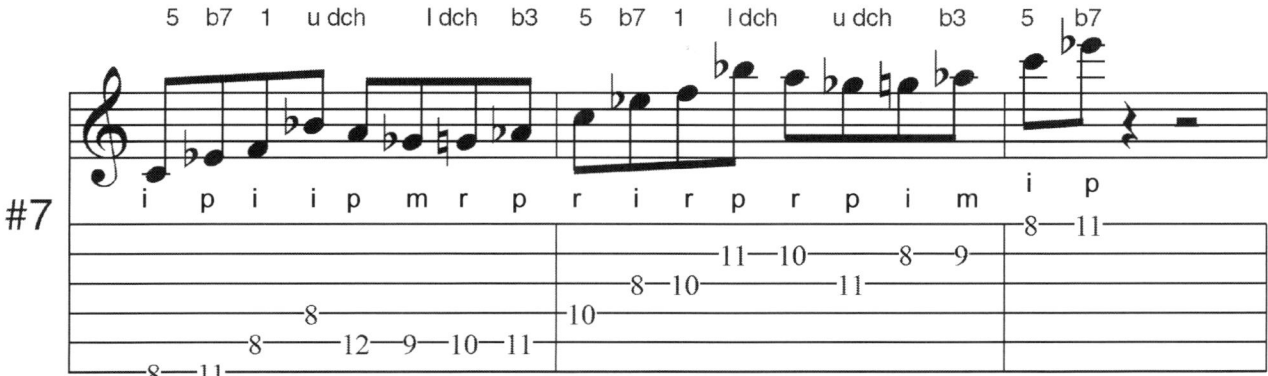

*Repeat Exercise #7 using lower double chrom. & upper double chrom. to b3

Ascending min. 7th arpeggio w/ upper double chrom. & lower double chrom. to 1

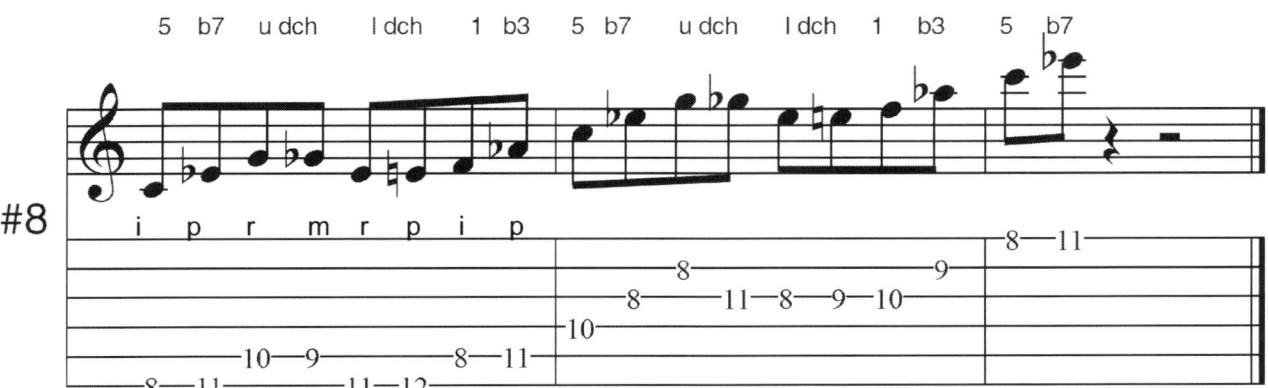

*Repeat Exercise #8 using lower double chrom. & upper double chrom. to 1

l dch = lower
double chromatic

u dch = upper
double chromatic

PAT. 5 DORIAN ARPEGGIO w/ 4 NOTE ENCLOSURES

Descending min. 7th arpeggio w/ lower double chrom. & upper double chrom. to b7

*Repeat Exercise #1 using upper double chrom. & lower double chrom. to b7

Descending min. 7th arpeggio w/ lower double chrom. & upper double chrom. to 5

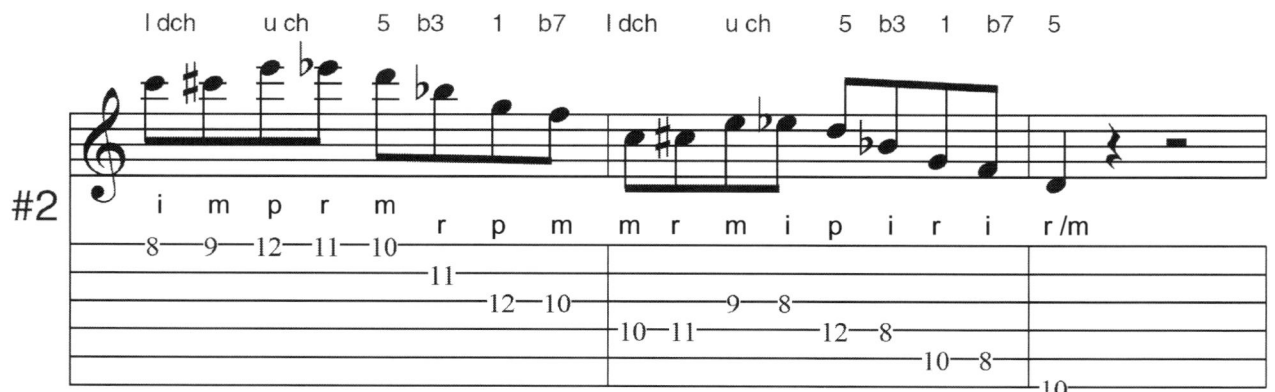

*Repeat Exercise #2 using upper double chrom. & lower double chrom. to 5

Descending min. 7th arpeggio w/ lower double chrom. & upper double chrom. to b3

*Repeat Exercise #3 using upper double chrom. & lower double chrom. to b3

PAT. 5 DORIAN ARPEGGIO w/ 4 NOTE ENCLOSURES

Descending min. 7th arpeggio w/ lower double chrom. & upper double chrom. to 1

*Repeat Exercise #4 using upper double chrom. & lower double chrom. to 1

Ascending min. 7th arpeggio w/ upper double chrom. & lower double chrom. to b7

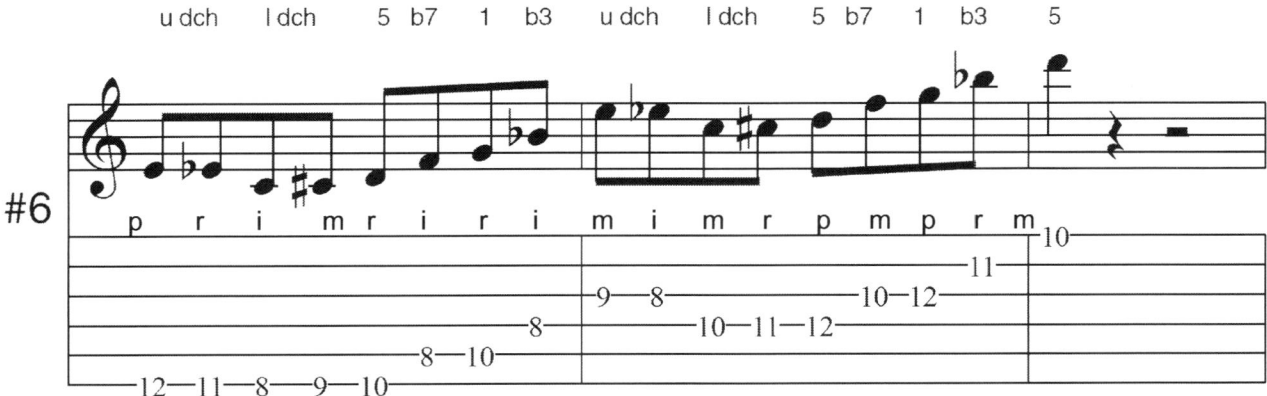

*Repeat Exercise #5 using lower double chrom. & upper double chrom. to b7

Ascending min. 7th arpeggio w/ upper double chrom. & lower double chrom. to 5

*Repeat Exercise #6 using lower double chrom. & upper double chrom. to 5

PAT. 5 DORIAN ARPEGGIO w/ 4 NOTE ENCLOSURES

Ascending min. 7th arpeggio w/ upper double chrom. & lower double chrom. to b3

*Repeat Exercise #7 using lower double chrom. & upper double chrom. to b3

Ascending min. 7th arpeggio w/ upper double chrom. & lower double chrom. to 1

*Repeat Exercise #8 using lower double chrom. & upper double chrom. to 1

SUMMARY OF BEBOP CALISTHENICS 6A

ARPEGGIOS WITH 4 NOTE ENCLOSURES

Dorian (1 - 2 - ♭3 - 4 - 5 - 6 - ♭7) Play each exercise descending and ascending ⬇ ⬆

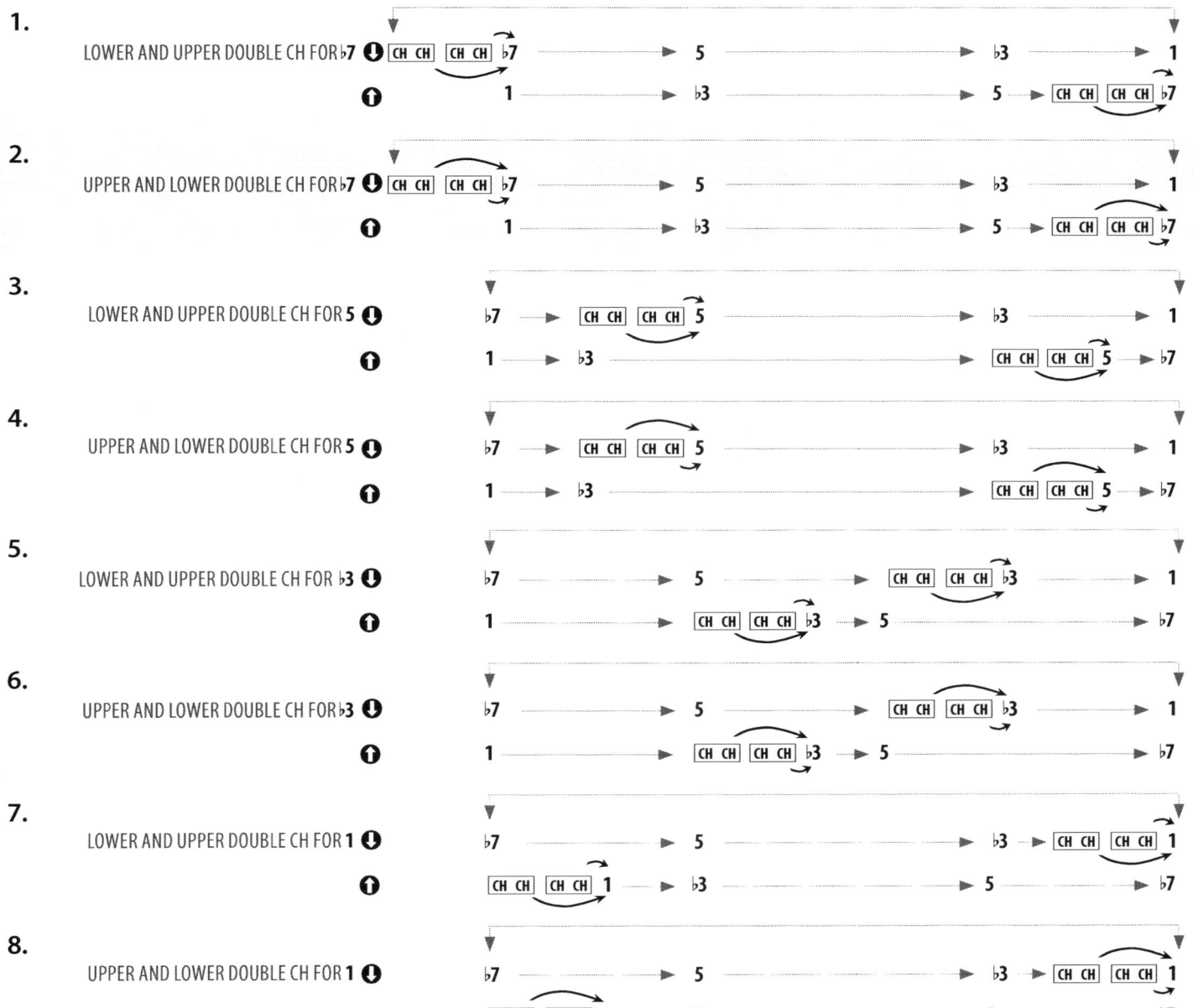

SUMMARY OF BEBOP CALISTHENICS 6B

ARPEGGIOS WITH 4 NOTE ENCLOSURES

Mixolydian (1 - 2 - 3 - 4 - 5 - 6 - ♭7) Play each exercise descending and ascending ⬇ ⬆

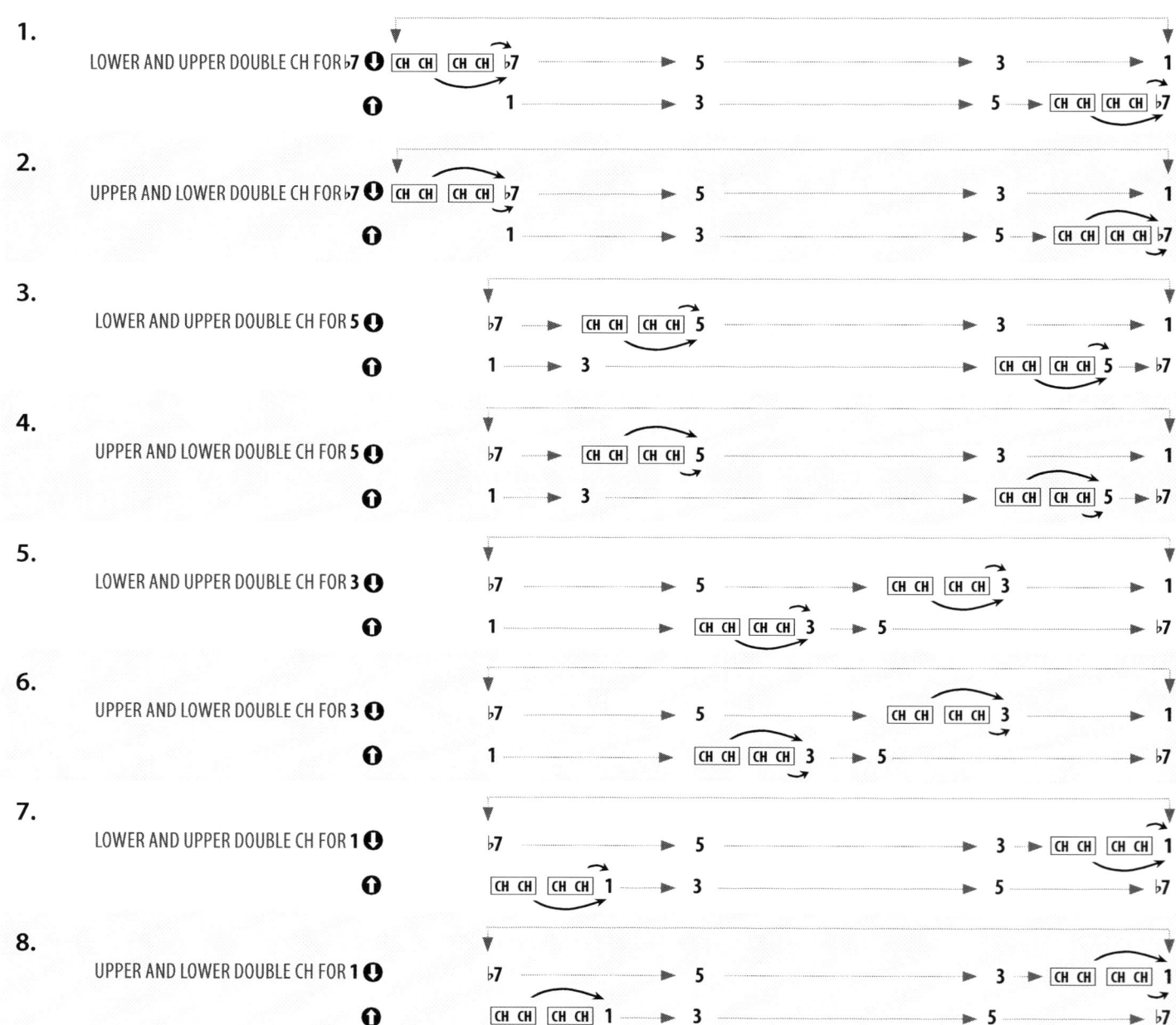

SUMMARY OF BEBOP CALISTHENICS 6C

ARPEGGIOS WITH 4 NOTE ENCLOSURES

Ionian (1 - 2 - 3 - 4 - 5 - 6 - 7) Play each exercise descending and ascending 🔽 🔼

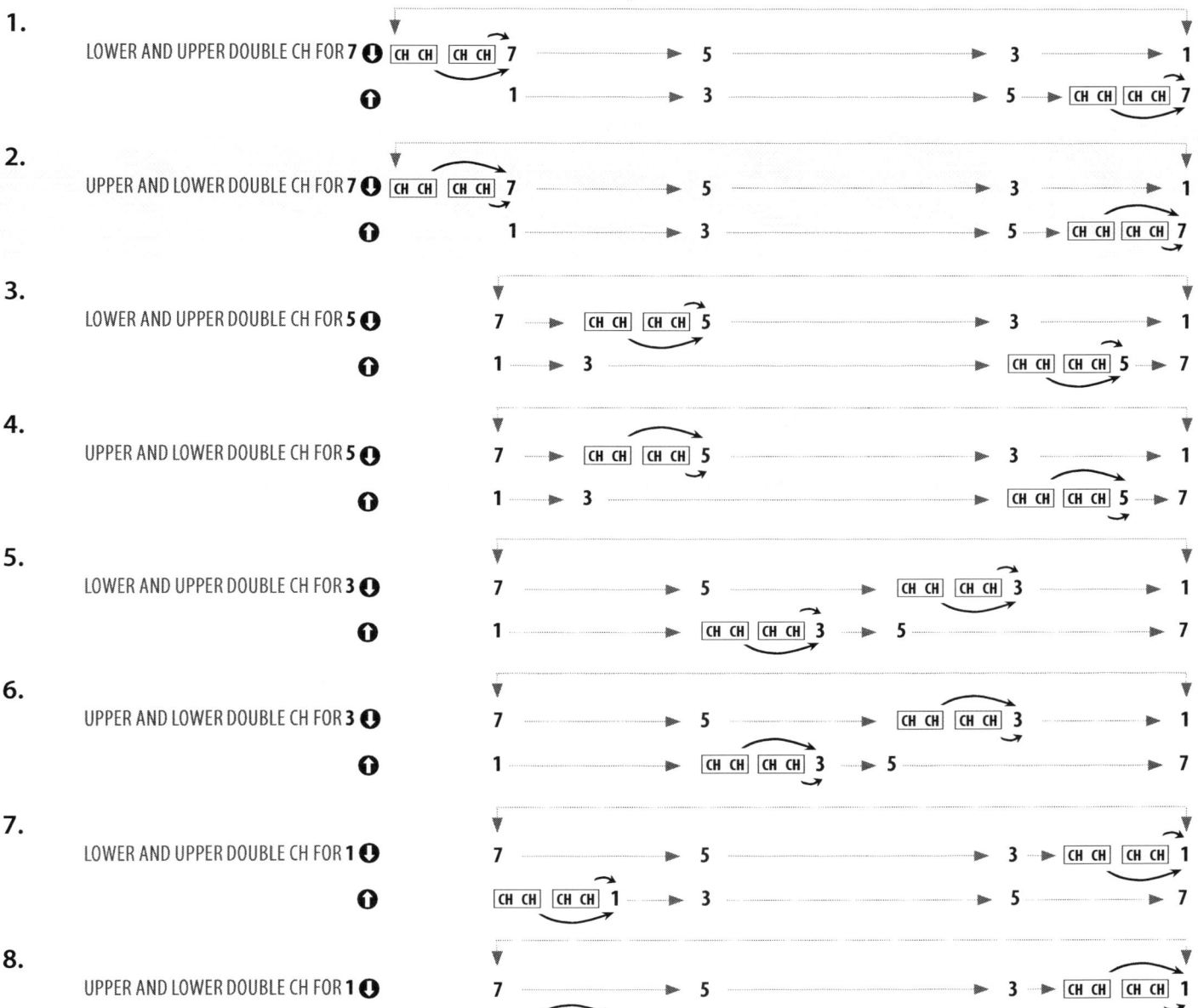

SUMMARY OF BEBOP CALISTHENICS 6D

ARPEGGIOS WITH 4 NOTE ENCLOSURES

Locrian (1 - ♭2 - ♭3 - 4 - ♭5 - ♭6 - ♭7) Play each exercise descending and ascending ❶ ❶

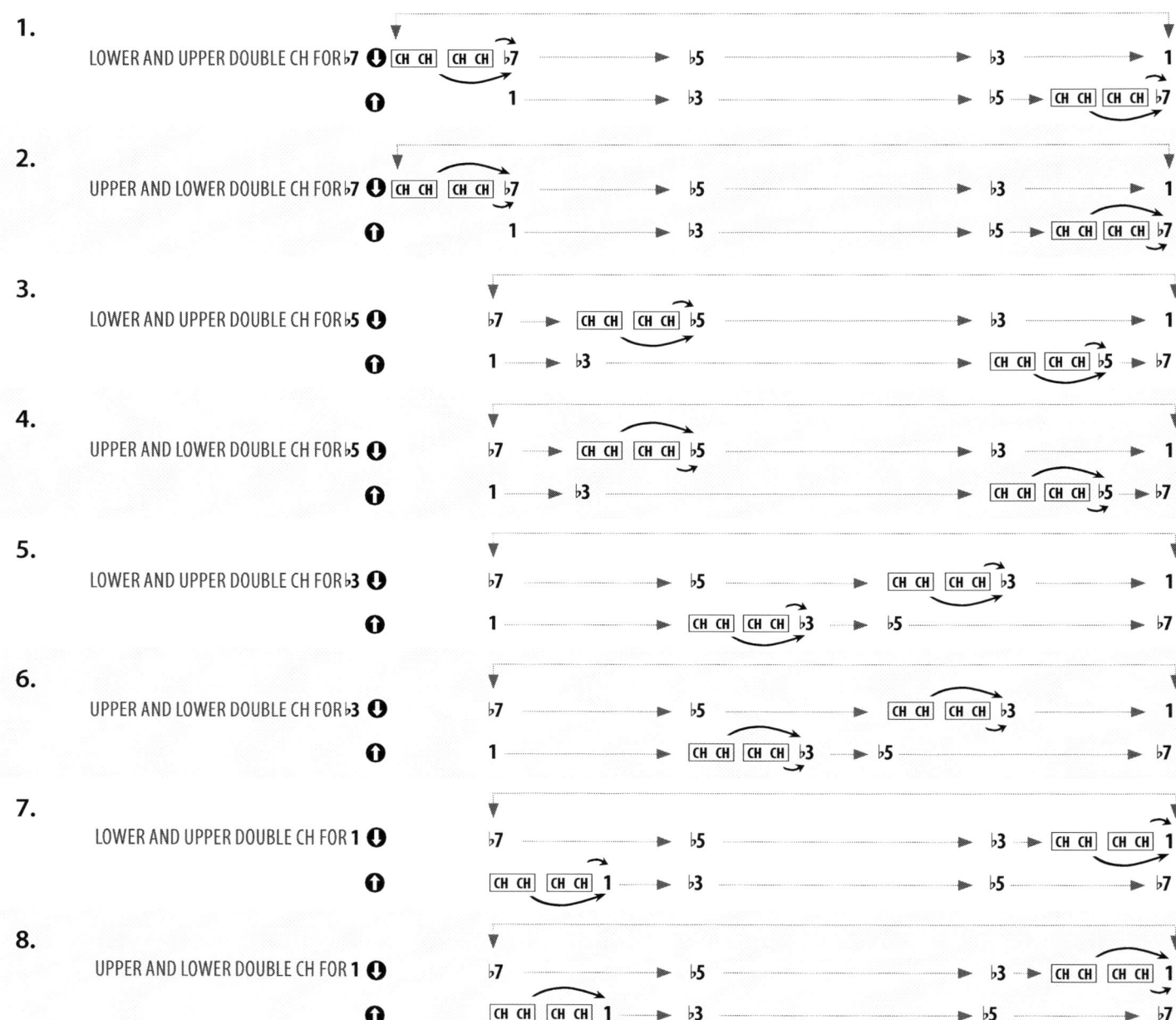

SUMMARY OF BEBOP CALISTHENICS 6C

ARPEGGIOS WITH 4 NOTE ENCLOSURES

Super Locrian (1 - ♭2 - ♯2 - 3 - ♯4 - ♯5 - ♭7) Play each exercise descending and ascending ⬇ ⬆

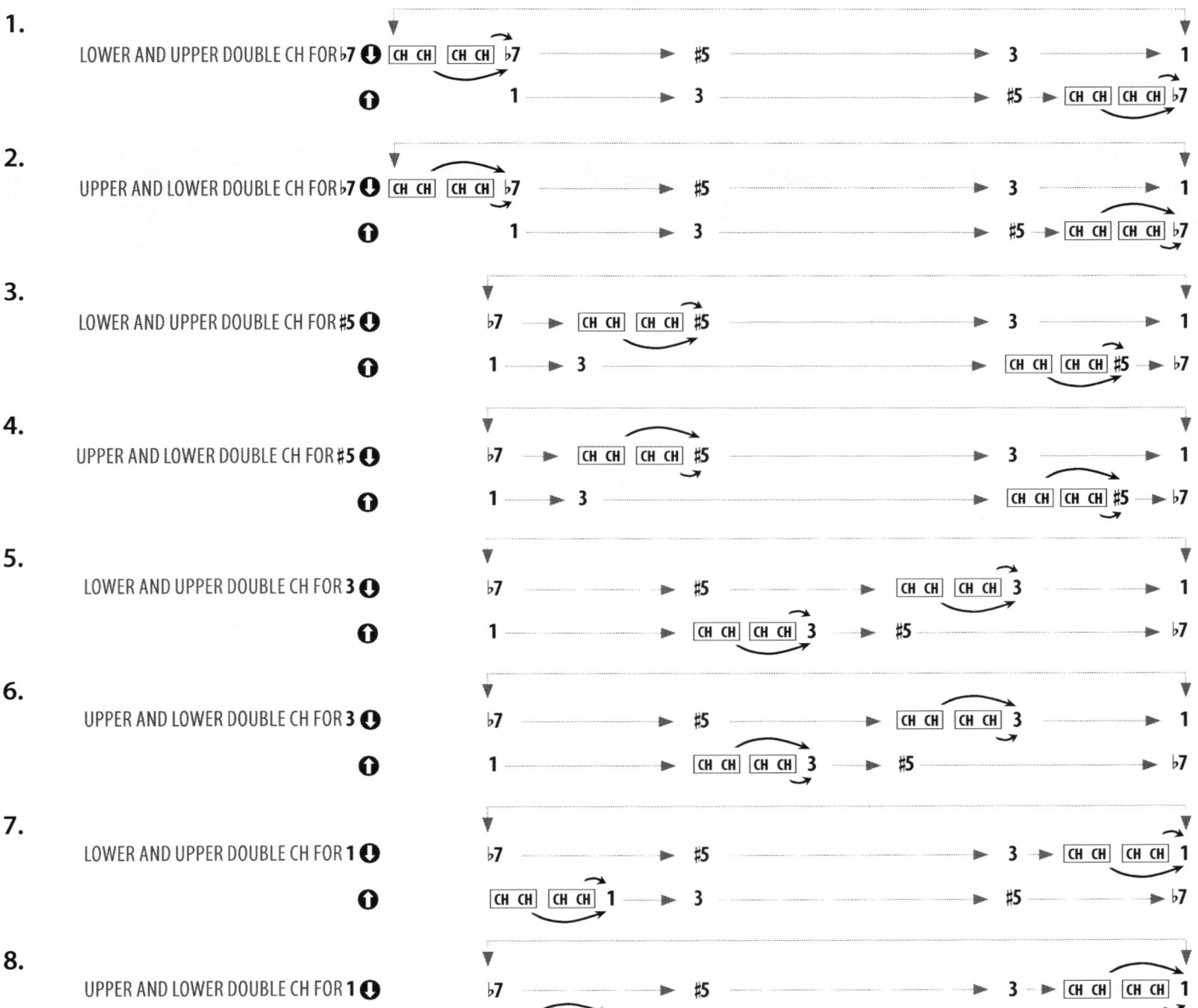

Appendix 1

HOW TO PRACTICE
USING THE SUMMARY OF
BEBOP
CALISTHENICS

HOW TO PRACTICE USING THE SUMMARY
OF BEBOP CALISTHENICS

The Summary of Bebop Calisthenics at the end of each section is based on the old adage that, «a picture tells a thousand stories». Each summary consists of a graphic depiction of the arpeggio's numerical cycle. It is designed to help you keep track of where you are within its structure at all times, and in turn help you *visualize* complex approach note events ahead of time.

A «summary» may direct you to execute the exercise through the arpeggio cycle in one of 3 ways:

1. Descending & Ascending. ❶ ❶
2. Descending only. ❶
3. Ascending only. ❶

Once the direction has been established, simply follow the arpeggio cycle accordingly and apply the approaches in the order specified for each event. Remember: «down arrows» signify that the prescribed approach will resolve *downward* to its target chord tone, while «up arrows» denote that the resolution will be *upwards*. All approaches will resolve by stepwise motion to its target.

To illustrate this concept let's take a look at the summary for *Bebop Calisthenic 1A / Exercise 1: Descending & ascending dominant seventh arpeggio with lower neighboring tone for 3 and b7* (see p.31).

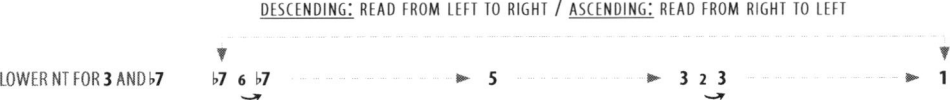

Note that the above is applicable to any fingering pattern using any rhythm or time signature! Here is the full procedure using Mixolydian Pattern 1:

1. When using Pattern 1, the cycle begins on «3» due to the fact that it is the highest available chord tone on the 1st string.

2. We then continue descending numerically through the cycle, executing the designated approach events. The 1st event occurs immediately after playing the initial «3». As a result, we are directed to play its lower NT which is «2», thereafter resolving upward back to «3».

As we continue descending through the arpeggio, we play the «1» (1st str.), the «b7» (2nd str.) followed by its lower NT which is «6», thereafter resolving upward back to «b7». We continue in the same direction next playing the 5 (2nd str.) until we reach the «3» on the 3rd string. Once again we encounter another approach event and thus play its lower NT or «2», followed by its resolution back to «3». Continuing in this same fashion, we should next play the «1» (4th str.), the «b7» (4th str.) with its lower NT which is «6» (5th str.) resolving back to «b7», the «5» (5th str.), again the «3» (6th str.) with its lower NT or «2», and finally the 1(lowest available chord tone on the 6th str.)

3. To finalize, we would repeat the exercise ascending numerically from the 6th string until we reach the highest available chord tone on the 1st string.

Appendix 2

FURTHER ADVENTURES
with
BEBOP
CALISTHENICS

FURTHER ADVENTURES WITH BEBOP CALISTHENICS

If you've played through several of the bebop calisthenics in this book, it is likely that you have occasionally thought to yourself , «part of this sounds like something I've heard in a jazz line before». That is indeed true because they contain most of the melodic components of the bebop idiom. Nonetheless, because they are solely exercises to internalize various melodic concepts and develop dexterity applying them, they lack rhythmic variety and are not in the context of a harmonic cadence (eg. I7-IV7, II-7-V7, etc.). As a result many students throughout the years I have been teaching these exercises, have inquired as to how they might be able to derive actual vocabulary from them. This is what we are going to explore next...

PROCEDURE TO DERIVE VOCABULARY FROM THE BEBOP CALISTHENICS

1. **Determine what fingering model you wish to use to construct your phrase.** In this example we will construct a 2 measure phrase over a I7 and IV7 and will use mixolydian patterns 1 and 4 correspondingly.

Keep in mind that this procedure can be used for any kind of progression, from a simple II-V-I all the way to a full fledged standard if you desire.

2. **Determine on which string you wish to begin your phrase.** For our example let's begin on the 2nd string using mixolydian pattern 1. Preferably we want to start with a guide tone or upper extension, so in this instance we will be using the b7.

3. **Determine whether the line will initially descend or ascend.** Because we are starting on the 2nd string, we have substantially more fretboard «real estate» if we choose to descend.

4. **From one of the calisthenic summaries, choose an arpeggio sequence with the «approach note» concept of your choice.** For the current example let's use descending dom. 7th arpeggio w/ lower neighboring tones for 3 and b7 (#2 on p.31/ Summary of Bebop Calisthenics #1a). Proceed to create a full measure in 8th notes using this sequence starting on the b7.

5. To begin the 2nd measure, determine which is the closest available guide tone in the new chord. Since we previously ended on the root of the I7, if we ascend, the closest guide tone of the IV7 turns out to be the b7 which is located on the 3rd string (pat 4).

6. Again, decide whether you will descend or ascend and choose an arpeggio sequence from one of the calisthenics. For our current example we will use ascending dom. 7th arpeggio w/ unprepared approaches from above to 1 and 5 (#8 on p. 53 / Summary of Bebop Calisthenics #2a).

* Notice in the 2nd measure above, that the range of pattern 4 ends on the next to last 8th note (b7 on the 1st string). This forces us again to descend in order to keep a continuous 8th note line to the very end of the measure.

7.   **Create rhythmic variations.** Eighth note lines will begin to sound mechanical and repetitious if over used, especially in the wrong context. To remedy this we are going to rhythmically alter the previous line and derive some alternative vocabulary from it. Here is a 2 step procedure to achieve this:

*1. Start by omitting a few notes from your original phrase, a technique known as «truncation».
Just the simple insertion of rests in place of the omitted notes will yield a new phrase !*

2. Assign new rhythms to the remaining notes. Make sure that your final outcome is equivalent to the full measure's time signature value (eg. 4/4, 3/4,etc), and don't hesitate to include some rests in order to allow your line to «breathe». Also, be sure that the last note at the point of chord change voice leads smoothly to the closest guide tone of the new chord. Here are 3 examples:

Variation 1:

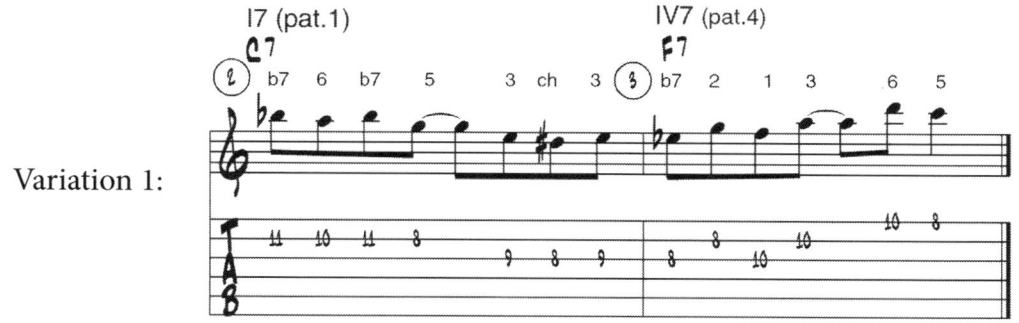

(RHYTHMIC VARIATIONS CONTINUED)

Variation 2:

Variation 3:

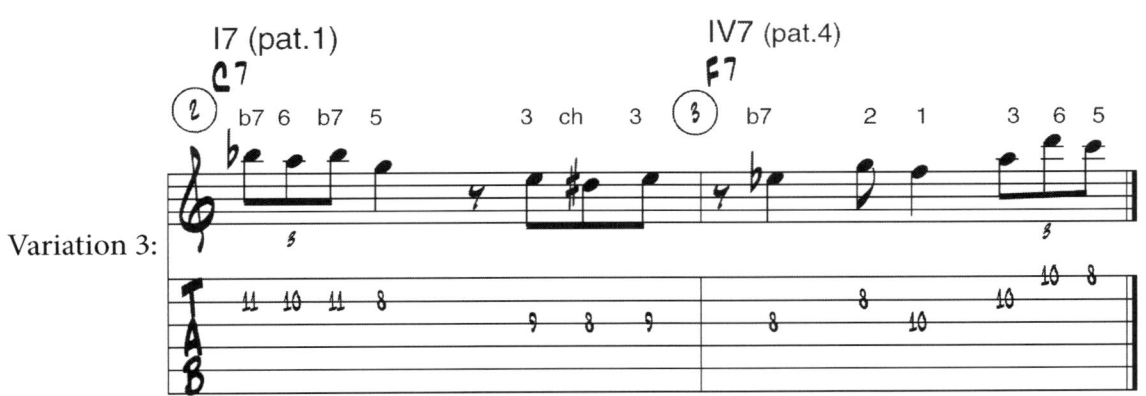

The Bebop Guitar Improv Series
by Richie Zellon

VOLUME 1

VOLUME 2

The Lesson Books

A step by step explanation of the most essential melodic, harmonic, & rhythmic elements that make up the bebop idiom, coupled with a total of 42 jazz etudes demonstrating their application in order of gradual difficulty.

The Scale & Arpeggio Book

To be used in conjunction with Volumes 1 and 2, the Scale & Arpeggio Book introduces the Heptatonic System of Fingering Patterns employed throughout the series.

It features a thorough explanation of the use of vertical and horizontal fingerings when improvising over chord changes. Regular notation, tab and diagrams are included.

The Workbooks

All the necessary exercises to develop the improvisational concepts introduced in both Lesson Book 1 and 2.

Be sure to check out the **Bebop Guitar Improv Series Online!**
Featuring hundreds of instructional videos, it is the perfect compliment to the book series.

For more info please visit *https://bebopguitar.richiezellon.com*

Printed in Great Britain
by Amazon

61180597R00068